The HeArt of Paris

A unique journey to pay homage to women who made the evolution of art possible

RENATE VAN NIJEN

ISBN 9789082452860

Published by Palcho Publications

info@renatevannijen.com / www.renatevannijen.com

Images in this book

Renate van Nijen is the creator of the images in this book. They are her impression of some of the women described in 'The HeArt of Paris'.

To see the original paintings in full colour, please visit www.renatevannijen.art

Contents

Preface

We used to meet at a café to talk about art, my paintings, my books, life in general, but also about Paris. Mario often spoke about his passion for literature and art; about the neighbourhood where he grew up in Montparnasse, in Paris. He told me how he discovered that the greatest avant-garde artists of the 20th century had lived very close to his house.

I always loved listening to these stories. Each time we met, it was like a never-ending waterfall of interesting art facts. Art wasn't just a passion or a hobby for Mario, it also was his refuge in a world he sometimes felt estranged from. For years, he had been jotting down everything he remembered and learned, referring to the lives of bohemian artists, scandals and miseries, that he could later use during his guided tours of Paris.

I told him he should write a book. He replied he wouldn't be able to. *"I'm not a writer,"* he said. I couldn't stop thinking about it, so I told him I could write this book. We knew there was a lot of material that could be interesting for future readers, but in the end, we decided the book would cover the period from Napoleon III to the end of the 1930s in Paris.

Gradually, our journey of art and literature became a reality. At first, we wanted to talk about the places that tourists hardly ever go to. But soon we realised women were present at every moment. Not just in the vast majority of the works exhibited in museums like the d'Orsay or the Petit Palais, often naked, but also serving as inspiration as models, and women giving their support to artists, like Degas, Toulouse-Lautrec, Gauguin and Delaunay, who would not have been such valued artists without these women.

They were their muses, their models, their courtesans. Like, for example, Manet's Olympia, Degas's dancers, or Émile Zola's Nana. Who were these women? We also realised there were many female artists, but the large majority of them struggled. Generally speaking, women were not allowed to create.

Mario and I relived almost eighty years of Parisian history. When I finally sat down to write this book, Mario sent me the audio recordings of the content, which I then translated into English. These recordings made me even more curious; I wanted to see what these women looked like, how they lived. I wanted to learn more about how they helped turn Paris into the capital of art, as pioneers of the major social changes at the end of the 19th and beginning of the 20th century.

Women who helped set aside academic art and revolutionised the avant-garde. I wanted to get to know them through portraits, photographs, in the images of silent cinema. I also watched a lot of filmed material and researched information online. I discovered even more amazing women, creators, and it was necessary to talk about them.

My close friend Jeanette Bos, who lives in Paris, became involved in the book from the first draft and was of great help; she was the person who could verify certain things. The entire process took a year and a half, but I loved every moment of it.

It was a very personal journey, a dialogue between friends who shared a fascination for art and, most importantly, an admiration for the women who managed to create and fight to be recognised. You could say *"Women who made the evolution of art possible"*.

We could not possibly cover all the artists, male and female, and influential people, such as gallery owners, collectors, etc. that put a stamp on this paramount important period in the history of art. And having included some stories found during our research, such as films, documentaries and written texts, I'd like to clarify that the information was sometimes contradictory. We had to make a choice based on our personal preferences.

I'd like to invite you to read this book with an open mind and heart. Just enjoy the journey. I very much hope reading this book may inspire you to get to know Paris through the eyes of the creatives who lived there.

Perhaps you will change your view, like Jeanette when she told me "*I've been living in Paris for over thirty years, but I can honestly say that I now look at the city with different eyes, almost rediscovering it, seeing things I had not noticed before or taken for granted.*"

And something happened to me too! As I started exploring the Parisian art world, I felt inspired to create portraits of several women featured in this book. Telling their stories through my paintings and through the written word. I want to honour them with my art like we are honouring them in this book.

The women in these portraits look straight into your eyes. They want to touch your soul, your awareness, ask you to see them for who they were, to acknowledge them.

My message with this book is one of hope, of understanding the power of the human spirit to survive in difficult times, using art to bring about change!

For more information about my art, I invite you to visit my website. www.renatevannijen.com

Renate

Introduction

Do you know that feeling of finding yourself in the middle of a large city, not really knowing where to go, and feeling lost? You came to visit landmarks, beautiful buildings, interesting sites, perhaps wanting to find out about art and history, visiting museums, but you don't even notice the beautiful architectural surroundings because you are too stressed out to find the right information, the correct metro, train or bus and you are overwhelmed by too much traffic, people, perhaps unknown smells? You stand out like a sore thumb as the tourist on a city break and it's not necessarily the shorts and flip-flops that give that away.

Would you like to explore Paris in a different way? Being guided by its history paved by great artists and in particular the women who once walked its streets? Have a really special experience, as if you are entering into the story? A story about the past, about the how and the why of the remarkable sites for you to visit. You will not be a tourist, rather a part of the stories, as you dive into the past and sense what it must have been like for the artists. Great painters, writers, musicians, and the women who inspired them.

You will learn about how most female artists didn't get the recognition they deserved. These men and women who turned Paris into the vibrant city it still is today.

You will discover a different Paris, in a unique, coloured way, sketched by words. Stories that will guide you through its avenues, parks and boulevards. You will climb into the minds of the protagonists that have been there before you. Those men and women who weren't famous when they walked the streets of Paris, like you are doing today, whether that is in person or from the comfort of your home.

So, who are you?

Are you a tourist or an adventurer? A tourist is a person who travels and visits places for pleasure and interest. The pleasure of visiting those impressive monuments, taking a few selfies next to the Eiffel tower and then sharing these photos on social media. A tourist travels and consumes a product, but doesn't necessarily live what they see. There is nothing wrong with that. Being a tourist can be great, just away from daily chores and obligations. But what would it be like to be a discoverer, a non-tourist?

Going on a trip full of surprises, sensing the essence of those who came to join a vibrant artist scene and of those who inspired these artists? A sense of the women who were brave enough to fight for their existence, who weren't heard and acknowledged, but were definitely seen. These women who left their soul in Paris.

What will you discover?

Firstly, we will guide you through the architectural landscape of Paris. This grand city where the stories in this book, which can be used as a guidebook, took place. Whilst you embark on this very special journey you will discover what Napoleon III and Hausmann did. You will learn about the bourgeoisie and their dislikes, yet fascination for arts and literature. You will find out about the different art movements and styles that were replacing the Romanticism era, which was based on the old Greek classics with large paintings showing historical combats, mythological scenes and later, portraits of important rulers and noblemen, and paintings of perfectly depicted women who don't look at the viewer of the painting. The Venuses of the time.

You will get to know the artists by their art and their muses, the women who were the source of their love, their inspiration, their existence, their hardship and their rise to fame, changing the landscape of art in an important time in history. Those women who weren't heard at the time. With this book I want to give them a name and a voice. I want to honour these women who you will get to know through the stories of artists you will have heard of. You will get to know their lives, the buildings they lived in and how they influenced this important change in art and literature in the Paris of their epoch.

How will you find out you might wonder?

Let me tell you a story. My name is Renate and I'm a Dutch artist and writer. I live in La Herradura, a small seaside village in Andalusia, Spain. My life as an artist and writer was, and is, about creating and diving into my soul to discover new avenues to explore. Getting inspired by observing my surroundings. The passers-by who became the protagonists in my stories, expressed with brushes and the written word. But I also realised that when I go to a museum, there usually is more art by men than by women. Especially art from the 'old days', artworks made by men that represent women. The woman is in the hands of the man who creates. She is the inspiration, but she also is a slave of the creation and I just felt there was something wrong with that, something was missing. Then I met Mario.

Mario was born in Paris as a child of Spanish immigrants. From a very young age he was interested in art. He was raised in a district where a lot of artists worked. He and his family lived on the seventh floor of a Hausmann building. His mother worked as a housekeeper for people with lots of money who lived on lower floors in the building.

Mario was often allowed to come with her. As a very young boy he remembers being fascinated by the abundance of paintings, shiny art objects and African masks, which were the height of fashion in the sixties in Paris. It sparked an interest in him that has never left him. From early in his life he felt he was born to find out, study and explore the great artists and the women who they met. Those men and women who had such a strong influence on the city of Paris, the city so many people love! He felt the desire to explain this to those who could not see, sense or understand the why of the minds of artists who lived in Paris from 1850 to 1940. Mario was born to collect this knowledge and share it with others and I am the writer who has become his 'vehicle'!

Why may this interest you?

You could say that art, in all its forms, including architecture, literature, music, etc. connects and divides. It can grab you, disgust you, fascinate you, tell stories, provoke, endear, record history. Art plays with reality and evokes an emotion, so who is the artist who created that emotion? Who was he or she inspired by? Who were those women who paved the way to freedom for other women, sometimes without even knowing it?

Perhaps you also like to discover their stories, to understand them, learn from them. But most of all I invite you to feel Paris, 'her' soul, past and present through the history of art and the amazing men and especially women who are showing us their power.

Mario and I will 'walk you' through the city and we will have conversations. This is a personal story of a magical visit to Paris! It's not a travel guide, but Mario is guiding me on this trip to Paris. Will you join us?

Haussmann's Paris

A décor for a new art world

Perhaps you've visited Paris before, or maybe this is your first time, but when you look around you, you may notice that the buildings along the avenues and boulevards of Paris all look very much alike. And you're right! Although these buildings are impressive and a triumph of the architecture of the time, it can be said that they have a certain charm and beauty, with their typical, elegantly twisted, cast-iron balconies. The monumental appearance, the dark-coloured roofs with dormers, the large rectangular windows and facades made of 'pierre de taille' give a sense of importance, of grandeur.

Haussmann-style buildings have six or seven floors, and each building had to be similar to the one next to it. Certainly, these buildings may seem uniform, and the details may not be obvious at first glance. It can even feel overwhelming, unless you delve into the history behind the why there are so many large buildings in the same style. When you understand the history behind a building or the reason for a certain architectural style, everything comes to life. You see things with different eyes.

We are in the Sèvres-Babylone district on boulevard Raspail, surrounded by Haussmann buildings and not far from the river Seine. It has started to rain and we decide to go to a café with the same name. The atmosphere in Café Raspail is warm and welcoming, with its elegant Art Deco interior and impressive 'trompe l'oeil' ceiling depicting a large plate of fruits, vegetables and kitchen utensils. We order a coffee with croissants and I listen to Mario.

"In order to understand this uniformity in the Haussmann buildings in Paris, we have to go back to the period before 1850. It was already a big city with around one million inhabitants, and growing rapidly, as more and more people flocked to Paris in search of work. However, it was a medieval city, with its labyrinthine, narrow, dirty, and poorly lit streets.

At the time, France was ruled by Napoleon III, Napoleon I's nephew, and he wanted to put an end to this. Noble as it may seem, he also had another reason for doing so. Napoleon III had previously visited London and was impressed by what he saw, including the architecture in steel and glass. Inspired by London, he wanted to go bigger and better and turn Paris into the symbol of imperial France, showcasing its greatness. To achieve this, Napoleon III commissioned Haussmann, who was the prefect of Paris, to carry out this enormous project. Haussmann met with urban planners and with bankers to secure large loans and Napoleon gave him carte blanche for this monumental project.

Paris was in the midst of the industrial revolution and apart from creating new buildings, they also built large train stations, such as Gare St. Lazare and Gare de Lyon, to facilitate the transportation of goods into the heart of Paris, Les Halles Baltard. This was a covered market with huge pavilions constructed in glass and metal, two signs of modernity. This is one of the great legacies of La Belle Époque and Haussmann's Paris. Les Halles Baltard no longer exists; it was destroyed, despite significant protests, and was replaced by a shopping centre.

Paris was creating its new history. The train stations also facilitated the travel of visitors, who started coming to Paris to visit what was becoming the capital of business, art, and pleasure. A lot of what we see in Paris nowadays, strolling along the avenues and boulevards that cross Paris from north to south, east to west, is related to the Paris of the mid-19th century. The most striking of the infrastructure are the straight lines.

A very clear example of the grandeur of the Haussmann project is the Paris Opera quarter, where you can find Palais Garnier, created by architect Charles Garnier in 1875. This impressive building houses a distinguished auditorium; its ceiling was painted by Marc Chagall in 1964. Its avenue connects it to the Louvre. The wide, tall buildings, very similar to each other, give the whole city a monumental appearance, as do department stores like Le Printemps and Le Bon Marché, turning Paris into the most modern capital of its time.

But it wasn't just about grandeur. Can you imagine how it was before, without a sewage system? People had to drink water from the Seine, and many even went there to wash themselves. It's no wonder it was an era of epidemics and cholera was one of the leading causes of death. To prevent these epidemics and ensure that all the dirty water left the city, Napoleon III decided to build a sewage network, unique in the world. They constructed kilometres of sewage canals beneath the city that allowed the water to flow out of Paris. These are still in use today. It was a significant undertaking, as you can imagine. Additionally, they created a gas and water system throughout the city. It was the triumph of the industrial revolution.

Existing houses had to make way for five to seven-story buildings to accommodate the growing number of people in Paris. From 1853 to 1870, thirty thousand properties were demolished, and forty thousand new buildings were built. Paris went from having twelve boroughs to the twenty that exist today, and its population grew by over five hundred thousand inhabitants. Haussmann's buildings were occupied by people from all social classes. The very modest and humble people lived on the upper floors. These were called 'chambre de bonnes', for domestic staff. They had their separate entrance to avoid mingling with the bourgeoisie, and of course, there were no elevators.

Later, when rents increased, the less privileged people had to move to the suburbs. The ground floor of the buildings was mainly used for commercial enterprises, such as clothing stores, tailors, and hat shops. The workshops for these shops were on the first floor. Wealthy people lived on the second and third floors. Haussmann was obsessed with straight lines in everything he built. He made all the avenues and boulevards straight, and many of them lead to impressive monuments.

There were good reasons for this. At the time, people used horse-drawn carriages, and the wide avenues facilitated access for those selling goods in the central market of Paris. But Paris was also a revolutionary city and the wide, long streets could impede the construction of barricades and facilitate the quick arrival of the army to conflict areas. This would also discourage crime and maintain public order.

Another vision of Napoleon III was to include plenty of green spaces in the city. Parks such as Les Buttes Chaumont and the Parc Montsouris. In fact, there is a park in every neighbourhood of Paris. Welcoming oases of fresh air and relative quietude in the midst of a modern city. When we visit Paris nowadays, we see something else that contrasts with the straight lines, the famous metro entrances designed by Hector Guimard. Apart from the train stations, an enormous metro network was created. The entrances have curved lines that imitate branches and plants, and some have glass roofs. The Porte Dauphine and Châtelet metro stations are two examples of this style.

It was a time of many changes, and Paris was also a city of many Expositions Universelles, which are world exhibitions, that showcased progress in science, technology, and industry. The construction of the metro was part of the 1900 world exhibition. It has to be said that the metro entrances were not only inspired by nature but also by feminine forms, with their elegant lines, sensual designs, featuring curves reminiscent of women. It was the beginning of the Art Nouveau period. The first world exhibition was in 1855, and some structures were created to showcase technological, scientific, and industrial advances to the world. It was an interesting time with many new inventions, such as electricity in 1906.

The Eiffel Tower, created in 1889, to be part of the 1900 world exhibition, is a great example. Interestingly, not many people know that this eye-catching tower was almost destroyed as entrepreneur Gustave Eiffel only had a twenty-year permit to use the land. However, they had installed a giant radio antenna on the tower, which literally saved it from destruction! At the time Paris became known as the 'La Ville Lumière' as there used to be magnificent light displays during the Expositions Universelles, but most of the buildings and structures were removed after the exhibitions."

How fascinating Mario. I'm one of those people who never really knew the history of the Eiffel Tower. It just was the symbol of Paris to me.

"I think that is the same for many people. But getting to know the history of a place brings it to life, I believe. Not sure whether that is the same for you?"

Yes, it certainly does.

"Although all the industrial advances and changes to the city may be impressive, it is fair to say that it also upset many people that the old town of the city had to disappear to a great extent. The city centre, where we can now find the Nôtre Dame, 'L'île de la cité' was almost completely destroyed. It received a lot of criticism, especially from writers, because Paris had a certain medieval charm. Nowadays, you can still find this architecture, with its narrow streets, around Le Marais, near the Jewish quarter of Paris.

One of these writers, who was quite specific about this, was Charles Baudelaire a French poet. He witnessed the destruction of much of Paris, including his own home in rue Hautefeuille where he was born. He reflected this in his poem *Le Cygne* as he states "*Le vieux Paris n'est plus*" (Paris is no more)… "*Ce qu'il y a d'enivrant dans le mauvais goût, c'est le plaisir aristocratique de déplaire*" (What is exhilarating in bad taste is the aristocratic pleasure of giving offense). He feels orphaned and a victim of change as according to him literary life was going to die in a society of pleasure and luxury, sonorous violence through the noise of modernity. It has to be said that Baudelaire, he himself born into a well-off family, always was a flâneur of Paris and known for his quote "*Je t'aime ô capitale infâme*" (I love you infamous capital city).

After Hausmann's death, at the age of eighty-two, the works continued until World War I. Certainly, one could say that the late 19th and early 20th centuries were times entirely dominated by men. The strong buildings of Haussmann and the grand avenues and boulevards give Paris a very masculine feel. But upon closer inspection, Paris also had a lot to do with women. The lush green parks that invited women to come with their families for a walk or a picnic. Lower-class prostitutes and courtesans attracted men from all over the world, and artists flocked to the city to find inspiration in female models."

Mario promises me that we will delve deeper into the influence of women on the design and architecture of Paris. After finishing breakfast, we leave the café and pass the house of sculptor Rodin, near the edge of the Seine, now a museum and worth a visit, both for its art collection and for its beautiful sculpture garden. We are also close to the Musée d'Orsay, the museum that showcases all the art of the Belle Époque. Walking to the left, Mario points out the magnificent Pont Alexandre III. Across the river, we see Le Grand Palais and Le Petit Palais. We are going to pay a short visit to Le Petit Palais.

I almost feel overwhelmed by the sheer beauty of the building itself, with its ionic columns and grand, golden porch. It was designed by Charles Girault and built for the 1900 world exhibition. It became a museum in 1902 and to this day you can admire its permanent collection free of charge. When we walk through the grand entrance, we go to the circular courtyard and garden. I love the stylish floors of the covered pavement terrace with the painted ceiling surrounding the garden, part of which is a welcoming café-restaurant, the Jardin du Petit Palais. What really caught my attention is the entrance with large white sculptures and big windows that flood the space with light. Inside Le Petit Palais there is also a lot of art, among others by painters of the Academic and the Realism style. For example, the painting *Le Sommeil* by Gustav Courbet of two women kissing and we are looking at a painting by Mary Cassat, called *Le Bain*. The permanent collection also contains furniture, sculptures and much more. It really is a very beautiful mixture of Academic and Realism art.

I'm fascinated, but there is so much more to see, so after our visit we walk to the Champs-Élysées Clemenceau metro station. We notice the statue of Georges Benjamin Clemenceau, who became the Prime Minister of France from 1906 to 1920. He was an important figure and close friends with Monet. We enter the metro station and emerge a few minutes later at one of the best examples of an Art Nouveau-style metro entrance, Châtelet.

Art Nouveau

Nature and women

When we exit the Châtelet metro station situated in the centre of Paris, near the Seine, I take a few pictures of the Art Nouveau style exit wondering about Hector Guimard, who designed it. Who was he? What inspired him? I admire the sensual shapes and forms, made of iron with stretches of glass, resembling tree branches and the wings of an insect. I have always liked Art Nouveau, and yes, I can say that it evokes emotions in me. Perhaps because my art and some of my stories are rather sensual, so I can identify with that. I'm curious to find out more about this art movement in Paris. Especially about the role women played during this period, as their presence can clearly be seen in art, sculptures, and the curves and feminine forms in Art Nouveau.

We are walking in the direction of the Musée des Arts Décoratifs. Just like the Châtelet exit, the museum is situated in rue de Rivoli and Mario is going to explain about Art Nouveau. It's very busy in the streets, but I feel like walking in the décor of a modern story revealing its past. I see a mixture of people going about their day and it is easy to spot the tourists. It is May, and the sun is pleasantly warm. I believe that the best time to visit Paris is either during spring time or autumn and I feel happy and privileged to get this private tour. Mario says...

"Paris is a city of abundance. You are surrounded by art; it's everywhere, and it's not just about visual arts like paintings. It's a very visual city in terms of its architecture, impressive lobbies, entrances, staircases, and interiors. There are plenty of shops that give you an idea of those old times when Paris was becoming an art city. Although many have visited the city of love, often depicted in travel guides and movies with romantic images of the Seine and world-famous monuments, not many truly immerse themselves in the soul of the city. Art Nouveau is a great example of art in Paris. But what exactly is Art Nouveau?

It is primarily a form of ornamental art, characterised by its organic lines and used mainly in interior design, architecture, illustration, and also in jewellery. You can find it in the interiors of Art Nouveau buildings with sensual staircases, ornaments, and furniture. It's almost like a musical style with all its curves. In Paris, you can visit some department stores, for example, Les Galeries Lafayette, which has many Art Nouveau features, especially in its interior, such as the impressive dome. If you haven't seen it yet, I highly recommend that you do.

This new art movement began around 1890 in Belgium. It emerged during a period of classical architecture, characterised by straight lines and technological advancements. In contrast, Art Nouveau drew inspiration from nature and feminine forms. It aimed to unite decoration and architecture in harmony, like a dream. It challenged classical art with its unconventional forms. The facades of buildings, balconies, staircases, portals, and furniture, all adorned with sensual and fantastical forms. It was also a rebellion against the dominant art of the time, which was of the old school, very realistic. In Belgium, architect Victor Pierre Horta was one of the founders of the Art Nouveau movement. For example, Hôtel Tassel is considered to be the first Art Nouveau house in Brussels.

In Paris, when someone mentions the name Hector Guimard, everyone knows that he was the designer of the metro entrances and exits and an architect and designer of this movement in France. We know that Guimard met Horta. Guimard was twenty-eight years old when he constructed a building called Castel Beranger, in 14 rue Jean de La Fontaine, featuring wallpaper, balconies, and windows in Art Nouveau style. Every detail, including the furniture, was carefully designed. He achieved early fame with this first Art Nouveau apartment building in Paris. In 1900, the construction of subway entrances was entrusted to Guimard, and he captured a perfect alliance of metal, glass, and lacquered lava.

Paris boasts magnificent examples of Art Nouveau, where women and nature are represented through curved and arabesque motifs. Some artists drew upon Japanese art to create their pieces, as seen in certain building entrances. Artists and designers used flowers, trees, lilies, ferns, poppies and often peacocks, a bird with a flower-like appearance, as well as insects in their designs. They felt inspired by these elements, creating masterpieces of decorative art. Some of them skilfully blending glass and metal. Glass was often used to create a thick, watery effect resembling the bottom of a pond. Actresses of the time also inspired this artistic movement. Some great actresses and courtesans were depicted as both light and perverse, frivolous and goddess-like.

The obsession with women was prevalent in Art Nouveau. Women with long hair and stylised arms, appearing as if they were dancing, were featured in posters by artists such as Alphonse Mucha, a Czechoslovak artist. Mucha moved to Paris in 1888. He used this art style for his theatre posters and soap packaging. He became well known in Paris in 1895 thanks to his theatre poster for Gismonda (1894), created for superstar Sarah Bernhardt. It marked the beginning of recognition for his distinctive style, known as the Mucha Style. This established him as an important artist. Sarah loved his work, and they became friends. She offered him a contract to create costume and set designs. He also produced six more posters for her productions. All these posters had the same elongated format. The actress appeared in a sort of shallow niche. Both the artist and Sarah benefited from their collaboration as his work helped elevate her to an iconic status. This is a great example of the influence of women in art.

It has to be said that Art Nouveau was not immediately accepted by the ruling classes and aristocrats. It was quite scandalous. It was called the work of the devil, and in a time of rampant anti-Semitism, it was referred to as Jewish art. It was also claimed that Guimard was of Jewish descent, but, interestingly, he had participated in a competition for the design of the Paris metro entrances and won. In itself a victory for art.

The undulating forms of Art Nouveau broke away from straight lines and this was seen as wild and unorthodox, without rules or codes to adhere to. There were even restrictions on young girls taking the subway,

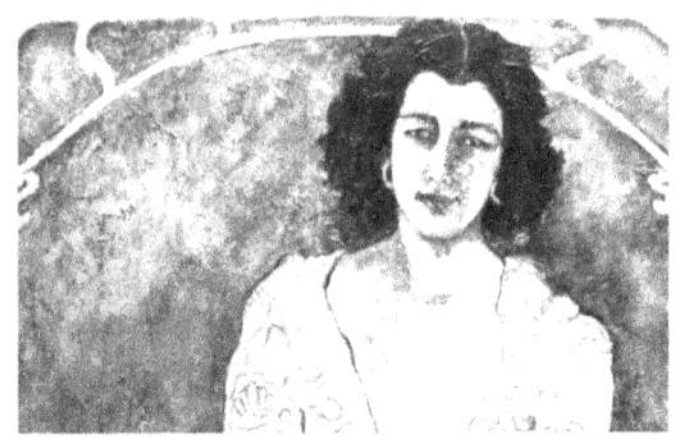

Sarah Bernhardt

because of the erotic appearance of the entrance, it was considered a sin. As women, at the time, were seen as both poisonous and alluring in a male-dominated society, it doesn't really come as a surprise that an art that celebrates the female form was felt like a threat.

Women were also seen as weak, fragile, and prone to nervous disorders. The famous neurologist Jean-Martin Charcot, associated the Art Nouveau movement with madness, labelling it as 'style nouille', a term that roughly translates to 'noodles'. For some it represented madness in motion. It was also seen as a manifestation of uncontrollable disorders. Therefore, it was considered a dangerous art form that could disrupt the established order and cause illness or degeneration in the French society at that time.

All this demonstrates how important art is, because Art Nouveau was a rebellious movement against the masculine style of art and architecture in the late eighteen hundreds. And it didn't take long for the bourgeoisie to fall in love with the curved shapes and forms with their arabesque influences. High-society women became consumers, purchasing Art Nouveau products from luxurious warehouses, such as Le Printemps, to decorate their homes. It became highly fashionable and influenced their fashion choices. The women of that time wore long dresses, feathers, flowers, and hats as part of their attire. It even extended to women's hairstyles, as they let their hair grow long, reminiscent of movement, the way it seems to fly with the wind. You could say that women embodied nature in their clothing, inspired by eastern cultures and Japan in particular. This contributed to the Western man's dreams of such sensual and exotic women.

Art Nouveau meant a change in women's clothing as well. During the first period the S-shape was still fashionable, which was created by wearing a corset to make the breasts and bottom stick out. But during the Art Nouveau period there were female designers who had started off with the S-shape but then abandoned the corset to create a more fluid silhouette. I will point out two of them who were very successful, also internationally.

Jeanne Paquin was one of them. She was a well-known fashion designer, famous for her luxurious lingerie and tango-style dresses. She was the most important female couturier of her time and you could see the influence of the Egyptian and Chinese culture in her designs. She was born Jeanne Marie Beckers. In 1891 she married Isidore René Jacob who owned Paquin Lalanne et cie, a couture house. In that same year, Jeanne and Isidore opened Maison de Couture at 3 rue de la Paix in Paris. Jeanne was very innovative and used strong colours. Black and red became her signature, which was interesting as traditionally black was seen as a colour of mourning. But she used to blend the black fabrics with colourful linings and trims.

Then there were also the Callot Soeurs, which became one of the leading fashion design houses by the end of the Art Nouveau period. They first opened their business in 1895 at 24, rue Taitbout in Paris. It was run by four sisters, Marie, Marthe, Regina and Joséphine. Marie, the eldest sister was actually trained as a dress-maker and they were all taught by their mother, who was a lacemaker. They were very successful and were at the forefront of changing the style of women's clothing into a more liberated style. This was especially obvious during the twenties, which is now known as the Art Deco period. These must have been strong women to be so successful in business in a time where women were not considered equal to men.

It is also important to realise that women had an indirect influence on the success of Art Nouveau at the time. Bourgeoise women started decorating their homes with lamps, jewellery, vases, and glass objects. For example, Art Nouveau vases by Emile Gallé who specialised in glass and porcelain vases, drawing inspiration from Japanese art, and who often engraved verses by poets on his works. But we should also mention René Lalique, well known for his creations of glass art, perfume bottles and jewellery. Examples of the magnificent works of both Gallé and Lalique can be admired today in the Musée des Arts Décoratifs, which we are about to visit.

We could say that Art Nouveau brought humans closer to nature in a world of technology and great advancements. This fusion was evident in the decoration of houses, especially those bourgeois homes. Sadly, Art Nouveau didn't last long. Its peak period ended around 1910. It was only in fashion for a relatively short time. It could be said that it went out of style, as is the case with many prominent architectural or design styles.

Even so, it made a comeback in the twenties and thirties when surrealist artists started to reclaim Art Nouveau. Surrealism also evokes dreams and fantasy, and they valued that. And more recently, in the sixties and seventies, the Underground movement, which was against the dominant culture, brought back this interesting style once again, which can be seen in concert posters like the 1969 Woodstock Rock Musique Festival poster. You could say that it was part of the hippie movement, especially in art and writing, with elegant and curvilinear lettering. During the eighties, Art Nouveau disappeared again as a style, but nowadays many still love and admire this fascinating art movement, much appreciated in the world of antiques."

That's true and I'm certainly one of these people. I love the elegance of it and, actually during the preparation for this trip I've started creating a series of paintings with a clear Art Nouveau influence. I'm really happy with the result. It started off with some faces of unknown women. I've never worked with models; everything springs from my imagination, so these women just 'appeared'. But I've now decided to honour the women that we will talk about in this, to me, very special journey, by painting my impression of them. I'm excited, not just for this trip and the artworks that it inspires me to create, but also for the book that might entice you to come and visit Paris and discover this fascinating art history and the women who helped create it, seen through the eyes of a Dutch artist.

On our way to the Museum of Decorative Arts we pass some interesting antique shops that also sell Japanese art and furniture, and we check out Galerie Vivienne, a covered shopping mall built in 1823, where we visit an oriental shop that sells paravents, Chinese figures and kimonos. This really brings me in the mood to learn about yet another interesting period that created a shift in the work of quite a few artists that we all know. We enter the Musée des Arts Décoratifs.

Japonisme

An inspiring new trend

The name of the Musée des Arts Décoratifs says it all, and I am excited to see examples of decorative art. You never stop learning when you're open to it. Today, Mario explains to me what Japonisme is. There are many things I didn't know, and the more I immerse myself in this journey, the more fascinated I am to learn about what art, and especially women in art, have done for Paris.

The museum covers different types of decorative art, including the bed of Valtesse de la Bigne, one of the famous and wealthy courtesans in late nineteen-century Paris. The bed is decorated with gilt bronze and green silk velvet. I've seen photos, but it will be a different experience to see it in person. Just imagine the stories that bed could tell. But right now, I'm going to learn about Japonisme and I expect to see some examples of Japanese decorative arts. In fact, since the founding of the museum in 1864, it has presented and preserved Japanese art in France. So what is Japonisme?

"In 1850, Japan started trading with the rest of the world. Before that, it was very isolated and the Japanese refused all contact with the outside world. In Paris, tea houses opened, and shops began selling Japanese art and prints. It became very fashionable, and both artists and writers collected Japanese prints and paintings. For example, Émile Zola, a French novelist and journalist, was known for his collection. We also know that Édouard Manet, a French painter who was one of the precursors of the Impressionist movement, liked to include Japanese-style imagery in his art, as did many other artists of the time. The department stores, like Le Bon Marché and La Samaritaine, started selling Japanese products such as prints, kimonos, embroidered dresses, decorative screens, and more.

It's important to remember that Academic art in France was inspired by Classical art. It was a very rational style of art, with a lot of balance and symmetry. Japanese art, on the other hand, was considered more childlike; it doesn't have a central focus and doesn't require symmetry or balance.

Now we refer to this art style as Japonisme. Japanese art and literature influenced many artists in Western Europe. It was an artistic style that was fashionable in Paris from 1870 to the early 19th century. It was during the same period that Art Nouveau became popular. In 1890, there was a significant exhibition featuring works by famous Japanese artists. They printed catalogues, books, magazines, prints, and it was highly successful.

The elite of that time were bored with the old French art and were always looking for something new. Artists were attracted to more primitive forms of art and found inspiration in exotic cultures, such as Polynesia, Eastern cultures, Japan, and Africa. This Japanese art style spread throughout Europe and particularly to Vienna. Art lovers in Vienna started buying Japanese art prints, and this greatly inspired artists like Klimt, who had a large collection of Japanese prints and created many artworks featuring women in kimonos. He even liked to wear a kimono himself.

Artists sought inspiration outside of France. For example, Gauguin, who went to Polynesia to find the primitive, dreamlike, and spiritual side of art. Japonisme is especially interesting for its influence on artists throughout Europe. Even music was inspired by it, with composers such as Charles-Camille Saint-Saëns writing symphonies dedicated to Japan, and the opera *Madame Butterfly* by Giacomo Puccini. You can also think of composers who created operettas, which are a type of light opera, partially sung and partially spoken. One of the most famous of the time was Gilbert and Sullivan's *The Mikado*.

Another great example of Japanese influence is the work of Vincent van Gogh."

I'm fascinated when Mario explains that from the more than nine hundred letters he wrote to his brother, we know that Van Gogh said that his entire body of work was based on Japanese art and that it was the beginning of Impressionism for him, representing a different use of colour and movement.

"That's right. His famous paintings of the starry sky clearly give the impression that they are inspired by the Japanese wave paintings of Katsushika Hokusai. In one of his paintings, *Portrait of Père Tanguy*, which Van Gogh painted when he was in Paris in 1887, Japonisme is very evident. He wrote that he wanted Japan to be within him. In 1888, he created a self-portrait with a partially shaved head, resembling a Buddhist monk, and in the background, you can see the blooming almond trees so typical of Japanese art. Van Gogh was actually a devoted follower of Zen Buddhism. He dreamt of creating a community of artists living like Japanese monks. Henri de Toulouse-Lautrec was also influenced by Japanese art, and a good example is his painting called *Le Divan Japonais*, which pays homage to the cabaret. Neither he nor Van Gogh ever visited Japan. Van Gogh moved to Arles in southern France, where he felt surrounded by the colours of Japan.

And the story continues. In 1990, Akira Kurosawa, a Japanese film director, created a movie called 'Dreams', consisting of eight parts. One of which is 'Crows'. It tells the story of a student who finds himself inside 'Korenveld met kraaien' (Wheatfield with Crows) a painting by Van Gogh.

Japonisme was important for artists in Paris back then, but even today, you can still sense this passion for Japan in Paris. A millionaire named Emile Guimet, who visited China, Japan, and India, created a museum of Japanese and Oriental art in Paris in a popular and elegant area, known as Musée Guimet, also referred to as the National Museum of Asian Arts. Worth mentioning is that there are three pagodas in Paris. A pagoda is a tiered tower with multiple eaves common to Nepal, China, Japan, Korea, Myanmar, Vietnam, and other parts of Asia. They were usually built for religious functions as seen in Buddhism and Taoism. One of the three pagodas in Paris, La Pagode was turned into a cinema and films were shown from 1931 to 2015. It was constructed by architect Alexandre Marcel in rue de Babylone, and was a gift from François-Émile Morin, the director of Le Bon Marché warehouse, to his wife.

It is clear that there were quite a few Japanese influences in Paris, and it's easy to see that artists of the time were influenced by this, including Paul Gauguin, Georges Seurat, and Paul Cézanne. We also know that Edgar Degas, Claude Monet, and James Tissot were fervent collectors of Japanese art.

Art was, and I would argue still is, dominated by male artists, and this certainly was true, even more so, during the times we talk about now. Nevertheless, there was one female artist known for being influenced by Japanese art as well. This was the American artist Mary Cassatt, who came to Paris in the late nineteenth century and made it her home. She was good friends with Edgar Degas, who created the artwork *Au Louvre*, depicting Mary Cassatt and another woman believed to be her older sister, Lydia. The sisters lived in a small apartment on rue de Laval, which is now rue Victor Massé. This street was a hotspot for artists' homes and studios. Although Mary is considered an impressionist artist, she, along with many of her artist colleagues, was inspired by woodblock prints by Japanese artists Katsushika Hokusai and Utagawa Hiroshige. We will delve deeper into Mary's story later."

We have discussed the Paris of the Haussmann's renovations, the renewal of Paris, and how Art Nouveau and Japonisme were significant movements. It's been a long day and we go back to our hotel, but there is still much more to learn and I'm eager to find out how artists and writers have changed the history of art. Not only in Paris but around the world!

Realism

A changing art world

After a good night's sleep, I meet Mario for an early breakfast at the hotel. It looks like it's going to be another sunny spring day. I'm grateful that I took my walking boots with me as today we will do quite a bit of walking.

We will pass through different types of neighbourhoods, to get the feel of the Paris of today, but also a feel for the Paris during La Belle Epoque. During our walk Mario will share information with me about Realism. I like these walks as I can see the beautiful buildings and impressive avenues where writers and artists used to either live, or come to, in order to get their inspiration.

We start in Place du Palais-Royal in 204 rue Saint-Honoré, in front of Palais Royal which was built in 1639. It was the residence of Cardinal Richelieu the Chief Minister to Louis XIII. It is eight o'clock in the morning and we pay a quick visit to get an impression of the galleries and gardens.

We then continue our walk and go to the east of Paris, in the direction of L'avenue de l'Opéra where we are going to pay a visit to Palais Garnier, also referred to as Le Opera de Paris. It is a great symbol of Haussmann's Paris.

We booked tickets for a guided tour in advance, which is recommendable. I feel like we have stepped into another era. The grandness of everything, it is a feast for the eyes, a challenge for the brain, well for my brain. How did they do all this? All this abundance, created by talented architects, artists and designers.

After our visit we continue our walk via boulevard Haussmann, which will turn into boulevard Montmartre, in the direction of place de la Republique where we will have our lunch break. On our way, there are many places of interest, such as a wax museum, Musée Grévin, but we decide to enter Passage Jouffroy, a covered arcade that takes you back in time. Its tiled floors, the glass ceiling and wrought iron details create a perfect setting for a variety of shops selling antiques, books and much more. There is even a hotel. Curiously, the exit of the Grévin wax Museum is located inside Passage Jouffroy. It's considered to be one of the nicest remaining Passages Couverts as they are called. It was built in 1846 and connected one boulevard to another. I can totally imagine the wealthy ladies and gentlemen of the time coming here to do some shopping.

It becomes obvious to me that, at the time, the bourgeoisie was living a life of wealth and luxury. We arrive at place de la Republique where we have our lunch at a pavement café. Mario points out the statue of a woman, referred to as Marianne. This is the symbol for the French republic. Isn't it interesting? Not a man but a woman.

After lunch we have to walk uphill, passing through the neighbourhood where the working classes lived during the Second Empire; a neighbourhood that inspired Realism of great artists and writers, such as Émile Zola and Victor Hugo. It's been quite a long walk, and I am delighted when we arrive at a magnificent park called Les Buttes Chaumont, which was created for the Exposition Universelle de 1867. Today things have changed, and the area has become a mixture of all layers of society. Previously, it was an abandoned and an unhealthy place to live. A place where duals took place and burglars would come to hide. It was also known as the place where executions of people sentenced to death took place.

Napoleon III had a lot of power, but also wanted to serve the people. He created this park on a former limestone excavation site so that the workers could have a space to go to, a place with clean air. They even created a waterfall, a grotto, a lookout point, and a pond. All artificial and very well done. Even today, it is pleasant to see the greenery and nature in such a busy city like Paris. We sit on one of the numerous benches, happy to give our legs a rest. It's very pleasant here, a wonderful atmosphere, and I love seeing a great variety of people enjoying the park. All the different races and backgrounds create a colourful scene on this sunny day. Mario begins to explain about an important movement in Paris.

"We have talked about the second half of the nineteenth century when France was in a period of great economic prosperity. The other side of all this was the social reality of the working classes who lived in the east of Paris, those who built the buildings, the grand boulevards, the metro network, and monuments like the Eiffel Tower. This inequality was depicted by great authors like Émile Zola and Guy de Maupassant, but also shown in the works of realist painters like Manet and Courbet. These works of art were quite scandalous since art and literature used to portray perfection. For example, in art, women were depicted in perfect sizes and shapes to appear beautiful. The dominant artistic style was highly academic.

There was also a big problem with alcohol. Many workers drowned their miserable existence in alcohol, and alcoholism spread like wildfire. Painters and writers reflected this in their works. It was like taking a photograph of these realities. Honoré de Balzac was one of the first writers to touch on this subject in the early 19th century, but the most famous author known for his Realism was Émile Zola, who came from a bourgeois family. There were also other writers like Gustave Flaubert who scandalised with his book *Madame Bovary*. Realism in literature and art was judged and rejected by the ruling classes. Showing their way of life, for example, the face of a worker with an intensely sad expression in a painting, and writing about or portraying their suffering and the effects of alcoholism, was seen as vulgar. That's why it was heavily criticised.

People like Émile Zola documented the injustices and what alcoholism did to entire families. The harsh life of women who felt they had to engage in prostitution to survive or feed their families, and the men who turned to crime just to try to stay alive. There was a double standard. Wealthy men visited prostitutes but practically ignored the suffering that occurred in these lower classes, but artists and writers made it clear that society would benefit if people received a good education. Zola was a highly committed writer and journalist, demonstrating that if you were born into a poverty-stricken family plagued by alcoholism, it was unlikely that you would find a way out. And most of the time, that pattern would continue.

The only escape for women in poverty was to become prostitutes and hope to find a rich man. Even women who were artists, painters, writers, or worked in the theatre usually depended entirely on a man or their wealthy family. Or they received such little money that they had to sell their bodies. In a sense, it could be said that all these women, many of them anonymous, were shaping Paris. By being the principal theme of artists, by satisfying the needs of men from Paris and beyond. Men coming from all over Europe, to enjoy themselves in the city where prostitution was everywhere. It was actually considered a normal part of life.

A very important painter of the Realism movement was Édouard Manet, famous for his paintings *Olympia* and *Le Déjeuner sur l'herbe*. Manet and Zola were friends. What is interesting, considering that they both came from upper-class families, is that Manet and Zola were republicans and against Napoleon III. Manet played a key role for future painters and in a way was seen as the master or inspiration of the Impressionism movement. He was an intriguing artist. At that time, Manet's work was seen as provocative as it was a blend of Realism and Romanticism. Eugène Delacroix was seen as the leader of the French Romantic style, but Manet represented with his work the end of an era and the birth of modern art.

Manet was born into a Parisian bourgeois family and received a musical and literary education. He was a complex character and at some point, grew disillusioned with France and went to Spain. This became an important period in his life. He felt inspired by other artists such as Velázquez and Goya and created paintings of flamenco dancers and bullfighters. Back in France, Manet became close friends with Zola, who became a great advocate for his work. During that time, it was important for artists to be friends with writers and journalists who supported their work. He had painted his two most famous paintings, *Olympia* and *Le Déjeuner sur l'herbe*, and sent them to the salons to be exhibited. There were important salons where the art of renowned artists was showcased. This was around 1860. Manet's art was rejected though, and Zola defended him. In fact, he told the jury that they made a mistake, pointing out that Manet's paintings were alive.

This rejection forced Napoleon III to create another exhibition salon for artists who were not accepted. Interestingly, many of these rejected artists became very famous and admired by all. Manet was, of course, one of them. He was also one of the first painters to work outdoors, often taking his easel to the countryside to work with natural light. He painted many scenes of people dancing in the streets, in gardens, often focusing on women. We will talk about those women later as they were very important. Even today, the art world seems to focus on those men who changed the art scene, but the reality is that they couldn't have done it without the influence of women. It is important to realise this, but it is also paramount to explain Manet's work as it was so significant for what we now know as Impressionism. We can assume that Manet enjoyed finding inspiration in his travels as he also went to Brazil. Sadly, he returned ill with syphilis. Towards the end of his life, knowing he was going to die, he could no longer paint large canvases and started painting flowers in vases, inspired by Japonisme. He didn't want to give up painting. What is considered his last painting, *Le suicidé*, depicts a man who shot himself and is believed to represent his impending death."

Being an artist myself, I can imagine that he found solace in his painting, in the creation of art. But it must have been challenging as an artist to denounce the ruling classes. And I love learning the stories behind those famous artworks that we can still visit in the museums of Paris.

"Indeed, Manet's paintings *Olympia* and *Le Déjeuner sur l'herbe*, as well as Courbet's work, for example, his *L'Origine du monde* (The Origin of the World), caused a great scandal. But let's analyse Olympia first. It was painted in 1863-1865. We see a naked woman lying on a bed. This woman's name was Victorine Meurent. She was a French model and painter, accepted by the Académie des Beaux-Arts in 1879 and in the exhibitions of 1885 and 1904. She exhibited up to six times. To support herself better, she was modelling for various painters, including Toulouse-Lautrec and Manet.

There are some unusual and quite revolutionary aspects in the painting *Olympia*. She is not perfect. Her legs appear short, she has a round belly, small shoulders, and a rather square face, which is not in line with what was considered classical beauty. She wears a ribbon around her neck, which suggests the influence of Velázquez, and a flower in her hair. But she also wears pearls, a bracelet, and elegant shoes. Her hands cover her intimate parts, but it is not entirely clear whether she innocently covers them or if she is pleasuring

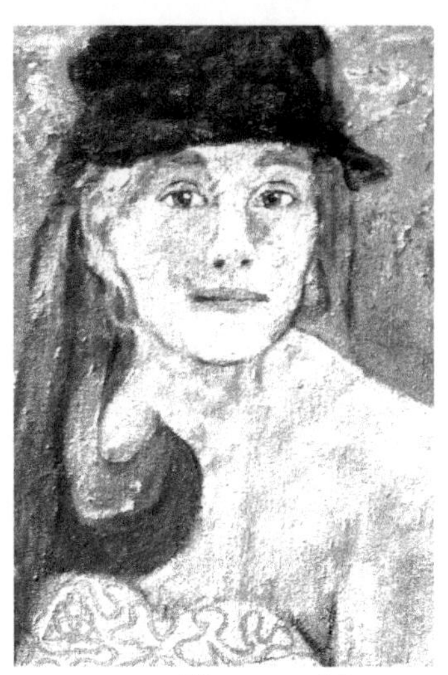

Victorine Meurent

herself. Behind her, we see a black woman, likely a servant, offering her a large bouquet of flowers. On the right, there is a black cat, which is significant as prostitutes were called 'chattes' (cats), and the woman's intimate part was also referred to as 'chatte' (pussy). Even more interesting is that she is looking directly into the viewer's eyes, who then becomes a participant by offering their reality. It is almost as if we become voyeurs, and that causes discomfort as it is a gaze of domination over the viewer.

Manet was seated when he painted *Olympia*, which creates more intimacy. This was also unusual as painters of the time always painted their scenes from above. The painting was ridiculed by the press and the art world in Paris. After Manet's death, his wife tried to sell *Olympia* to a wealthy American, but his artist friends gathered enough money to buy the painting and keep it in France. The painting represents the reality of the relationship between prostitutes and the upper class. In a sense, his painting *Le Déjeuner sur l'herbe*, originally titled *Le Bain*, which was created before *Olympia*, carries a similar message. Again, there is a naked woman looking directly into the viewer's eyes. This painting is set in the outdoors, believed to be near the Seine and his family's property in Gennevilliers. A picnic basket with some scattered food suggests that they are having a picnic. But no one is eating. There are two elegantly dressed men and another woman in the background. Among the trees next to a pond, a woman is bathing. This woman was a friend of Manet and later became the wife of Zola. The woman in the foreground is Victorine Meurent. Manet used images of people he knew in his paintings. One of the two men is said to be a combination of his two brothers, and the other man in the centre is his brother-in-law, the Dutch sculptor and painter Ferdinand Leenhoff.

The scandal of this painting is that it is not painted in a mythological or historical style, which was the prevailing and accepted trend of Romanticism at the time. It is also unusually large, which makes it even more intimate. It measures two hundred and eight by two hundred and sixty-four centimetres; this size was only used for historical, religious, or mythological paintings. When you look at the painting you may feel uncomfortable. Especially because the two men are fully dressed in dark colours as a total contrast to the naked whiteness of the female figure. The men talk to each other, she looks at us. Manet did not hide his brushstrokes, and even the painting appears somewhat unfinished in parts of the scene. He did not necessarily aim to provoke with his art but it had that effect. We actually know that he was a cheerful man.

As we mentioned, he was a friend of Émile Zola. Let's talk about the *Portrait de Émile Zola* that Manet painted in 1868. It is a fairly large painting as well, measuring one hundred and forty-six by one hundred and forty centimetres, and depicts the writer approximately a year after publishing his first novel, *Thérèse Raquin*. Interestingly, in this novel in the eleventh chapter, the scene from Manet's *Le Déjeuner sur l'herbe* is evoked in the crime scene, describing how the characters go out for the day in Saint-Ouen. This painting is an interesting work of art and, in a sense, a collaboration between two important figures in art and literature. In fact, after *Olympia* and *Le Déjeuner sur l'herbe* were rejected by the Salon, Zola created the catalogue for Manet's solo exhibition, and it is believed that the *Portrait of Émile Zola* is a gift of gratitude from Manet.

The painting shows Émile Zola sitting at a table with a book in his hands. On the left, we see a Japanese screen, in reference to the role that Far Eastern art and design played in revolutionising perspective and colour in the art of European painters. We also see a print of a Japanese wrestler by Utagawa Kuniaki II, an engraving of Velázquez's painting showing Manet's fascination with Spanish art, and underneath, we see a black and white print of *Olympia*. But when you look closely, you can see that the model is looking at Zola and not straight ahead like in the original painting. Overall, this artwork gives an excellent idea of the interests of these friends.

On the table, we see an oriental inkwell and a variety of papers and books, indicating that Zola was an avid writer. For example, the *Les Rougon-Macquart* series is a set of twenty novels, it tells the life of a family in the Second Empire. Stories about miners, alcohol, etc. In his extensive work, Zola reflected the life of the bourgeoisie and the working class. He was known for defending social injustice both in his books and as a journalist. At the time, anti-Semitism was increasing in France.

One story makes this very clear, now known as the *Dreyfus Affair*, which became a political scandal. In 1894, Captain Alfred Dreyfus, a thirty-five-year-old artillery officer of Jewish descent, was accused and convicted of treason. He was then imprisoned for communicating French military secrets to the German embassy in Paris. He was sent to Devil's Island in French Guiana, where he was held for almost five years. It was the year 1896 when George Picquart, who was the head of counter intelligence, identified a French army major, Ferdinand Walsin Esterhazy, as the true culprit. This evidence was later suppressed by high-ranking military officials, and Esterhazy was acquitted. Then, Émile Zola wrote an open letter, *J'accuse*, which was published in the newspaper *L'Aurore*, pressuring the government to reopen the case. In 1899, Dreyfus returned to France but was sentenced again to another ten years in a new trial. But, in 1906, Dreyfus was exonerated and reinstated as a major in the French army. He died in 1935.

Zola's outspoken opinion had created many enemies. He died under suspicious circumstances. Some claim that issues with the chimney, which caused Zola to die from asphyxiation while in bed with his wife, were not accidental. He was sixty-two years old at the time of his death. His wife survived him.

Another important artist at that time was Jean Désiré Gustave Courbet, a French painter and the most representative of Realism. He remained steadfast in painting only what he saw and rejected the Romanticism of the era. His favourite subject was painting the life of peasants, but his painting *L'Origine du monde* remains the most famous and scandalous.

Courbet began painting at a very young age. At the age of twenty, he would visit the Louvre Museum and copy works by Titian and Rubens. He was also studying law, but he did not complete it. He exhibited at the Salon in 1844 and even received a gold medal from the Salon jury for *L'Après-dînée à Ornans*, a work that preceded a large number of paintings depicting life in Ornans. Among them is *Un enterrement à Ornans*, a very large size painting, over three by six metres, depicting the funeral of an ordinary person. We don't even know who he or she is. The people in the image are not beautiful or perfect. The painting was criticised because it wasn't a historical or mythological scene. Courbet was committed to showing the reality of ordinary people's lives.

The painting for which he is most famous, *L'Origine du monde*, offering a very realistic view between the wide-open legs of a woman lying on her back, was created in 1866, but it wasn't a scandal right away. It was a commissioned work for a millionaire. It was never intended to be part of an exhibition. It remained in a private collection and was hidden for a long time. It is believed to have been later bought by a sultan and eventually ended up in the collection of the famous French psychoanalyst Jacques Lacan, considered the most controversial psychoanalyst since Freud. When *L'Origine du monde* came into public hands, it became a major scandal and remains controversial to this day.

Courbet was a deeply committed person and believed he could change the world. He was known for being anticlerical. He defended the working class, and his political activism - he was a republican socialist - meant that he was also against Napoleon III. His paintings depicted the reality of how humble people lived. He also participated in the Paris Commune; he and others supported the destruction of the column that stands in place Vendôme, which was a symbol of Napoleon's power. Due to his political involvement in the Commune, which was a French revolutionary government that seized power in Paris during the Franco-Prussian War from 18 March to 28 May 1871, Courbet lived in poverty until his death because he had to pay for the damages caused and the reconstruction of the column. These paintings by Manet and Courbet that we have just described are still in Paris and can be seen in the Musée d'Orsay."

It has been a long, but great day, with lots of impressions and learning about these artists that I knew little about. I feel like I am expanding my horizon, my creative horizon. That makes me feel happy.

Prostitution during the Belle Époque

A means to survive

We start our day at the Notre-Dame de Lorette, a Roman Catholic church in a neo-classical architectural style, located in 18 rue de Châteaudun and we are going to walk in the direction of the Champs-Élysées, to visit Hotel la Paiva. This is the part of Paris that used to be known for its many so-called maisons closes or brothels. On our way we are passing the Église de la Madeleine, a church in Parthenon style. It feels like a very wealthy area, and it used to be, but it was also a place where prostitution thrived.

Sometimes it was difficult to distinguish a prostitute from a bourgeoise woman, as we can see in some of the paintings by Jean Béraud, a French painter who was known for painting life in Paris. Paintings of elegant women, strolling along the boulevards, such as the Champs-Élysées and Montmartre. Images of people in large parks or at the race courses, and along the river Seine or in cafés. Detailing every day Parisian life during the Belle Époque, including apparent prostitutes waiting for a client. Mario explains why we started our day in front of the Notre-Dame de Lorette.

"Prostitution was widespread in Paris in the late 19th and early 20th centuries. It was the final period of the Belle Époque. One could say that Paris was the brothel of the world considering the number of prostitutes there. High-class courtesans captivated thousands of men. Of course, the many prostitutes also created business opportunities, think of the fashion industry. There were different types of prostitutes, and they were given names. For example, there were prostitutes working near Notre-Dame de Lorette, and those women were called *Les Lorettes*. There was also a student neighbourhood, and the women who worked there were called *Les Étudiantes*. Those who worked on the grand boulevards were called *Les Boulevardières*.

Many of these women also had other jobs such as waitressing, dancing, or even acting. Women were not allowed to sell themselves on the street by approaching men; that was prohibited, but men could recognize them by the way they dressed. Such as not wearing a hat, or taking off their hat and making specific gestures. Slightly lifting up their skirts and wearing excessive makeup, also distinguished them from non-prostitute women.

Prostitution was quite accepted as part of society. Middle-class and upper-class men would marry women, preferably from well-to-do families, to create heirs for their fortune. So, women at home were taking care of the children, and it was not uncommon for them to not mind if their husband visited a prostitute because they already had several children, they didn't use contraceptives, and they didn't want to have more.

It is clear that during the Second Empire and until 1914 Paris was the capital of pleasure and luxury. There were two hundred and fifty brothels in Paris. It was a frivolous city that attracted princes and businessmen from all over the world. The working class frequented the closes, where prostitutes, who were completely dependent on older women who had also been prostitutes, worked. They earned money but lived in these brothels. They slept in bunk beds and had to pay for everything, from food to clothing. For many women, it was the only means to survive and escape total poverty. Some of them were having up to thirty clients a day. This intense activity of the sex trade contributed to the worldwide reputation of Paris as a city of indulgence and entertainment.

The maisons closes were required to have a large house number on the front door and keep a light on at all times to distinguish them. From 1836 many of the brothels were allowed to exist, in order to control prostitution. Prostitutes had to go to the hospital when they had venereal diseases; they were interned in these hospitals that felt like prisons. They had to register with the police and undergo medical check-ups. At the time syphilis was widespread. It is estimated that one-fifth of the population of Paris suffered from the disease. When these women were interned in these prison-like hospitals, they were actually treated with mercury, but when the symptoms disappeared, they would return to the streets, causing the disease to spread again.

The most well-known of these hospitals was Maison St Lazare. It is estimated that around ten thousand women were submitted here at some point. They were supervised by the sisters and nuns of Marie-Josèphe. Around thirteen hundred women were permanently residing in the three buildings of the hospital. They could be held there from forty-five days up to three months. The authorities, we could say hypocritically, wanted to protect but also to control these women.

Prostitution was considered a necessary evil, but it also played a significant role in art, showcasing a reality of life through painting, photography, and literature. We already know about Courbet and Manet, but other artists also depicted the female body in a distinctive way; they painted ordinary women. Edgar Degas, Henri de Toulouse-Lautrec, Vincent Van Gogh, and many more artists used prostitutes as models.

Writers of the time also took an interest in and drew inspiration from this world. For example, Guy de Maupassant portrayed these women as heroines in his stories, such as *Boule de Suif*. Zola, the naturalist writer, wrote about it in a novel called *L'Assommoir* set in a working-class enclave in Paris, where the protagonist, Gervaise, is a woman living with an alcoholic. Her life is full of misfortune. In the end, when her husband dies in an accident falling from a roof, she falls into alcoholism and prostitution. The daughter of Gervaise, from *L'Assommoir* becomes the protagonist of Zola's next novel, *Nana*.

We know that the principal character of *Nana* was inspired by the life of Blanche Dantigny, a mediocre actress who became a famous courtesan. Like many courtesans, also called *Cocottes*, they served as models for artists. Blanche had a rather scandalous life, but we can see her in a painting by Gustave Courbet named *La Dame aux bijoux*. After leading a quite eventful life, when the war between France and Prussia broke out, she became a nurse. Sadly, she then died from smallpox. Even in death, she could inspire artists like Zola, who used the story of her death to complete the novel *Nana*.

Zola was an observer of his time and went to the extent of reproducing what others had experienced. Not only did Blanche Dantigny inspire Zola for the novel *Nana*, he was also inspired by the famous courtesan named Valtesse de la Bigne, whose bed we saw in Musée des Arts Décoratifs. Other artists, like Henri Gervex, had also painted her."

You know Mario, I really like hearing the stories of who these women were, those women who inspired great writers and artists at that time. We perhaps look at a work of art, admiring the composition and the colours for example, or we might be intrigued by a story in a book, but often we have no idea who actually inspired these stories. I'm finding this very interesting.

"Yes, I do too. Valtesse had a striking history. She was raped in the streets when she was only thirteen years old. It is not clear whether she worked as a laundress or in a dressmaking workshop when she was young, but her father was violent and an alcoholic. She posed as a model for the painter Camille Corot and later began practicing clandestine prostitution.

She was arrested several times by the police, but, as was the case with many women engaged in prostitution, she had ambitions of living a better life and started associating with wealthy clients. She met a man with whom she had two children, but she continued in prostitution. One of the men she met was Jacques Offenbach, a French composer of German Jewish descent. He was considered one of the creators of the 'operetta'. As a composer he was very representative of the era. He offered Valtesse a role in one of his operas *called Orpheus in the Underworld*, and Valtesse became his lover. She actually had several lovers, and one of them built her a mansion at 98 boulevard Malesherbes.

Valtesse became interested in art and literature and even wrote her own autobiography, but she reinvented herself and created a past where she concealed her humble and unfortunate origins. One day, Zola visited her at her house and was amazed when he saw her bedroom. It was a luxurious bedroom with the ornate bed that we saw at the Museum of Decorative Arts. Zola describes this chamber in his novel *Nana*. When Valtesse read the book, she told Zola that she didn't recognize herself in the novel. She said that the Nana she saw in the book was a vulgar and stupid woman. Valtesse died from a haemorrhage in 1910."

So women played a much more significant role in the art scene in Paris than they are often attributed. Can you imagine these artists without women... without models, without their muses? It would be difficult, right?

"Degas is also a good example. He was a French impressionist painter, although he preferred to refer to himself as a realist painter. He created pastel drawings and oil paintings, but he is known for his fascination with ballet dancers. Degas painted the movements of dance in his artworks and depicted the dancers, some of whom were also prostitutes, during rehearsals. He was known for portraying what happened behind the scenes. For example, the dancers before going on stage. He also depicted the dark world of mothers selling their daughters to men, who usually appear dressed in black in the painter's artworks. These men were seeking young dancers who would later become their lovers.

After his death, numerous artworks were found, including many drawings of prostitutes. They depicted women with grotesque and obscene bodies in great detail, showing women waiting for clients in clubs and brothels. When Napoleon III's reign ended, many of these brothels closed, and some turned into luxury establishments to attract wealthier clients."

Mario explains more about Degas to me, but I must admit I have mixed feelings about these older men, like Degas and Gauguin, painting very young girls. Gauguin is well known for his images of girls in Tahiti and it is said that he is the reason why many very young girls on the island contracted syphilis. If this were to happen in today's world, he would surely be condemned, but we must not forget that it was a different time. This is not an excuse, just a reality. A rather dark reality from my point of view. The fact that so many women had to sell their bodies created an opportunity for artists to find willing models to undress.

As a woman, I struggle with the idea that Degas was only interested in these young ballet dancers from an artistic perspective. I suppose we will never know, and I ask Mario for his opinion.

"From what I have studied, I have the impression that Degas was not abusive, but some suggest that he was a misogynist and found pleasure in seeing people suffer. Without having been there, I suppose it's just an assumption. However, Degas was an interesting artist. He never married and wanted his life to be private.

In addition to painting dancers, he also painted quite a few portraits, including the art model Emma Dobigny. Her real name was Marie Emma Thuilleux, and Degas met her between 1865 and 1869 when he lived in Montmartre. She was only fifteen years old when he painted her first portrait. He always portrayed her with dignity. It's not known if she was that special person in his life, but his paintings of her seem quite serene.

From Degas's extensive body of work, we can conclude that he was quite obsessed with ballet dancers and cabaret artists. Sadly, these women were not seen as respectable women. Dancers were associated with prostitution, and it was believed that these young ballet dancers worked as prostitutes. Cabaret and ballet shows were frequented mainly by men and courtesans who hoped to find their next patron.

Degas also created some sculptures, but he was more of a painter than a sculptor. Nevertheless, one of his sculptures became world famous. It is called *La Petite Danseuse de Quatorze Ans*, depicting a fourteen-year-old dancer. When Degas created this sculpture, he was already forty-five years old. He made many drawings of the girl. The sculpture received a lot of criticism because it did not conform to the aesthetic standards of the time. It was truly an innovative sculpture. Furthermore, it was made of wax, and Degas used real hair and real clothing for the statue. He was a perfectionist, so it's interesting to see that he reworked this statue several times and made her head appear quite harsh, with a reduced forehead, giving her a more primitive look. People considered it ugly and ridiculed the statue. But in reality, it was the first sculpture of modern art and it created an evolution in the art world."

When I look at the statue, I don't see that ugliness, Her name was Marie Van Goethem; she was originally from Belgium. Mario tells me that we can take a look at the house where she lived with her family.

"When Marie was born in 1865, the family moved to an apartment building on rue Notre-Dame de Lorette, known as Place Bréda, which is close to Degas's studio on rue Saint-Georges. This neighbourhood was one of the poorest and most squalid areas of Paris associated with prostitution. In 1880, after frequently changing their address, which is probably a sign that they couldn't afford the rent, the family finally settled on rue Fontaine.

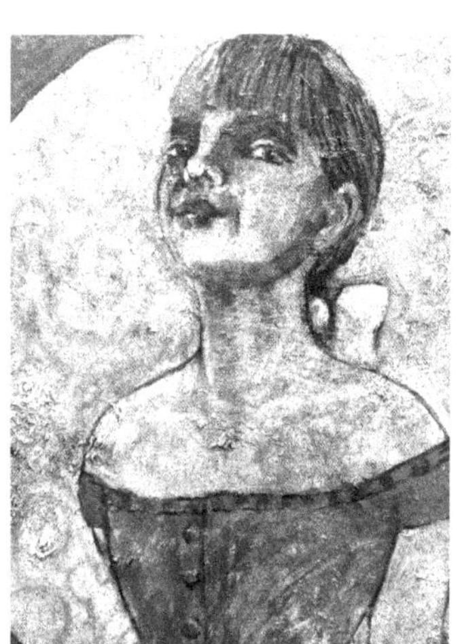

Marie van Goethem

When the statue was first exhibited, Marie was already working in a famous cabaret called Le Chat Noir in Montmartre. Le Chat Noir became the symbol of Bohemia at the end of the 19th century. Marie was around sixteen years old at that time. She was one of three sisters. One of her sisters, apparently became a thief, and she had an older sister named Charlotte who became an established dancer. But Marie turned to prostitution.

Although many in the art world know this famous statue, very few know her name. Not much is known about her life as a teenager, nor do we know when she died or where she is buried. We can only assume that she had a fairly harsh and miserable life. Degas never intended for the statue to become a bronze sculpture and created several wax models in different sizes before creating the finished statue. He only displayed the final statue, with real hair and clothing, to the public once, in 1881. The reason he made this wax statue is that he felt it was more lifelike that way, with the skin appearing almost real. It is believed that he kept the wax statue in his house until his death. Afterwards, his family created twenty-two bronze copies of the statue, which can now be seen in prestigious museum collections worldwide."

I personally want to honour her, and for this reason I created my impression of Marie in a painting. Speaking of painting... I know that Vincent van Gogh lived in Paris for two years, and there was an important woman in his life during that time.

"Yes, Paris was an attractive city for many artists from around the world. Vincent van Gogh also went to Paris in 1886 and eventually stayed there for two years. He visited brothels and painted prostitutes, but he mainly painted scenes from the brothels. Women waiting in the living room for a client to arrive or having a drink with a client. He didn't paint nude women, but it is almost certain that he had a prostitute who modelled for him, but we don't know who she was.

However, Van Gogh fell in love while he was in Paris. He must have felt happy when he found a place to exhibit his work. It was at the café Le Tambourin, a restaurant first located at 27 rue de Richelieu and later reopened at 62 boulevard de Clichy. It was close to the home of his brother Theo, where he stayed during his time in Paris. Van Gogh was a regular visitor and thirty-two years old when he had a brief relationship with the owner, Agostina Segatori.

She was born in Ancona, Italy, and at first made a living posing for artists. Many well-known artists, including Manet, used her as a model. She saved the money she earned to open the café. It became very popular among writers, artists, and critics.

Agostina allowed the artists who frequented Le Tambourin to exhibit their work there. The place was filled with extravagant decorations and artworks that were often used as a form of payment. Van Gogh also paid for food with some of his paintings. During that same period, he became very good friends with Paul Gauguin, who claimed that Van Gogh was deeply in love with Agostina. In fact, they were seeing each other for four months, and during that time, Van Gogh created some paintings of courting couples.

Agostina allowed him to have an exhibition of his work at the café, and it's likely that the painting Van Gogh created of her, an interesting portrait of Agostina called *Agostina Segatori Assis au Café du Tambourin*, was created there. She is sitting on a stool with a glass of beer on a table in front of her, holding a cigarette in her hand. Behind her, on the wall, we see one of Van Gogh's works. Drinking and smoking were highly inappropriate for respectable women at that time and were associated with artistic individuals and prostitutes. Now we know that Agostina was a modern and progressive woman who earned her own money with the café. She was an independent woman, which was unusual in those days. When Van Gogh and Agostina split up, he wanted his paintings back, but unfortunately, Le Tambourin went bankrupt and was sold with his paintings included in the sale.

It's interesting to see how artists met and interacted in local cafés, isn't it? There is even a portrait of Van Gogh sitting in Café du Tambourin by Toulouse Lautrec. When we talk about prostitution and art, we have to mention Lautrec, as he is well known for his paintings of women in brothels, but of course, he also created other artworks. Let's talk about his most renowned genre. He himself frequented brothels and even lived for a while in a room in a brothel called *La Fleur Blanche* in rue du Moulin.

He started painting prostitutes, both on cardboard with gouache and pastels and in oils. He didn't depict the explicit and dark side of prostitution but rather portrayed a lively atmosphere. He felt at home in the brothels, and the women who worked there were his family. He painted women with vibrant colours, and it is evident that he did not despise women like some other artists did. He didn't paint their genitalia, but in his works, we see them eating, playing cards, or sleeping. He captured a part of these women's lives when they weren't selling their bodies, without focusing on their work, like receiving the doctor to check for gonorrhoea or syphilis. He also painted women sleeping together, showing intimacy but always with great respect. He didn't portray them as something threatening but rather gave aesthetic and sentimental value to women whom society considered vulgar. Lautrec didn't judge those women; he was a liberal man who loved freedom and loved women."

We will dedicate a chapter to Lautrec and his women because it's fascinating to see who these women were. I have to say that I like Lautrec. His art, and now getting to know him a bit better, also the man he was. And I can understand why women felt compelled to engage in prostitution as a means of survival, and how being a model may have been a good way to make some money.

"It is important to realise that it was seen as normal for a man to frequent a courtesan. These courtesans were called *Les Cocottes*. They were the courtesans of the latter part of the Belle Époque, from 1890 to 1914. They were prostitutes who had a lot of money and were not the typical prostitutes controlled by a man. They could choose their clients, and their prices were very high.

One of the most famous courtesans of the time was a Spanish woman named La Belle Otero. She managed to amass a fortune equivalent to forty million euros in today's money. These women owned palaces and were very powerful. They were considered the first feminists, but today's feminists would probably have a different opinion on that. They were also called *the horizontals*, but they were very independent. What we do know about these women is that most of them grew up without a father figure or were violated by a relative. They possibly hated men and used them to climb up the social ladder, hoping to find powerful men from high society, such as politicians, businessmen, and high-ranking military officials.

They were elegant and intelligent women. Interestingly, some of them were lesbians. They sought power over men and wanted to enrich themselves. In those times, it was normal for wealthy men to have their own courtesan, and these women had several of those high society men. They earned a lot of money, but they also needed to spend a lot. They had to buy expensive clothing and change outfits frequently. They had their own carriages and many jewels. It was not uncommon for these courtesans to wear more elegant clothing than high society women. For men, it was actually a symbol of status and power to be able to afford and be seen with a high-class courtesan.

These women had to seek out their clients by walking the streets. They would go to parks and places where these wealthy men gathered. Many had photos taken of themselves and placed ads in local newspapers, inviting men to come to their homes to see their collection of jewellery or paintings. The photos served as their calling cards. There were also restaurants that were famous for having women to 'entertain' men. The most famous one, which you can still visit in Paris, is Maxim's restaurant, located near the Place de la Concorde. There were 'working rooms' upstairs, but the restaurant itself was beautifully decorated with Art Nouveau-style lamps and other objects, featuring women as the main theme.

By that time Napoleon III was gone, and France had become a republic. In a sense, the *Cocottes* were a symbol of sexual freedom in a still very puritanical world. However, there was a double standard. Women who were more liberal were seen as vulgar and quickly labelled as prostitutes. Manet painted *Olympia*, and they said she must be a prostitute. But we know that his model, Victorine Meurent, was also a painter and earned some extra money by posing for artists. It could be said that the way women were represented in art brought about a significant change in the art world itself.

Think of Art Nouveau, with its feminine curves. The importance of women in art was not only evident in painting and decoration but also in theatre and opera. Great examples of this are those courtesans who became famous actresses, singers, and dancers. We will talk about some of them in the next chapter. It's easy to see why Paris has become the city to go to for both business and pleasure."

As a woman, all of this makes me feel somewhat uncomfortable. The fact that women were seen as objects of sexual pleasure, but at the same time, I understand the inspiration and influence on art. I can understand the power that becoming a prostitute holds for some women. I want to learn more about women like La Belle Otero, and I would love to visit the houses where these women used to live in Paris.

We have now arrived at the Champs-Élysées, where we can see the house of one of these powerful courtesans. I'm happy that we managed to get a special permit to see the inside of this impressive building, which is now a luxurious hotel, Hôtel de la Païva.

The Art of Seduction

"There were several very famous and powerful courtesans in Paris and one of them was La Païva, also known as 'the queen of kept women'. She was born in a Russian ghetto in Moscow in 1819. Her parents were Polish and German Jews, and life was tough. Her father was a weaver, but not much is known about La Païva's education. At the age of seventeen, she married a tailor with whom she had her first child, a boy. But she decided to leave her husband and baby behind and began traveling to many European cities.

During this time, she called herself Terese, but she was still legally married. Her goal was to become rich, so she settled in Paris, where she lived in a cheap hotel, a so-called maison de passe, a place where prostitutes worked. She was intelligent and planned to attract wealthy men. To do this, she bought fake jewellery and beautiful clothes. When she was twenty, she met Henri Herz, a wealthy pianist, who introduced her to the artistic society of Europe. Although she couldn't marry Herz, she had a daughter with him. When Herz went to work in the United States, she spent most of his money, and his parents kicked her out. She left, but she left her daughter with them.

Terese fell back into poverty and was forced to return to prostitution. She first went to London because it was known that there were wealthy men who paid a lot of money to be with women. She seduced an aristocrat named Edward Henri Stanley, the 15th Earl of Derby, and became his mistress. She also became the mistress of many other men. As her demand grew, she raised her prices and quickly became rich and a famous courtesan. In 1848, Terese returned to Paris and met Araújo de Païva, a wealthy Portuguese heir. When her first husband died, she married Araújo, but left him shortly after. The marriage arrangements included her husband giving her over five million in today's money, making her a very wealthy woman. Araújo also gave her the house on rue Rossini.

At the age of thirty-three, she met and seduced Count Guido Henckel von Donnersmarck, a twenty-two-year-old Prussian industrialist. She became his mistress, and he shared his fortune with her. He gave her the Château de Pontchartrain near Paris and built a mansion for her at 25 avenue des Champs-Élysées, which was later nicknamed the *Louvre of the ass*. Nowadays the building is a luxurious hotel; Hotel de la Païva. Auguste Rodin was one of the sculptors involved in designing the interiors."

I'm delighted that we have a special permit to visit the interior of the hotel.

"Yes, me too. It has beautiful features, such as a central staircase, made of very expensive Algerian yellow onyx, luxurious furniture and a bathroom with Arabic tiles and details. The bath itself is clad in silver bronze and has three taps, one was for champagne and one for milk. From 1904 the hotel was used as a gentlemen's club and Terese, who became known as La Païva, hosted many lavish dinners. Her salon was frequented by writers like Gustave Flaubert and Émile Zola, as well as painters and many other influential men.

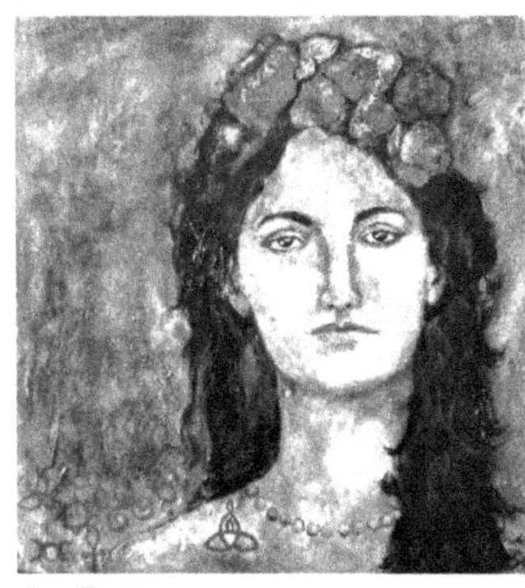

La Païva

When she was fifty-two years old, her marriage to Araújo was annulled and two months later she married the love of her life, Count Henckel. Araújo lost all his money due to bad investments and gambling debts, and committed suicide. During the Anglo-Prussian War, people began to turn against La Païva and Henckel, due to their Jewish origin. And like other courtesans, she was accused of being a spy. She and her husband decided to leave Paris and returned to his manor house in southern Poland. La Païva died in 1884 when she was sixty-four years old. Henckel apparently deeply mourned his wife and preserved her body in the attic in embalming fluid. He remarried four years later and his new wife, according to some sources, discovered her body.

The history of other famous courtesans is also very interesting to mention as these women were more than just courtesans. Most of them had an artistic career as well. We will discover the lives of some of them.

La Belle Otero who was Spanish, Mata Hari who was Dutch, Sarah Bernhardt who was born in France and Apollonie Sabatier who was also born in France. Many of the courtesans had an absent father who either left or died. They all had some kind of trauma in their childhood. For example, La Belle Otero was raped at the age of eleven. It's unimaginable the pain it created in a girl of that age. Gaining power over men by seducing them might have been a way to turn that disdain into an advantage. These successful courtesans used men's weakness and sexual desire to their benefit and amassed great amounts of money. Just as Paris attracted international artists, mostly men, in search of fortune, it did the same with women.

It must be said that women were objects of obsession at that time. They were seen as a lesser species and for the most part, women's art and literature were not taken seriously. Nevertheless, the main theme in the art and design created by men, was women. So, in a way, society was dominated by man's obsession with women and on the other hand some women dominated these same powerful men.

Everything took the shape of a woman, as can be seen in sculptures, paintings, building facades, and even furniture. It was common to see women with open arms, displaying their bare chests in decorative art. It was accepted by the bourgeois ruling class."

I do wonder what the life of a bourgeoise woman during that time looked like. Women who married a wealthy man when they were still young.

"They were destined to be the mother of that man's future children, his heirs. These women were not educated to seduce a man; that was the role of the *Cocottes*, something completely accepted in society, and not only in France. The *Cocottes* were special. They were rising above the misery of poor women who had to sell their bodies to survive, although often these courtesans came from a poor background.

Let's talk about the most seductive of them all. La Belle Otero. Agustina del Carmen Otero was born in 1868 in the village of Valga, in northern Spain. She was raised by her single mother as her father, who she claimed was a Greek army officer, was absent. She grew up in poverty and never received a proper education. In fact, she was illiterate, but she did everything she could to learn to read and write and overcome her misfortune. After working as a domestic servant in Santiago de Compostela, she moved to Lisbon at the age of fourteen with her boyfriend and dance partner, where she worked as a dancer and singer. When she was twenty years old, she met Ernest Jurgens, who became her first patron, and they moved to Marseille with the intention of starting her career as a dancer in France.

The relationship didn't last long, and she adopted the stage name *La Belle Otero*. In no time, she became the star of the *Folies Bergère* productions in Paris. Her Spanish roots gave her a mysterious and charismatic look. She had captivating dark eyes, an attractive figure, and she was confident, intelligent, and seductive. She became known as a flamenco dancer but had developed her own unique style. She travelled all over the world, including the United States.

From the very beginning, la Belle Otero had a goal in her life. She wanted to marry a prince. Her authentic style of dance had earned her a lot of fame and she performed in the most famous venues, among which is Maxim's in Paris. She was invited by important figures like kings, nobles, and even the Grand Duke of Russia. Men who gifted her expensive jewellery, cars, houses, and more.

She became one of the most sought-after courtesans in Paris, even in Europe, but it was known that she chose her lovers carefully. Some of her wealthy admirers were Kaiser Wilhelm II, Prince Albert I of Monaco, the kings of Spain, including the Duke of Westminster, and the writer Gabriele D'Annunzio. She was also loved and admired by writers, painters, poets, and politicians. Apparently, at least six lovers committed suicide after she left them.

At the age of fifty, she was still sought after. She and other great courtesans of the time were seen and treated as celebrities. Then, in the early 1920s, she was involved in a car accident and decided it was time to retire. She moved to a grand mansion in Nice, in the south of France. She had accumulated the equivalent of about four hundred million euros during her career but became addicted to gambling. She lost almost everything, and in the final years of her life, she lived in a room of a hotel in Nice, apparently paid for by the director of the Monte-Carlo casino. She died at the age of ninety-five from a heart attack and was also buried in Nice.

When we see paintings of the atmosphere in Paris, it's an environment of parties in restaurants, salons, and the opera. It's quite difficult to distinguish who is the courtesan, seeking a man to support her, and the married woman, because the courtesans dressed very elegantly. It's not easy to recognise them in this era obsessed with virtue and morality, and at the same time, with prostitution. We already know that many men of the time frequented brothels, even Napoleon III had his own mistresses. Paris was the capital of sex and had over one hundred thousand women engaged in prostitution. It was a city where everyone came to enrich themselves and have fun.

But let's talk about art again. Art depicted the truth of society. There's a sculpture called *Femme piquée par un serpent* by Auguste Clésinger, and the model who posed for it was Apollonie Sabatier. The sculpture caused a scandal but made Auguste and Apollonie famous. It was commissioned by a Belgian tycoon named Alfred Mosselman, who was Apollonie's long-time lover. The statue, which can be seen in the Orsay Museum in Paris, depicts a very realistic female body; a woman apparently in agony. But the expression of the sculpture suggests she is also thoroughly enjoying herself.

Apollonie was a French entertainer and courtesan who had lovers such as Alexandre Dumas and Charles Baudelaire. What happened with these women was that, when they were painted and used as models for sculptures, people, especially the men who frequented them, immediately recognised them. In *Femme piquée par un serpent*, they recognised Apollonie.

She was born as Aglaé Joséphine Sabatier in 1822. Her mother was a laundress for Aglaé's biological father, Count Louis Harmand d'Abancourt, who arranged for her mother to marry André Sabatier, an army sergeant who became her stepfather. The family moved to Paris, and Apollonie started singing at the Opéra Garnier. It was during this time that she changed her name to Apollonie. She became a muse to many French painters and writers in the 1850s in Paris, but she also became a salon hostess. This salon was in avenue Frochot, near place Pigalle. This is where she met many of the French artists of the time, including Gustave Flaubert, Victor Hugo, and Édouard Manet.

Apollonie and Baudelaire were lovers from 1857 to 1862. She was described as a well-proportioned woman who seemed to have a halo of happiness around her. She dressed in her own style, without following the fashion trends of the time, apparently advised by her artist friends. After the death of Alfred Mosselman, Apollonie became the mistress of art collector Richard Wallace. Apollonie Sabatier died in Neuilly-sur-Seine from influenza in 1890."

I'm impressed by the stories of these powerful women. I'm also curious about Mata Hari. It's possible to visit the building where Mata Hari was arrested; it was the Elysée Palace Hotel on the Champs-Élysées, but today we have a long day ahead and whilst Mario explains about Mata Hari, we are crossing the river Seine via the Pont de la Concorde bridge, walking in the direction of Musée de l'Orangerie in place de la Concorde.

"Mata Hari has become a mythical legend, and unlike women like La Païva and Sarah Bernhardt, her name sounds familiar to many people. She was born in Leeuwarden in the Netherlands as Margaretha Geertruida Zelle in 1876. Her father was a sought-after hatter but lost the family fortune when Margaretha was still a teenager. Her parents later divorced, and when her mother died when Margaretha was fifteen years old, she went to live with relatives. She attended a teacher training school but later married Rudolph MacLeod at the age of nineteen, who was an officer in the Dutch colonial army. He is said to have been abusive and infected her with syphilis.

They moved to Java and also lived in Sumatra. They had two children, but their son died at a young age. Some say it was due to the mercury treatment for her syphilis, which he had contracted from his parents. After returning to Europe when Margaretha was twenty-six, they separated and later divorced in 1906, a year after she went to Paris. Although she had custody of her daughter Jeanne Louise MacLeod, who was called Non, Rudolph refused to provide financial support, forcing her to leave the child in his care. Margaretha had learned East Indian dances and began dancing professionally in the hope of earning enough money to be reunited with her daughter.

She renamed herself Mata Hari, which means 'Eye of the Day' or 'Sun' in Malay. She was tall and very attractive as an exotic dancer and was willing to appear nude in public. She was an instant success in Paris and other major cities. She became a well-known courtesan and had numerous lovers, many of whom were military officers. One of them apparently bit off one of her nipples. I suppose you could say that her association with military officers led to her downfall.

Although widely known as a spy during World War I, her espionage activities are not very clear. She was arrested and charged with spying at the age of forty-one at the Elysée Palace Hotel. She admitted to accepting money from a German officer but claimed that she had only provided outdated information. Some information suggests that she had agreed to act as a French spy in German-occupied Belgium but had not been forthcoming about her prior arrangement with the Germans. She was executed by firing squad in October 1917. Some say she refused to wear a blindfold and blew kisses to her executioners, while others deny it. However, her guilt was widely questioned, and the German government exonerated her in 1930. Later, it was discovered that French documents seemed to confirm her innocence and that she had been used as a scapegoat for French setbacks during the war.

What remains is that her name, Mata Hari, now equates to a spy and has become the subject of numerous books and films. Although she was Dutch, she was buried in France at the Vincennes Cemetery on avenue Victor-Hugo in Fontenay-sous-Bois."

It's interesting to me that Mata Hari's daughter went to university in the city of Arnhem, which is the city where I was born. It feels somewhat strange that her daughter walked the streets where I grew up. Two years after her mother's execution, she was about to start working as a teacher in the Dutch East Indies, but she suddenly died before leaving in 1919. It's unclear how she died.

"There was another great courtesan named Sarah Bernhardt, who was very famous at that time and is still well known in the film industry today. In fact, she is the first French actress to receive a star on the Hollywood Walk of Fame. So, who was this fascinating woman?

She was born in 1844, although this is disputed by some because in 1871 there was a fire at the Hôtel de Ville, which is the city hall in Paris, during the uprising known as *Le Commune*. Sarah's birth records were burned in the fire, and it is believed that she put a later date on her birth certificate to appear younger.

She was one of the superstars of her time and gained international fame. We know that she was the illegitimate daughter of a Dutch Jewish courtesan named Judith Bernard. Sarah later changed her name to Sarah Bernhardt. Her father was unknown for a long time, but he is now known as a lawyer from Le Havre. It is said that his family paid for her education and insisted that she be baptised as a Catholic. Her mother travelled a lot but also ran a salon frequented by important men, including the half-brother of Emperor Napoleon, writers, and musicians. Her mother was a high-end prostitute and taught her daughters to be the same. Sarah was only thirteen when she supposedly began working as a prostitute. But Sarah was not considered beautiful by the standards of that time. She was seen as rather ugly, very thin, and with a pale face. She didn't want to become a prostitute but dreamed of becoming an abbess in a convent, but life had other plans for her.

At the age of seventeen, she studied acting at the Conservatoire for one or two years. Her teachers were two prominent actors, Joseph-Isidore Samson and Jean-Baptiste Provost from the Comédie-Française, but Sarah felt that she wasn't very good, and as a perfectionist, she didn't want to be the second or third best in her class. She wanted to be the best. She started working as an actress at the Comédie-Française, which at the time was considered a great privilege, but by the age of eighteen, she no longer enjoyed it and left. Interestingly, ten years later, the Comédie-Française asked her to return, as by then she had made a name for herself. She had a rather high-pitched voice, which meant that she couldn't play the more serious roles, and she was usually cast as a princess or a naïve girl. She simply didn't have a powerful enough voice for the theatre. But Sarah fascinated people with her gaze, gestures, attitude, and charisma. She was very stylish, even in her private life. The way she moved, ate, and spoke was very elegant. She was like a plant, as if floating in the wind like vines, the way she draped herself on a chair.

This truly inspired Alphonse Mucha, and you can see it in his work. It could be said that she was his muse. But Sarah was also a very talented painter and sculptor herself, although she is not recognised as an artist. That was the fate of many female artists. Men were predominantly influencing the art scene.

During her life, Sarah had many lovers and continued to be a courtesan in addition to being an actress. Many important men were received in her bedroom, including Napoleon III, who was her lover. Interestingly, she was also the mistress of one of Napoleon's enemies, Victor Hugo. She was able to seduce many men, including bankers and the Prince of Wales, but she didn't want these men to fall in love with her. She could ask around fifteen hundred French francs for a night with one of these men. For her work as an actress, although she was well known, she only received two-thousand francs a year. This makes it easier to understand why Sarah chose to continue her courtesan work even after becoming internationally famous for her theatrical work. At that time, women were paid very little compared to men; an actress earned half the salary of an average worker.

But Sarah was loved in many ways and became very wealthy. One of her greatest admirers, who as I mentioned before also became her lover, was Victor Hugo. He gave her a teardrop-shaped pearl to thank her for her performance in one of his important plays called Hernani.

When she was fifty-five years old, Sarah opened the Sarah Bernhardt Theatre, of which she was the director for twenty-four years. You can still visit this theatre, which hasn't changed much, as it remains in the Italian theatre style, decorated with grey and gold touches, which was very unusual at a time when most theatres used red as the main colour. She was already a superstar, and everything she did inspired other artists and people in design, even in fashion. It can certainly be said that she revolutionised the theatre of the time, including the use of art and incorporating horses on stage.

Sarah also played male roles, and it is known that she did so in *Shakespeare's Hamlet*. In fact, she was the only actress in history to play both Ophelia and Hamlet! At some point, she was 'living' the theatre; her life was a theatre. She controlled everything and would stay there until the early hours of the morning. She wanted to do everything herself, and everything had to be perfect. In a sense, she was the author and protagonist of her own theatrical life. A hardworking, intelligent woman, but also extreme. At one point, she asked a surgeon to transplant a real tiger's tail onto her body. He refused and told her it would result in her death. This may suggest that Sarah liked to dominate men, as she apparently dreamed of striking men with her tiger's tail. What also drew the attention of many is that she cared for her dying sister in her house on rue de Rome. In the room where her sister's bed was, there was already a coffin, and Sarah slept in the coffin to keep her sister company. Sarah was thirty-five years old at the time."

What an incredible woman. But in a coffin? That's a bit morbid, isn't it? Goodness. I suppose there was a fascination with those kinds of things. But if she lived only for the theatre, it seems she didn't have a private life or a family. Was she ever married? Did she have children?

"There was certainly a fascination with the morbid and death. There was a lot of interest in spiritualist seances. This fascination with death is also notable in the art of the time. Presumably, with many diseases and a lot of people dying, it could explain the desire for there to be something more after death. Sarah's private life may be less discussed, but she had an illegitimate son named Maurice Bernhardt, who became a notable play writer and theatre director, and after Sarah's death, he took care of her theatre.

At the age of thirty-eight, Sarah met a very handsome Greek diplomat named Aristide Damala. He was eleven years younger than her and a notorious womaniser. They married in 1882 in London, and Sarah offered him roles in her plays. He continued his affairs with other women and was not well-received as an actor. He was also addicted to morphine, and their relationship was unstable. They separated, but as a Catholic, Sarah did not want to divorce him. Only eight years after they married, Damala took an overdose of morphine while he was in Marseille, and she rushed to take care of him until he died in August 1889 at the age of only thirty-four. He was then buried in Athens. A bust, which she had made herself, was placed on his tomb, and whenever she could, she made a detour in her travels to visit his grave. She did this until the end of her life and referred to herself as Damala's widow.

She was a strong and kind-hearted woman and was considered one of the early feminists. She loved helping women, but during the Franco-Prussian War, she also opened the doors of her theatre, the Odeon in Paris, and turned it into a makeshift hospital for wounded soldiers. And during the *Commune*, the civil war in Paris, she used her own money to organise ambulances and even created a farm where animals were raised to feed the soldiers. She was quite active in the *Commune* and then helped many women who had been arrested during the uprising and returned to Paris with nothing. In fact, she was an activist.

Sarah was unstoppable, full of energy, and when she was seventy-one years old and needed an operation for bone tuberculosis in her knee, which resulted in the amputation of her right leg, she continued working on stage until the end of her life, using stage props for support to be able to perform.

She was widely adored and performed on stages all around the world, including in the United States, and it is said that she journeyed across the United States in her own train, named *Le Sarah Bernhardt*. She graced both theatre and film screens, appearing in eight movies over a span of sixty years. In many ways, she was a trailblazer of celebrity culture. Sarah continued acting until the very end of her life in 1923, while still working on her eighth film, *La Voyante*. She is a great example of an independent and emancipated woman, who has left her mark in many ways. She passed away in her Paris mansion, held by her son Maurice, succumbing to uraemia."

It is truly remarkable to learn about these women. For me, it's difficult to fathom a life like theirs. I believe that women in our time often feel more secure and capable of facing challenges, but these women, considering the era they lived in, belonged to a different class. Personally, having travelled and lived in five different countries, I feel quite privileged considering how relatively easy my life has been and continues to be. For me, learning about these women from the past is truly inspiring. These women who had to face so many challenges and limitations and yet they managed to defy societal norms and made their mark on history.

Of course, in today's world women have more opportunities, rights, and freedoms, but much of what we have now is built upon the achievements of women like Sarah Bernhardt and others who fought for equality and recognition.

We arrive at the Musée de l'Orangerie and we will delve into the world of Impressionism; a groundbreaking movement that challenged traditional artistic views and created a fresh perspective on the way to create atmosphere in a painting, through the use of light and colour. I'm really looking forward to continuing this explorative journey and getting up close to some of the works by iconic artists like Claude Monet and Pierre-Auguste Renoir.

Impressionism

The end of Academic art

We are entering the Musée de l'Orangerie, a relatively small museum but very much worth a visit. You can spend a good hour of your time admiring its collection of art by famous artists such as Matisse, Renoir, Picasso, Utrillo and yes, of course, Monet! The basement is an oval hall exclusively dedicated to Monet's waterlilies. We are silently contemplating the extraordinary achievement of this great painter, surrounded by his floating waterlilies.

After our visit to the museum, we sit down at one of the cafés for a drink and a small bite, whilst Mario is going to explain about the style of art that I personally like very much. Impressionism.

In the world of contemporary art, Impressionism is often referred to as the art of impression. That makes sense, doesn't it? One could say that the artist is not trying to paint a faithful reflection of real life, a scene, a person, or an object, but rather an impression. Created with light, colours, atmosphere, and in a fluid manner. That's how I've always interpreted it, and in the past, I have described my own work as impressionist. Although now, thanks to Mario, I know that especially my latest artworks, are better described as Fauvist Expressionism with a touch of Symbolism. I don't really know where the term originated from nor what the description of Impressionism was at that time. I'm about to find out.

"Impressionism started around the 1860s. Monet and Renoir were two of the French artists who were at the forefront of Impressionism and they became close friends. They often painted together, setting up their easels side by side. The young Monet and Renoir, together with other artists such as Frédéric Bazille and Alfred Sisley, shared an interest in painting out in the open air, in other words, in real life. Especially Monet is, to this day, considered the leading figure in the Impressionism movement and most people will have heard of Monet and his famous paintings of water lilies.

Actually, it is interesting how the term came about. In 1872, Monet created a painting called *Impression, soleil levant*. This painting was exhibited at the first impressionist exhibition. It was in 1874 when Nadar, an important photographer of the time, offered his studio in boulevard des Capucines for this exhibition, as the impressionists were not accepted by the salons in Paris. An art critic saw Monet's painting and said, "*Well, I'm certainly impressed with this impression*". It was a mockery, like an insult, but this very painting gave rise to the name Impressionism.

The painters of that time were trying to move away from the dominant style of Academic art. Impressionism was a revolt of those painters. Courbet, Manet, and Degas were already on this path. It is important to remember that photography had been invented, so there was no longer a great need for portrait painters. The impressionist painters of the time were fascinated by colour and light, but each had their specialty. It all began around 1858. Monet met a fellow artist Eugène Boudin, who inspired and encouraged Monet to develop his impressionist techniques in order to free his style. He taught him the technique known as 'en plein air' (outdoors). There were also other artists who were exploring this new technique. For example Van Gogh who also was an impressionist and became obsessed with colour and loose brushstrokes.

What was new at the time was that these impressionists, as they went out to paint outdoors, had to get a portable easel and paints that wouldn't dry out in the open air. The solution came from an American oil painter, John Goffe Rand, who invented the metal paint tube. Most impressionist artists didn't paint from memory and didn't work in their homes with models coming to their studios. They could paint anywhere outdoors. At the same time, a new type of brush was invented. The flat brush, which was wide at the top and not round, ending in a point.

These brushes were great for painting waves and painting faster. That was important because working outdoors meant they had to capture the fleeting light of the moment, which constantly changes. Claude Monet is probably the most well-known impressionist artist. We can admire many of his works at the Musée d'Orsay but if you have time, do also pay a visit to the Musée Marmottan Monet in 2 rue Louis Boilly, where you will find a large collection of Monet's and Berthe Morisot's work.

Monet had a strong desire to capture the light in his artwork, which seems essential in everything he created. He loved capturing this light outdoors at different times of the day. He was fascinated by modern developments of his time as well. He made quite a few paintings of train stations, one of which was the Gare Saint-Lazare, which he painted in early 1877. This train station still exists. He liked to depict the changing light due to the steam emitted by the locomotives. Monet did visit London and was enchanted by the fog when he stayed there from 1870 to 1871. At some point, he told Rene Gimpel, an art dealer, "*Without the fog, London would not be a beautiful city. It is the fog that gives it its magnificent vastness.*" Some say that Impressionism was born out of pollution, due to the fogs and vapours that industrialisation brought to the air.

Monet frequently visited the north of France as well. Although he was born in Paris, his family moved to Le Havre on the coast of Normandy when he was a young child. He loved painting the cliffs and the changing light over the landscape. When he painted his work *La Femme à l'ombrelle*, the painting was accepted by the Impressionist Salon. It is quite a remarkable painting because it combines landscape and portrait, capturing movement and light.

Life wasn't always easy for Monet, and there was a time during his bohemian years when he even contemplated suicide. But around 1883, his life changed, and he was able to settle in Giverny, Normandy. He bought a house with some land. It was the ideal place for Monet, and it was here that he created many of his landscape paintings. He even built the pond and the Japanese bridge which inspired many of his artworks. But let's talk about Monet and the women in his life and learn how these women shaped it and influenced his art."

Listening to the stories of these great artists everything about them almost makes me wish I had lived in Paris as an artist during that time. But I realise that life for women artists was surely not as easy as it was for men. So, who was Monet as a man? Was he married or did he love someone? Is there a woman behind this great artist who supported and inspired him?

"Monet's love life is interesting, and there was indeed a woman whom he loved deeply. Her name was Camille-Léonie Doncieux. Camille was Monet's primary model. His family did not want him to marry her, but he did so anyway. It must have been true love. They got married in 1870, and he created a series of paintings of her. One of the first portraits of Camille was created in 1866, showing a woman in a green dress. It is a very large oil painting, measuring two metres and thirty centimetres by one and a half metres. The artwork was presented in an art salon with great success.

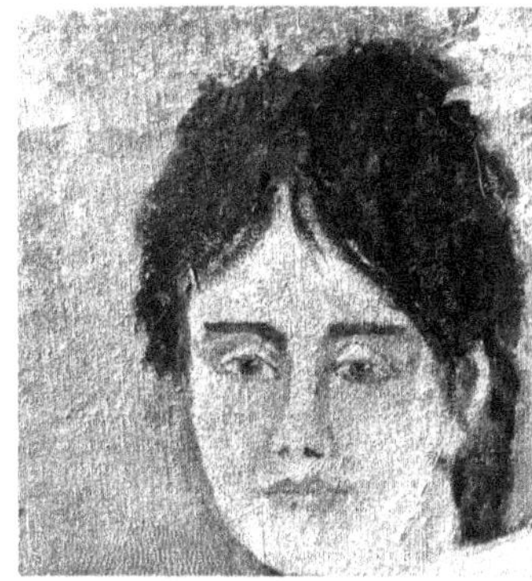

Camille Doncieux

Zola said it was the best piece in the exhibition. Camille appeared in many more of Monet's paintings. She was clearly his muse. One of them depicts her in a Japanese outfit with blonde hair, showing the influence of Japonisme in his work. The painting is called *La Japonaise*. They were quite poor before Monet made a name for himself in the art world, and they would acquire cheap Japanese dresses and objects that he could then use in his art.

Worth mentioning is his painting called *Déjeuner sur l'herbe*. Of course, it is quite similar to Manet's *Le Déjeuner sur l'herbe*, and he even gave it the same name. It is not known exactly why Monet created this large painting. Was it a provocation? Or just a study? Monet was only twenty-five years old when he created the work, and some think he wanted to paint a canvas as large as Manet had done. Monet was certainly influenced by the fame and possibly the infamy of Manet's work."

I am excited to go and see both paintings at the Musée d'Orsay later. Mario explains:

"Monet's painting measures four by six metes and depicts about a dozen people having lunch on the grass in a forest. In this painting, we also see Courbet and Camille, she is in the centre of the composition. The painting was damaged while Monet was still alive. Presumably, because he couldn't pay the rent for his house. He left this work as a collateral to his landlord, who he would then pay at a later stage. Sadly, the landlord did not take care of the painting, and one-third of the canvas was damaged and lost.

From Monet's body of work, it can be said that Camille was important in his art. But she was also posing for other artists, like Renoir and Manet. Manet, in fact, painted Monet's family in his garden. Renoir also painted Camille in a garden with her son and a scene where Camille is reading a book. Another work by Manet depicts Monet and Camille sitting in a boat, and Monet is painting.

When Camille had her first child, they discovered she had uterine cancer; yet she had another child. She was very fragile. That's why Monet had a lover. Her name was Alice Hoschedé, a married woman. Alice took care of Camille until her death in 1879. There's a painting that Monet created of Camille after she had already died. It's called *Camille Monet sur son lit de mort*. She was only thirty-two years old when she died. The painting of Camille dead in bed shows Monet's pain. It's a quite striking image and can be seen at the Musée d'Orsay.

After Camille's death, Monet lost the intensity in his paintings of women and he started painting more landscapes. Alice Hoschedé, who had cared for Camille, was the wife of Ernest Hoschedé, a department store magnate and art collector, with whom she had six children, although some believe that their son Jacques was actually Monet's child, but this has not been confirmed. Alice was a jealous woman, and unfortunately, after Camille's death, she destroyed all the photos and letters of Camille, as if to erase all memories of her. Only one photo was saved.

But how did Alice and Monet actually meet you might wonder. That's quite an interesting story too. In 1876, Ernest Hoschedé commissioned Monet to paint decorative panels for Château de Rottembourg. This may have been when Monet and Alice met and began an affair. When Ernest Hoschedé went bankrupt in 1877, he, his wife, and children moved in with Monet, but Ernest spent a lot of time in Paris trying to regain his fortune. In 1886, he came to collect his wife and children, but Alice refused to go with him and stayed with Monet. After Ernest Hoschedé's death in 1891, Alice agreed to marry Monet in 1892.

Alice died in 1911. Interestingly, her daughter, Blanche Hoschedé, became an impressionist artist. She received her education from Monet and became his assistant when she was only seventeen years old. She also married Monet's son, Jean. Her painting style was very similar to Monet's. She stayed with Monet in Giverny until his passing in 1926, where she continued to live and create art. The village named one of its streets in her honour, acknowledging her work."

I very much enjoy learning about impressionist artists and am curious to find out about other female impressionist artists. Mario will talk about that whilst we cross the river Seine once again to complete our day with a visit to one of the best-known museums in Paris. Musée d'Orsay, with a large collection of art, dating from 1848 to 1914, including paintings and sculptures by artists that we are discussing during this trip. The museum, where you could easily spend hours and hours of time, is situated on the left bank of the Seine.

Female impressionist painters

Defying the odds

We've arrived at Musée d'Orsay which exhibits one of the largest collections of impressionist and post-impressionist paintings in the world. I'm stunned about the exterior. A fine example of 19th century architecture as the museum is housed in a former railway station called le Gare d'Orsay. According to Mario this is the place where you can learn about and view the works of most of the artists that we are talking about. And apart from masterpieces by Renoir, Van Gogh and Monet, we will also be able to see the work of some female artists up close.

As we step inside, sunlight is pouring through the ornate glass windows, creating a warm, golden glow. It is very spacious inside with white walls and large white marble sculptures. What a great place to learn that at least some women were recognised as impressionist painters, described by art critic Gustave Geffroy in 1894 as the *"three great ladies of Impressionism"*: Marie Bracquemond, Mary Cassatt, and perhaps the most important female impressionist painter of the time, Berthe Morisot.

"Also worth mentioning is impressionist artist Eva Gonzalès, who was born in Paris, but had Monegasque and Spanish ancestry. For a long time, Eva was known for being a model for painters such as Manet, but she was also a painter herself. She in fact learned the basic techniques from Manet, who was her art teacher. She knew Berthe Morisot, who was also taught by Manet. You can see his influence in Eva's art until around 1870.

In 1871, her art took a different direction, inspired by the work of Edgar Degas. She never intended to exhibit her work. Coming from an affluent family, we can assume that creating art was not a means of survival for her. Eva married Henri Guérad, an engraver, in 1879. She continued working as an artist, and her talent was recognised by Parisian critics. Sadly, Eva died from an embolism due to complications from giving birth to her baby daughter, Julie. She was only thirty-four years old. This happened just five days after Manet's death. However, she was not forgotten. Her fellow artists organised a posthumous exhibition for Eva in 1885, two years after her death, at the La vie Moderne Salon. Her spirit remains in Montmartre in Paris as she is actually buried in the Montmartre cemetery.

Marie Bracquemond, born in 1841, also was a French impressionist painter. Marie developed her drawing skills as a child and began exhibiting her work at the Salón de París during her teenage years. Although she didn't receive formal art training, she received some basic tips and advice from Jean-Auguste Ingres who became the president of the École des Beaux-Arts, and also from Paul Gauguin, whose influence can be seen in her art.

Marie became the wife of Félix Bracquemond, a printmaker who played a significant role in popularising Japanese art in France. They met when she was copying Old Masters in the Louvre, which a lot of artists did in those days, and their love blossomed. The couple collaborated at the Haviland studio in the Auteuil quarter of Paris, where Félix was the artistic director and Marie designed plates for dinner services, among other things. He also taught her to create etchings, but she didn't produce many etchings herself.

Under the influence of impressionist painters, Marie's artistic style began to evolve. She started using larger canvases and more vibrant colours. She also embraced 'plein air' painting and often worked outdoors. Both Monet and Degas became her mentors. According to Marie and Félix's son Pierre, who later wrote an unpublished short biography titled *La Vie de Félix et Marie Bracquemond*, his father did not approve of the impressionist movement, because he was jealous of his wife's excellence in this style of painting. He even refused to show her work to visitors.

In 1886, Félix met Gauguin, who was financially struggling, and brought him into their marital home. Gauguin undoubtedly influenced Marie, providing guidance on canvas preparation techniques to achieve more intense colours. Marie did participate in three major impressionist exhibitions, and some of her drawings were published in *La Vie Moderne.* She also exhibited five of her works at the Dudley Gallery in London in 1881. Sadly, the constant lack of interest and discouragement from her husband led her to abandon painting, except for a few private works. In total, she produced around hundred and sixty artworks, but only thirty-one of them are currently located and catalogued in art collections.

Some of her best-known pieces include *Le Dame en blanc*, *Le goûter*, and *Sur la terrasse à Sèvres*. Marie passed away in Paris in 1916. Art critic Arsène Alexandre wrote about her in the *Le Figaro* newspaper, stating, *"she was one of those ignored artists whose talent and deliberate self-imposed obscurity will astonish future generations."* He praised her as an exquisite painter.

The third female impressionist painter we will discuss is Mary Cassatt. She was actually an American painter and printmaker who spent a significant part of her adult life in France. Her family believed that travel was an important aspect of education, and they visited several European capitals, including Paris. While her parents did not intend for her to pursue a career as an artist, Mary Cassatt began painting at the age of fifteen at the Pennsylvania Academy of the Fine Arts in Philadelphia. Creating art, particularly for women, was only regarded as a socially valuable skill, and not more than twenty percent of the students were female.

However, Mary and many of her friends were strong advocates for gender equality, which was quite remarkable during her lifetime. She was determined to establish herself as a professional artist and even chose to study the old masters independently. Apparently, she stated that there was no teaching at the academy for female students, who could not use live models until much later, and the primary training focused on drawing from casts."

I feel very fortunate that today we are able to see one of her artworks here in Musée d'Orsay. It's called *Jeune Fille au Jardin* and was painted in 1882. It clearly shows her talent. Perfectly depicting the young girls face and hands in soft colours in a freely painted style, sitting in front of a bed of red flowers in an almost abstract background. It makes me want to make up her story, reveal the mystery. Why is she there? What is she thinking? Who was this girl? But right now, I want to learn more about Mary.

"In 1866, she moved to Paris with her mother and some family friends accompanying her. She began studying art privately with Jean-Léon Gérôme, who taught a hyper-realistic technique. Her training involved daily copying of art at the Louvre Museum, for which she obtained the necessary permission. It was a time of change, with radical artists like Manet and Courbet breaking away from the Academic tradition. Artists were seeking new ways to paint. However, Mary Cassatt continued to work in the traditional style at first.

At the onset of the Franco-Prussian War, she and her family returned to the United States in the summer of 1870. Her father only provided for her basic needs, not for her art supplies, but Mary never considered giving up on art. In 1871, she returned to Europe. Within months Mary's career began to improve. Her painting *Two Women Throwing Flowers During Carnival* received a positive reception at the Salon of 1872 in Parma, Italy, and was sold. The art community supported and encouraged her. She subsequently travelled to Madrid and Seville, but in 1874, she made the decision to live in France. Her sister Lydia joined her, and they shared an apartment.

Mary then opened her own studio in Paris. In 1868, her painting *A Mandoline Player* was accepted by the Paris Salon. Mary preferred to depict the social and private lives of women, often portraying them with their children. She can be seen as an early feminist, as she initiated the creation of images of 'a new woman' from a female perspective. She was clearly positively influenced by her mother, Katherine Cassatt, who believed that women should be socially active and knowledgeable. In 1878, Mary created a painting of her mother titled *Reading the Figaro*.

Although Mary's work doesn't really express explicit statements about women's rights, she portrayed them with dignity, showcasing their meaningful inner lives. She never married because she believed it would restrict her professional freedom. Mary Cassatt was outspoken in her advocacy for women's equality and actively campaigned with her friends for equal travel scholarships for students and the right to vote for women.

As an artist, she greatly admired Degas, and later mentioned that his pastels had a profound impact on her, transforming her life. She developed a friendship with Degas and quickly became involved in the impressionist movement. Degas was often seen with Mary and her sister Lydia, studying artworks at the Louvre. Mary Cassatt's frequent strolls through the Louvre fascinated Degas, leading him to create a substantial body of work, including prints, drawings, pastels, and two paintings on this subject. As an artist, Mary is often compared to Degas due to their shared interest in capturing movement and light. Their studios were just a five-minute walk apart, and Degas would regularly visit her studio to offer advice. They collaborated for many years, sharing a high-society background, similar literary and artistic tastes, independence, and having studied painting in Italy.

Their friendship proved mutually beneficial. Degas introduced Mary to pastel and engraving techniques, while Mary assisted Degas in selling and promoting his artwork in the United States. Mary's body of work demonstrates that the 1890s were her busiest and most creative years. Although the impressionist group eventually disbanded, Mary maintained connections with Renoir, Monet and Pissarro. Today, one can still find a memorial plaque on the house in rue de Marignan, Paris, where she resided from 1887 until her death in 1926.

Now let's talk about Berthe Morisot, perhaps best known of them all. I admire the works of these extraordinary women, and I am fascinated by Berthe Morisot. Her art is so freely painted and yet so delicate. In many of her paintings, she uses very light pastel colours that appear soft, but upon closer inspection, you can see the bold brushstrokes that fit together perfectly."

I'm not an art critic, and I've never studied art, so I hadn't even heard of her and some of the other female artists before. But now, having walked the streets of Paris where these powerful women used to live, and thanks to all the information Mario is providing, a whole new and very interesting world is opening up to me. And I'm excited that we are going to see the work of Berthe Morisot and some of these female artists in Musée d'Orsay.

It has to be said though, in the large permanent collection of art, there appear to be only works of a few female impressionist and post-impressionist artists, and then just some of their works. I'm surprised that there are no works of Suzanne Valadon for example, an important female post-impressionist artist.

So let's give these often 'unseen' women a voice! It couldn't have been easy for them to establish themselves as artists. Women painters and other genres of art were not taken seriously, and sometimes I wonder if it's still the same today. The art world seems to be predominantly led by men, with seemingly fifty percent more men becoming famous. But at least nowadays it is more accepted for a woman to be an artist.

"You are right Renate, but let's get back to Berthe Morisot. She was born into a bourgeois family, and like many girls from upper-class families, she received art lessons. Women were not allowed to attend the official Academy of Fine Arts. Berthe was very close to her sister Edma, and they often painted together. They received private art classes from Joseph Guichard and Geoffroy-Alphonse Chocarne. Her sister Edma got married and stopped painting. We know this from the correspondence between the two sisters. Berthe was a rebel. She didn't want to marry; she wanted to become a successful painter.

Part of her artistic education involved copying paintings at the Louvre, where she met other artists, including Monet and Manet, with whom she became close friends. She also met Jean-Baptiste Corot, a landscape painter who introduced her to outdoor painting. It was at that time that she began to model for other artists as well, especially for Manet, who created quite a few artworks featuring her. One of the artworks where we can see Berthe Morisot is called *Le balcon*. It's a well-known painting created by Manet, exhibited in 1869 at the Salon de Paris. Curiously, Manet kept the painting at his home until his death."

We are now standing in front of the painting as it is part of the art collection of the museum. It is interesting to see the woman we are talking about portrayed by such a great master, as if we get to know her in person.

"The friendship between Berthe and Manet lasted for fifteen years. Many believe they were in a relationship. Manet, at that time, was already known for his scandals, and having a lover wouldn't be out of the question, but there isn't a single letter that proves it. However, it is known that Berthe once told a friend that all their love letters had to be burned. Additionally, Manet painted a picture of her with a bouquet of violets, and violets were a symbol of secret love.

Berthe was a modern woman, and at that time, it was not normal for a woman to go alone to an artist's house to model. They had to be accompanied, but Berthe visited Manet's studio on her own many times. In 1874, she married Manet's brother, Eugene Manet. Perhaps she married the brother to be close to Manet, but we don't know for sure. Unlike many other women, Berthe did not stop painting. Berthe and Eugene had a daughter, Julie, whom she painted frequently. Berthe did not have a studio, so she painted at her home. She created many outdoor scenes, such as garden scenes, many featuring her family. She claimed she couldn't live without painting.

At the beginning of her artistic career, Berthe faced criticism when she had an exhibition at one of the impressionist art salons. She was criticised for painting garden and family scenes, even by other impressionists. An art critic said her work was simple and entertaining but not worth taking seriously.

She also criticised herself, but she persevered. In 1864, she exhibited for the first time at the Salon de Paris. Later on, her work was selected for six more Salon exhibitions. In 1874, Berthe joined the first exhibition of the 'rejected' impressionists. Her fellow artists were Claude Monet, Edgar Degas, Paul Cézanne, Camille Pissarro, Alfred Sisley, and Pierre-Auguste Renoir. The exhibition took place at Nadar's studio, a well-known photographer. So, we can certainly say that she was in good company.

Berthe then continued to participate in most of the subsequent impressionist exhibitions. Unfortunately, being a perfectionist, she destroyed many of her paintings. Although she often painted tranquil scenes, she also depicted some tormented women. She herself sometimes felt tormented and knew she had to work hard in her art to continue exhibiting in the male-dominated art world.

The fact that a woman wanted to be a painter and live outside the family like men did was very unusual. Artists were considered to lead a bohemian life and women aspiring to live the life of artists were believed to be leading a disorderly life, even being promiscuous. This is probably why most women chose not to take the step of becoming full-time artists; it was poorly regarded. However, being married and being a mother didn't mean Berthe was going to sacrifice her life as an artist; she was both.

One could say she was a woman ahead of her time, with both a family and a job. Berthe didn't want to be seen as a woman painter but simply as a painter. She had many friends who were artists, musicians, and writers and to this day, she is well-loved. Unfortunately, most of her artwork is in the hands of private collectors, so it's not easy to see her work in a museum. But as we walk through the galleries of the museum, Mario points me to one of Berthe's paintings titled *Le Berceau*. This is one of her best-known works showing her sister Edma lovingly looking at her daughter Blanche. It's a very serene image and just watching it, can make you feel connected to the artist, who is so very capable of capturing intimacy and emotion in her work.

After her husband Eugene died, when he was only forty-eight years old, Berthe's work changed. She mainly created portraits of her daughter, her niece and some self-portraits. She wasn't a successful artist during her lifetime, but towards the end of her career in 1894, she had a solo exhibition at Galerie Durand-Ruel which was a success. Critics finally recognised her talent. She was still a relatively young woman when she died at the age of fifty-four. She is buried in the Passy Cemetery in Paris."

I feel inspired by the lives of these female impressionist artists who are examples of talented and courageous women who defied the norms of their time and left a significant impact on the art world. They were showing the art critics that creativity and talent are genderless. I'm so glad that today I was able to get a glimpse into the lives of some of these great women. May their legacy live on and may more women artists find their voice and be recognised for their art.

It has been a long day with a lot of impressions. But I have to say that it's wonderful to walk the streets of Paris, knowing that these women walked here before us, and are still here in spirit through their art. It's an enriching and unforgettable experience. Time to go back to our hotel. I feel tired but inspired. I can't wait to get home and continue my own art journey. However, this week I will continue my discovery of art in Paris, and tomorrow we will go to Montmartre.

Toulouse Lautrec

And the women in his life

We've just come out of the Abbesses metro, a beautiful example of Art Nouveau, and walk in the direction of the Moulin Rouge, a cabaret and party establishment which has become a world-famous tourist attraction. The neighbourhood still oozes with excitement, with its strange mixture of tourism and sex-shops. Of course, when we are talking about the Moulin Rouge Henri de Toulouse Lautrec springs to mind as arguably his most famous works are the cabaret posters commissioned by the Moulin Rouge.

"In the previous chapter, we talked about Impressionism which started around the 1860s. This was also when Montmartre became the go-to place for artists. Painters like Claude Monet, Camille Pissarro, Pierre-Auguste Renoir and Edgar Degas lived close to, or even in Montmartre. Mary Cassatt, Pablo Picasso, and Vincent van Gogh lived there as well at some point during their artistic career. There were many more artists who also did. It surely was a lively place with an abundance of scenes to be inspired by, as there were a lot of dance halls and cafés where the artists met. A good example is one of Renoir's paintings called *Moulin de la Galette*, which shows young people dancing. But today we will talk about Lautrec and the women who inspired him, as Montmartre became his home as well."

Whilst Mario tells me more about this interesting painter, we are climbing the steep steps in the direction of the Sacré-Coeur, an area with lots of narrow streets that used to be countryside with grapevines. Today there still is a grapevine that produces wine every year.

This promises to be truly intriguing. I must admit that I am learning many new things and I find everything interesting. We are going to find out about the women in Lautrec's life. Mario has already told me a lot about how he painted women; with respect, without any object of desire or obscenity, even though he often painted prostitutes.

"Let's not forget that he was the son of aristocrats and he started by painting his mother and the bourgeois environment which he grew up in. His mother was his model and you can see the admiration he had for her through the sensitivity in his work.

His parents were actually full cousins, and this was presumably the reason why Lautrec had a growth problem. The family did have another child, a boy, who died when he was only one-year-old. This must have affected his parents greatly as they separated soon after that. Lautrec was looked after by a nanny, but when he was eight years old, he went to live with his mother in Paris. From a very young age he used to draw and make caricatures. His mother was truly supportive. Perhaps that's where his sensitivity and respect for women in his paintings originate from.

Despite coming from a bourgeois family, Lautrec developed an affection for women living marginalised lives, such as the prostitutes he painted, who became like a family to him."

I wonder if much is known about these women. Do we know their names, their backgrounds, why they were doing what they did?

"Let's start with Cha-U-Kao. We don't know what her real name was. She used Cha-U-Kao as her stage name as she was a French entertainer who regularly performed at the Moulin Rouge. Apparently, Cha-U-Kao is derived from the word 'chahut', which means chaos and noise. It was also referred to as an acrobatic dance, similar to the can-can. Lautrec made a series of paintings of this eccentric woman, who used to be an agile gymnast and openly declared that she was lesbian. In fact, she became one of his favourite models.

Yesterday we were able to admire the painting *Clownesse–Cha-U-Kao* in the Musée d'Orsay. It portrays Cha-U-Kao in her dressing room at the Moulin Rouge, already relatively old, a declining artist. Despite the bright yellow contrasting her dark-coloured dress and red sofa – I presume it's a sofa – it feels a bit sad to me. He created some artworks of Cha-U-Kao with her partner who is believed to be Gabriele, a dancer who modelled for Lautrec as well.

One of the brothels frequented by Lautrec was in the rue d'Amboise, and one of the working girls there was Mireille. He was very fond of her. A well-known painting in which we can see Mireille is called *Salon de la rue des Moulins*. She is the woman sitting in the front, in a semi-profile position, with her hand around her leg. The painting depicts the women waiting for their clients, and their Madame keeping a close eye on them. Mireille also visited his studio to model for him. Apparently, after she left and went to Argentina, Lautrec stopped going to the brothel in rue d'Amboise. We don't know what happened to Mireille after that.

In 1885, Lautrec met Suzanne Valadon. She was actually Degas' model. He painted several portraits of her, but he also supported her ambition as an artist. People say they were lovers and that she would have loved to marry him. When their relationship ended, she actually attempted suicide. This was in 1888. I think we should be grateful that she didn't go through with it, as she herself became an incredible artist who should not be forgotten.

Lautrec was not only interested in painting women in brothels. He also loved the world of the circus and portrayed many women who worked there. One of the best-known circuses of the time was the Fernando circus. Lautrec, among other paintings, created a very famous artwork of a woman riding a horse, capturing the horse's movement very well. It is called *Equestrienne*. It has been suggested that the woman on the horse is Suzanne Valadon, who used to briefly work as a trapeze artist in a circus.

He enjoyed painting the working class with great attention to detail but in an open style, especially the women who used to work in the Montmartre area. One could say he was a painter of real life. He even created paintings depicting the sadness of alcohol abuse and paintings of women consuming absinthe, a very strong alcoholic drink. Lautrec had a problem with alcohol himself as well.

Some of the women he painted were famous, like Yvette Guilbert, a well-known singer and cabaret actress. Lautrec met her at the Moulin Rouge, which was the largest nightclub in Paris at the time. Yvette was born into a poor family in Paris and she started singing when she was a very young girl. At the age of sixteen, she began working at the Printemps department store as a model and was discovered by a journalist. She then took acting and singing lessons and eventually became a well-known star in Paris' nightlife scene. Sometimes she wrote her own lyrics, which could be filled with lost loves, tragedies, and even obscene texts, based on the poverty she had experienced herself. Lautrec made many portraits and caricatures of Yvette and even dedicated his second album of drawings to her.

People loved her, and she received many positive reviews, including from Sigmund Freud, who attended one of her shows in Vienna. She became known outside of France too; Yvette has performed in the United Kingdom, Germany, and even at the New York City's Carnegie Hall. She was also invited to perform for the Prince of Wales (by then King Edward VII) at a private party, which demonstrates her fame and how much she was admired. Her audience loved her imitations and songs about ordinary people in France. George Bernard Shaw, an Irish playwright, critic, and political activist who had a great influence on theatre and Western culture, wrote a very good review about her.

Yvette later married a businessman named Max Schiller and became an actress in silent films. In her later years she wrote about the Belle Époque, and two of her novels, *La Vedette* and *Les Demi-vieilles* were published. In 1920, she wrote another book with a catchy title *L'art de chanter une chanson*, which means 'the art of singing a song'.

I don't like creating lists of people's achievements as it can be a bit boring, but can a woman like Yvette Guilbert be boring? She truly was a remarkable woman as she also established schools for girls in both Paris and New York. I like the fact that she was honoured as the Ambassador of French Song in 1932. She passed away at the age of seventy-nine and is buried in the Père Lachaise Cemetery in Paris.

It's quite evident from Lautrec's work that he loved red-haired women, and Yvette was indeed a redhead. Another one of these women was Jane Avril, who was an important figure in his life.

Lautrec didn't live to an old age. He suffered a stroke in 1901, which may have been a result of his alcoholism and syphilis. He was partially paralysed and was taken to his mother's chateau in Saint-André-du-Bois. Unfortunately, shortly after that, he passed away in his mother's arms. He was only thirty-six years old. Yet in Paris, it was as if his spirit continued to live on, even to this day. Tourists often buy souvenirs of Paris featuring images of Toulouse-Lautrec. His artist friends did not forget him either. We know that Picasso made drawings of Yvette Guilbert and asked Jane Avril to speak about her friend Lautrec."

I'm getting a much better idea of who Lautrec was and in particular who some of these women were. I can imagine what it must have been like. I can almost sense it, now, here in Montmartre. Parties into the early morning hours, artists soaking up the inspiration, people dancing, but also drunks, desperation, prostitutes working out of necessity. It must have been intense.

We have finally arrived at Le Moulin de la Galette, which was painted by Renoir and many others, and is now a restaurant. It is also close to place du Tertre and the Sacré-Cœur. We decide to walk to the place du Tertre for a break. It is at the heart of the old Montmartre. I can feel my legs from walking uphill, as Montmartre is situated on a hill, the highest in Paris, also referred to as la Butte Montmartre.

Most people have heard about Montmartre, I certainly have. I am reminded of my trip to Paris so many years ago. I was seventeen years old when I visited the city with my parents, my brother and his girlfriend. I remember what I was wearing, a long skirt that I made from some old jeans and corduroy trousers, and a black T-shirt. Strangely, I didn't remember much about this trip, but now that I'm here, the memories resurface. The smells, the sensations and the atmosphere transport me back in time, back to when I came here as a tourist, with my face sketched by one of the street artists.

It must be said it is very touristic and to this day, painters come here with their easels to showcase their art. After our break we will go to the Sacré-Coeur and Mario will tell me more about Jane Avril and La Goulue. It promises to be an interesting story.

Jane Avril y La Goulue

A life of dance

What better place to talk about Jane Avril than Montmartre. I'm thinking back to the time when she walked these streets. Jane Avril is arguably most famous for her image on many of Toulouse Lautrec's posters, which turned her into an iconic figure, representing a world of dancers, cabaret singers and prostitutes.

Mario and I are looking at one of the tourist shops with souvenirs, with Lautrec's art on mugs, T-shirts and many other objects. But do tourists know who Jane was in real life? I am happy that we are going to find out who she was, and how she became a model for quite a few artists as well as a famous dancer. Who was this elegant woman who was often portrayed in a melancholic light?

"We know of Jane that she was a can-can dancer at the Moulin Rouge and other cabarets. Her real name was Jeanne Beaudon, daughter of a courtesan named Léontine Beaudon. Her mother was better known by the name La Belle Élise and it is believed that she was in a relationship with Marquis Luigi Defant, who some say could be Jane's father. When Jane was only two years old, he left her and her mother. Jane was sent to live with her grandparents in the country and received her education from the nuns of a local convent. Soon after, both grandparents died, and initially Jane continued to live in the care of the nuns. However, when she was only nine years old, her mother came looking for her with the intention of turning her into a prostitute.

Her mother was no longer a glamorous, sought after courtesan. She had less distinguished and less generous clients. Léontine forced Jane to work the streets, and a life of abuse and exploitation followed. Her mother was also extremely abusive towards her, which made Jane run away from home when she was only thirteen years old. She was then taken in by the mother of Mr. Hutt, a former lover of La Belle Élise. But Jane was always afraid that her mother would find her.

It is quite possible that this was the time that she developed a nervous condition and began to experience muscle spasms that were uncontrollable. In 1882 she was admitted to La Salpêtrière, a hospital specialising in neuropsychiatry and better known at the time as the 'insane asylum'. Jane was diagnosed with Sydenham syndrome, or Saint Vitus dance, characterised by rapid uncoordinated movements, swaying and nervous tics in the face, hands and feet. At the time they also referred to this as 'female hysteria'.

Jane was only fourteen years old, but she was there with adults, mostly women, many of whom had a mental illness. But the hospital staff took good care of Jane. She was treated by Dr. Jean-Martin Charcot, a neurologist who was an expert in 'female hysteria'. He was head of the Department of Neurology and Psychiatry and famous for his liberal approach regarding the human mind. Students from all over the world came to study his findings and to attend his clinical demonstrations, including Sigmund Freud.

It is important to remember that at the time diseases such as epilepsy and depression were considered a crazy and hysterical neurological problem. It was assumed that mainly women would have this problem. At the Salpêtrière Hospital there were very few men, possibly only twenty percent of the patients.

However, Charcot was able to verify that men were also affected by certain types of hysteria, and this caused a change in the world view of neurological diseases. Jane was safe in the hospital and received various treatments, including hypnosis, gymnastics lessons, and education. She supposedly spent two happy years there. Her mother visited her several times, but each time she did, Jane's condition worsened and Dr. Charcot forbade her to visit her daughter.

The hospital was also known for its annual celebration called *Le bal des folles*. It was authorised by the hospital management and organised by patients and staff. People from outside the hospital were invited as well. At the time it was not unusual to host parties. Paris was a hotspot for social events and festivities. Theatres and music halls flourished and even the lower classes organised parties on the banks of the Seine, as shown in the works of various impressionist artists."

I realise how important art can be in history and I wonder if my art and books will also leave a legacy. Perhaps help others realise that art, in all its forms, can bring about powerful change. At least I feel very inspired by this trip to Paris.

I had also never heard of *Le bal des folles* in La Salpêtrière. It was thought that these kinds of 'lunatic' hospitals were places where people were chained by their ankles and rats ran free around them. According to Mario, thanks to *Le bal des folles* we know that it wasn't so bad. Artists, journalists and women who defended women's rights were invited to attend these annual dance events in the hospital.

"We know that writers such as Émile Zola and Guy de Maupassant were among them. Without a doubt, the 'ball' influenced some of the stories written by de Maupassant.

The ball itself was a happy event and it is here that Jane flourished and received attention. She had used her eccentricity in her dance due to her nervous condition. A Belgian author, Frantz Jourdain, described her as *"an exquisite, neurotic and nervous creature, like a captivating flower of artistic corruption and sick grace."*

When Jane was sixteen, she was released from the Salpêtrière hospital, apparently after an affair with a young doctor came to a halt. She did not want to go back to her mother and was homeless. When she was attacked in the street, she sought the help of a group of women who took her to Madame Marcelle's brothel, where she was treated kindly and allowed to stay. She was invited to accompany them on one of the visits to Le Jardin Bullier, a popular music club, where Parisians came to listen to the orchestra, and women came to offer their services. There was also a dance floor and one day Jane spontaneously started dancing to the delight of the audience."

Is this how she began her career as a dancer?

"Yes, she went from club to club and was then invited to come to Le Chat Noir in Montmartre. In fact, the first modern cabaret bar, where visitors sat at the tables, enjoyed alcoholic drinks and watched the variety shows on stage. It was especially popular with artists including Claude Debussy, Erik Satie, and Lautrec. Jane became a much-loved attraction and also got to know other famous visitors who frequented the club, such as Oscar Wilde and Stéphane Mallarmé.

It was here where Jane, at the time still called Jeanne, met Robert Sherard, who was Oscar Wilde's biographer. It was Robert who suggested Jane adopt the more exotic stage name 'Jane Avril'. She was subsequently hired by Charles Joseph Zidler, co-founder of the Moulin Rouge Cabaret Club, and became the new headlining act. Jane replaced the legendary dancer Louise Weber, called La Goulue, who was the pioneer of the exotic can-can dance."

I'm curious to know who La Goulue is. Surely, she deserves a mention too and I'm happy Mario will explain more about her later.

"For now, we go back to Jane when she became popular for her unusual, jerky and very distinctive way of dancing. It was described as *"an orchid in a frenzy"*. Zidler had become Jane's impresario, allowing her liberties that other dancers didn't have. She would choreograph her own dances and design her own costumes.

In 1893, when Jane was preparing for a great ball, called the *Garden of Paris*, held on the Champs-Élysées, Zidler commissioned Lautrec to create the poster for the show. It was then that Jane and Lautrec became close friends. Becoming his muse also helped Jane increase her reputation and appeal in the entertainment field. Jane and Lautrec were not lovers, they had a friendship and work relationship, but we can safely say that

Lautrec was closer to Jane than to his other models and she remained his friend until he died.

Jane fell in love many times and did have a son whose father is unknown. Due to her job, she allowed him to grow up with foster parents. Nevertheless, she kept in touch and visited him regularly. She later met, and then married, French graphic artist Maurice Biais in 1911 when she was forty-two years old. He officially adopted her son and Jane stopped her career as a dancer. Unfortunately, their happiness was short-lived as Maurice lost his job and became addicted to gambling, losing much of Jane's fortune.

Maurice was later injured during his military service in the war and became seriously ill with a lung disease. He died in 1926 and at first Jane lived in near poverty, but later received financial help from Maurices' sisters that would make her life more comfortable. She died when she was seventy-five years old, during the German occupation of Paris. Her remains rest in the Père Lachaise cemetery, in the Biais family pantheon."

But who was this lady that Jane replaced in the Moulin Rouge? As I am still looking at some of Lautrec's artworks on objects in one of the many tourist souvenir shops in Montmartre, I also spot a picture of La Goulue. This is not her real name, but a name based on her apparent habit of drinking quite a bit of alcohol, downing the drinks of the clubgoers, while dancing there, when she was still a teenager. She was born as Louise Weber, but little is known about her early childhood.

I wonder how a girl like that could end up being referred to as the *"Queen of Montmartre"*.

"We know that her mother worked in a laundry and that at the age of sixteen Louise had to help out. It is said that she loved to dance and enjoyed dressing up in the fancy clothes of clients, often sneaking off to a ballroom in a 'borrowed' dress! She then ended up dancing in small clubs all over Paris and became popular for her rather bold behaviour as a dancer. She is known for teasing the men in the audience, lifting her dress in a swirl and revealing a heart that was embroidered on her briefs.

She met Pierre-Auguste Renoir, who introduced her to painters and photographers for whom she began to model. Louise also began dancing with Jacques Renaudin, who was a wine merchant who worked as a dancer as well, under the stage name Valentin Le Désossé. They ended up dancing at the Moulin Rouge together. Louise and Valentin performed the 'chahut', which is an earlier form of the can-can. They were an immediate success and were booked as a permanent show. In fact, La Goulue became the face of the can-can and the Moulin Rouge. She also became one of Lautrec's favourite models and can still be seen on several of his posters.

At the height of her dancing career Louise left the Moulin Rouge in 1895 to start her own traveling can-can show that was part of a fair. Unfortunately, it was not a success and she lost the money she had invested and had to close the show. She disappeared from the scene and was living in a caravan in poverty in Neuilly-sur-Marne. She was apparently suffering from depression and alcohol abuse. In 1928 she was seen again in Montmartre, unrecognizable by most people due to her severe overweight. She had to make a living selling cigarettes and peanuts on a street corner near the Moulin Rouge. La Goulue died just a year later, when she was sixty-two years old. But somehow, she still is in Montmartre as her remains can be found in the Cimetière Montmartre."

Before continuing our walk, I quickly pick up two small souvenirs from one of the Montmartre shops with images of Jane Avril and La Goulue, made by Lautrec. We are walking in the direction of rue Cortot.

Suzanne Valadon

Surviving in a male dominated art world

C lose to the place du Tertre Mario points out three gardens, which surround the museum we are about to visit. The gardens are named after Auguste Renoir, who lived and worked in the building between 1875 and 1877. In this period, he painted several of his masterpieces, which include *Jardin de la rue Cortot*. It is also the place where many other artists worked and lived.

We are about to enter the Musée de Montmartre in rue Cortot 12 which also houses the former apartment and studio of Suzanne Valadon. It is here where she created so many of her works, met her lovers, protected her son and lived a life dedicated to art. I'm excited as Mario has often told me that my work reminds him of Suzanne's art. I had never seen her work before he told me this. Perhaps I was somehow, unconsciously, connected to her spirit? I don't know, it doesn't matter. We're stepping into history.

Before I started this adventure in Paris. I used to say that I like to create art, not study it, but now that I'm on this fascinating journey with Mario things start to shift for me. Especially hearing about all these incredible women who lived in Paris in the late eighteen and early nineteen hundreds. I try to imagine what life must have been like for them, but of course I can't. Not really. We are in Montmartre, in our modern, busy, fast-paced time, surrounded by tourists who possibly haven't heard about this female artist either.

Suzanne Valadon was her artist's name, but she was born Marie-Clémentine Valadon. She must have been a courageous woman, a painter who made a name for herself in an art world dominated by men. So, who was this lady? Hers is an interesting story. She has been a circus acrobat, a model, an art student, a mother, but most of all, a successful artist, which was, considering the time she lived in, an exceptional achievement.

As we enter the museum, I'm pleasantly overwhelmed by the energy transmitted by the artworks. I believe that art, made by a real person, something that needs to be specified these days, can positively change the energy in a home or workspace.

Although we will of course admire the fantastic artworks by great masters exhibited in the museum, our focus will be on this eccentric woman with ambition.

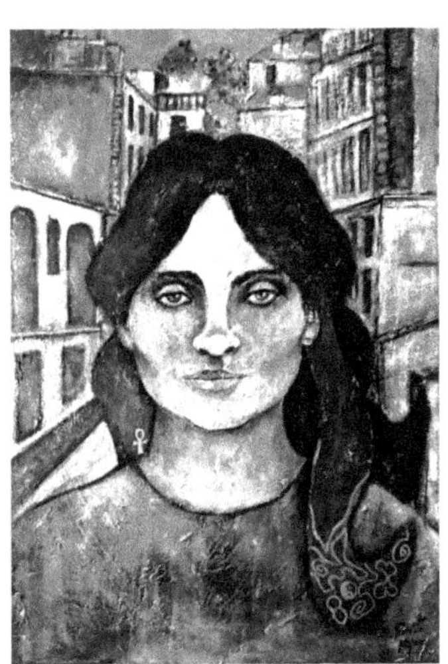
Suzanne Valadon

"Suzanne Valadon has been portrayed by various artists. She was first a model but later became a painter herself. She met great artists such as Chagall, Renoir and Lautrec and she was the muse of Pierre Puvis de Chavannes, a French painter whose work influenced many other artists. He became a confidant and close friend of Suzanne. She often went to his studio in Neuilly where she posed for his neo-classical paintings, and together they would visit Place Pigalle, which was a known place for artist's studios and literary cafés. Later on, Chavannes became the co-founder and president of the Société Nationale des Beaux Arts.

Suzanne became the first woman to be admitted to the Beaux Arts. Her work was admired by other artists as well, for example, Degas and Picasso."

To me her work comes across as quite daring, often using strong colours and loose brush strokes. Suzanne Valadon's life could have been a great story for any of Émile Zola's books.

"She was a typical example of the condition of women of that time, becoming a mother at the very early age of eighteen. She had a pretty hectic love life and nothing is known about the father. When Maurice was seven years old, Suzanne met Utrillo, a Spanish man who was an artist and a businessman. He recognised Maurice as his son.

Suzanne Valadon herself didn't know who her father was either. Her mother worked in a laundry, and Suzanne also had to work cleaning clothes. But apparently, she was rebellious and had various other jobs such as selling vegetables, serving as a waitress. At the age of fifteen she began performing as an acrobat in a circus. She then met two symbolist painters, Antoine de La Rochefoucauld and Theo Wagner, who were decorating a circus in Medrano. This was possibly her first introduction into the art world. It was custom for many artists to visit the circus, including Lautrec and Berthe Morisot for whom Valadon is believed to have been the inspiration for her 1880 drawing of a tightrope walker.

After having worked in the circus for a year, Suzanne injured her back as a result of a fall from a trapeze and had to stop working there. She was very pretty and started posing for different artists. Renoir has created several paintings of her. She also met Lautrec, probably in Montmartre. He fell in love with her and started using her as a model as well. He also suggested to her to change her name and call herself Suzanne instead of Marie-Clémentine. Not just Lautrec, but many men felt attracted to her and the famous musician Erik Satie also fell in love with her.

Suzanne met him when she was also seeing Paul Mousis, a wealthy financier who wanted to marry her. However, Suzanne turned him down as she did not want to lose her independence, but she agreed to become his mistress. Suzanne, Mousis and Satie often went out together. They were referred to as being involved in a love triangle. The affair with Mousis lasted a long time and Suzanne even moved in with him. Satie was devastated. Apparently, their affair had only lasted six months and it was Satie's one and only love affair. After his death, many unsent letters to Suzanne were found in his apartment.

During the time that she posed for painters like Renoir and Lautrec, she learned a lot about painting, but it has to be said that neither Lautrec nor Renoir encouraged her to paint. It was the sculptor and painter

Paul-Albert Bartholomé who saw her drawings and introduced her to Edgar Degas in 1894. When Degas saw her drawings, he told her that she drew like him and apparently said *"you are one of us"*!

It's quite interesting that she never posed for Degas. He was the first to value Suzanne's art and regularly bought works from her. In a way, he supported her in everything, and they became close friends. You can see his influence in her work as some of her paintings and drawings are similar to his ballerinas. In a way she was a woman of character who was way ahead of her time. She did what she wanted and cared very little about what others thought of her."

We are standing in front of Suzanne Valadon's self-portrait *Autoportrait*. Suzanne's artworks can be found in collections and museums all over the world, but I'm glad we can at least view her self-portrait. To get a better idea about her art I take a look at her work on my phone. I really love it and I feel so happy to now being able to get a glimpse of what her life must have been like.

Designer Hubert Le Gall and his team have created a faithful reconstruction in the museum of the atelier-apartment where Suzanne and her son lived. They were able to do so thanks to letters, writings and photographs of that time. We now enter this studio. Maybe I'm making this up, but I sense her energy. I'm glad it's only me and Mario in the space and for a moment we don't speak. I need to take it all in. The large mirror reflecting a window. The flowery, dark green wallpaper, the chairs... I feel that I can become her and I imagine her chatting to Maurice. We enter her studio, flooded with light from a window and half glass-ceiling. A few easels are scattered around the place. It's easy to imagine her working there with her son. I feel so privileged.

"Maurice was a very important part of Suzanne's life, but her life being so hectic with many lovers and being dedicated to painting, she left him in the care of his grandmother. That's when problems started for Maurice. The grandmother could not properly educate the grandson and so Maurice, already thirteen years old by that time, had problems at school and began to drink alcohol. It was easy for him to get it as he lived in Montmartre where alcohol was cheap, accessible and everywhere.

Maurice started behaving strangely. He would sometimes walk around naked and in 1904 he was admitted to a clinic with delirium tremens. This clinic was a place where he supposedly had a pretty bad time because he was surrounded by seriously mentally ill and some violent people. Maurice was sent there to protect himself, but in a sense also to protect society from his erratic behaviour. That was part of the function for those types of hospitals at the time.

When Suzanne realised that her son had become an alcoholic, she decided to do everything in her power to try to cure him. She forced him to paint in order to stop his habit of excessive alcohol consumption. He actually didn't drink while he was painting, it was a kind of therapy, but it didn't stop him drinking.

Maurice turned out to be very gifted. It is interesting and important to know that he did not paint portraits, he painted the streets and what he saw from his window in Montmartre. He considered the portrait artist to be his mother. There is a period called the white period between 1909 and 1914, which is somewhat naïve, a bit childish, but very meticulous. In addition, he used plaster as a painting material. That is why it is called the white period, because there are many white walls and buildings in the paintings. All his paintings have interesting perspectives. It almost seems that there is no end to the streets and there is usually someone walking down the street. These people are not defined, they are like shadows.

His relationship with his mother was special. Maurice had great admiration for her, and she painted some portraits of him while he was painting. Suzanne was very proud of her son, and he in turn considered his mother to be the greatest painter of her time.

As an artist, Suzanne Valadon was exceptional because she was doing something quite daring for her time. Her art is both feminine and brutal. She painted a lot of female and male nudes, which was considered quite scandalous. She also painted and drew her son when he was little, sometimes naked and she painted herself naked as well. In one of her paintings, we see an Adam and Eve scene and the man in this painting would later become her long-time partner. His name was André Utter, and they met in 1909. Utter was a friend of Maurice; he was also a painter.

One day Maurice introduced him to his mother. Utter fell totally in love despite the fact that she was a lot older than him. He and Suzanne began a relationship, which was rather unseemly at the time because of the age difference between them. He was three years younger than Maurice. Utter is best known today for being the manager and second husband of Suzanne Valadon and, as the stepfather of her son.

They called them the *'trinité maudite'* due to their many fights, reconciliations and alcohol abuse. Maurice continued painting and with great success. After a while he started to feel jealous of Suzanne and Utter's relationship. Living with Suzanne and her son at some point bothered Utter as well, because living with Maurice was quite complicated.

Maurice, better known as an artist under the name Utrillo, began to sell a lot of his artworks and became very successful, surpassing the success of his mother. Thanks to the sales of his paintings, they were able to buy a castle, the Château de Saint-Bernard in Saint-Bernard, where they lived for some time. In 1925 Utrillo was already very famous outside France as well.

Although he regularly was in trouble with the police because of fights, possibly due to his drinking problem, Utrillo was very productive and created many paintings. I'm finding it rather strange though that he doesn't seem to be remembered or seen as a great artist today, unlike for example Renoir and Lautrec. Yet nowadays, if you go to the Place du Tertre in Montmartre, there are many painters imitating Utrillo.

There also is a curiosity... in many of Utrillo's paintings he signed them at the bottom right with Maurice Utrillo, V. The V is for Valadon, obviously referring to his mother. At the height of his success Suzanne and Utter no longer had feelings for each other and separated, but they remained friends until she died.

It must have been hard for Suzanne Valadon. After her separation she possibly felt worn out and she started looking for a woman for her son. A woman who could take care of him after she had died. Suzanne also started drinking a lot, and it appears that the last years of her life were rather sad and lonely, but she always remained the great artist that she was. Around 1922 there was a retrospective exhibition of her work which was very successful, though only a few paintings were sold.

Suzanne died in 1938 and she is buried in the Cimetière Parisien de Saint-Ouen in Paris. André Utter died thirteen years after her and was then laid to rest together with Suzanne. She always said that the most important thing in life was to love, give and paint. Suzanne died of a cerebral haemorrhage. Many people were present at her funeral to pay her the last honours but Utrillo was so upset that he could not go. After his mother's death he became very religious and started to frequent churches. He did not stop painting though. He was married to Lucie Pauwels by that time so he did have someone taking care of him."

Suzanne Valadon isn't the only female artist we're rediscovering thanks to our trip to Paris and I'm really looking forward to learning about more of them. Brave women who had to survive in a world where women were admired but at the same time considered to be a lesser species.

I've said it before, but I'm saying it again. I feel really inspired by the great artists that we have seen and discussed so far. I absolutely loved admiring both Suzanne's and Utrillo's art. Her work appealing to me more because of her use of colours, and free-style. But I also like the mystery and gentle storytelling in Utrillo's art, even though I'm normally not a great fan of landscapes and city scenes in art, but that is just me.

We decide to go for a break in Café Renoir in the garden of the museum. It is a great place for a drink and a bite, away from the hustle and bustle of Montmartre, and to contemplate what we have just seen. For me, getting to know Suzanne Valadon especially, has been an amazing experience and I love her famous quote: *"I had great masters. I took the best of them, of their teachings, of their examples. I found myself, I made myself and I said what I had to say."*

Artist and literary cafés in Paris

We wake up to a cloudy day. The sky is grey and it's drizzling with rain. But in Paris rain doesn't mean that you have to stay indoors. Actually, it gives the city a certain charm, the streets, statues and old buildings seem to shine when the light reflects on them. We decide to go to one of the oldest cafés in Paris, Le Procope in rue de l'Ancienne Comédie in the Latin quarter. It is in fact known to be the first literary café in the world and dates from 1686. It was established by an Italian chef from Sicily, called Francesco Procopio, who introduced ice-cream to the French public.

When we arrive, it has stopped raining and we decide to sit outside at one of the tables. I take a peek inside and the ambience certainly is special. Again, like already quite a few times during this journey, I feel like being transported back in time. The black and white tiled floor, the elegant stairway, red walls with lots of golden touches. Beautifully set tables, with white table cloths and shiny glasses, are inviting to enjoy lunch or dinner. It is also like a mini-museum with works of art, sculptures, framed manuscripts and more.

Mario takes a sip of his coffee and starts talking...

"In its early days it was a place where philosophers such as Voltaire, Diderot and Montesquieu went. Most likely it was also popular because there was a fireplace and light. Writers and poets were given white paper and ink and would spend hours and hours in this literary café, where language was a means of conversation, of communication.

The traditional cafés in Paris are famous for their waiters, which were known as 'garcons', in typical Parisian waiter outfits. They inspired philosophers such as Jean Paul Sartre. It's easy to imagine writers coming here to exchange their ideas, in different eras, most certainly without the white table cloths, chatting about life in Paris.

So, why are we going to talk about the cafés in Paris? Well, they were really important for social life and for artists and writers to meet and get inspiration. During the period we are describing, but also before and after the Second World War as we learn from French photographer Robert Doisneau who photographed the streets and many cafés during the 1930s. In his work we can see the merchants, the owners of the cafés and people with accordions all giving a good impression of what it must have been like to visit these places. Important to know is that artists who had been rejected by the official Salon created so-called 'cabarets artistiques'. The cafés became like clubs where the painters, novelists, poets and composers joined to present their work and discuss the social and political conditions in Paris.

Of course, the cafés in Paris were also depicted in paintings by artists such as Béraud, Lautrec, Degas and Renoir. Through their eyes these cafés almost become like a theatre. Scenes where people talk, get drunk, and leave. Lautrec's paintings of the Moulin Rouge really bring this to life.

Cafés are also great to isolate oneself, observe and get a coffee or a drink and allow the inspiration to flow."

I can actually relate to that as one of my books, Cheers, was practically written in one. I used to walk my dog along the seafront and then go to a local café to have some coffee and breakfast. Sitting there with my notebook the words seemed to flow much easier than at home where there often were so many things to do and I became easily distracted. Now here, on the outdoor terrace of Le Procope, I feel stories bubbling up as well.

"Back in the days of the late 1800s and early 1900s the bar-restaurants were the place to go for artists and art critics. It also was quite common for the owners of these establishments to purchase art directly from the artists, something that is still done to this day. A great example was Italian born Rosalie, better known as mère Rosalie, who opened a small restaurant called Chez Rosalie, in Montparnasse. It was frequented by many artists and some of them painted the walls in exchange for food. Modigliani went here often when he was staying in Montparnasse, which was around 1920.

Towards the end of the 19th century Montmartre was like a town in a town as it was sort of inside and outside of Paris with its vineyards and fields with mills. Alcohol was cheap and it was an environment of freedom, a less expensive life which we can see in some

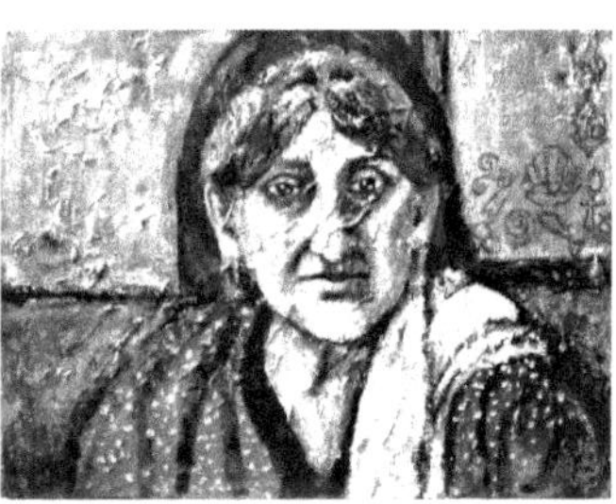

Mère Rosalie

of Renoir's works of art. One of the most famous places to go to was the Moulin de la Galette where people came to drink and dance, painted by several impressionist artists. You can sense and breathe the joy and the freedom when you look at these paintings. We already spoke about Van Gogh coming to Montmartre and going to Café du Tamburin but it is interesting to know that there were quite a few of these types of cafés. It must have been such a marvellous time to be an artist.

Another famous café, which no longer exists, was called Café Guerbois on avenue Clichy. We know that this was a café frequented by many artists, including Édouard Manet. He was part of a group of young avant-garde painters called *Le groupe des Batignolles*. The name comes from the Batignolles neighbourhood where these artists used to meet. Quite a few of them later became known for their impressionist art. They used to meet at the café, which was also a popular place for writers and art lovers, among whom was Émile Zola. We also know that it was frequented by Edgar Degas, Claude Monet, Auguste Renoir and sometimes they were joined by Paul Cézanne and Camille Pissarro.

Worth mentioning as well is Café de la Nouvelle-Athènes which was located at 66 rue Pigalle in place Pigalle, in the residential La Nouvelle Athènes district. Many artists and musicians lived there, such as Frédéric

Chopin, Guillaume Apollinaire, but also George Sand, a French female journalist and novelist. In the late 1800s and early 1900s the café was the centre of literary and artistic creation and regulars included Van Gogh, Matisse and Degas. Artists were also permitted to showcase their paintings. Some say that it was here where the first impressionist exhibition was planned."

Mario explains that when we were at the d'Orsay museum, we saw the painting *In a Café* (the original name was *Absinthe*), created in 1875 by Degas. It's an interesting work of art as he used a model and a friend to depict two figures drinking the rather destructive beverage absinthe. They seem to just stare into the distance, as if not aware of each other. The colour scheme gives the impression of a sad story about their existence. But I presume it was a lot livelier in the café when it was full of artists socialising and discussing daily life, and composer Erik Satie playing the piano in the background.

"During the Second World War the café was a striptease club visited by the nazis. It remained an interesting place as in the sixties it became a lesbian cabaret and later a rock venue. Sadly, the building that housed the former café was destroyed by a fire in 2004 and despite protests they could not save it. It was demolished.

More or less in front of La Nouvelle Athènes was Le Café du Rat Mort, which is now a bank. This was a favourite place of poets and writers, for example, Paul Verlaine and Arthur Rimbaud. These two men were always together, and they were also lovers. The place soon became a meeting point for artists who were seeking models. The clientele of Le Café du Rat Mort was very bohemian. Lautrec's famous painting *Au Rat Mort* was situated in the café. It is said to portray Lucy Jourdain, an infamous courtesan, in a private room where intimate liaisons took place. She seems to grin at the painter, whilst the male companion sitting next to her is half cut out of the frame, and looking away.

Some suggest that Lautrec went on a three-month bender with Lucy who, interestingly, was a lesbian. He created this painting in his studio close to the café in 15 avenue Frochot, after he suffered from alcohol poisoning and a mental breakdown. He did go to a sanatorium and subsequently spent some time in the province to recover from his addiction. But when he returned to Paris he started drinking again.

Some of these types of café-restaurants still exist and they serve food at a reasonable price. Current owners have kept the Belle Époque decoration. They are certainly interesting to pay a visit to soak up the atmosphere and perhaps enjoy a meal. There are still quite a few, around a dozen or more, of these types of restaurants left in Paris. They are referred to as *Les Bouillon Chartier*.

Montmartre certainly was a buoyant place at the time. Au Lapin Agile, which you can still visit today and Le Divan Japonais, both restaurants were examples of very popular cabaret cafés frequented by artists of the time. The owner of Au Lapin Agile used to serve a free meal to artists once a week. Both places served a lot of cheap wine that came from the vineyards that were practically next door. Jane Avril is also said to have performed in these establishments.

To be honest, the list goes on and a part of me would love to time travel into the past to just spend a few days watching the artists and their muses get together in these places that jointly formed the 'heart' of Montmartre. It's difficult to pick just a few to talk about, but there are four more cafés that are worth knowing about.

Firstly, there was Le Chat Noir which we have already mentioned in a previous chapter. It was famous and popular and opened its doors in 1881. It sits at the foot of the Montmartre hill. It was a cabaret café and a meeting place, like the others mentioned above, for artists and writers. Then there was La Cigale, which dates from 1887 and started as a café and concert establishment to later also include dance and comedy. Both are great examples of venues where poets, writers and artists came to have a bite and a drink. They often weren't charged for their consumptions in exchange for art, for example, cabaret posters or articles for the café's newspaper. It was very common for each café to have their own art and literacy newspaper. It is also interesting to know that the first movie screening took place in a café."

But I do wonder what it must have been like for women. Were they allowed to go to these establishments? From some of the photos that we have looked at these places were predominantly visited by men.

"Yes I think we can conclude that people at that time frowned upon a woman on her own sitting in a bar, but there were a few exceptions. For example, L'Auberge du Clou which was located at 30 avenue Trudaine is considered to be quite an iconic place and became known among the artists as a literary and artistic sanctuary. It was frequented by many artists that we get to know during this trip, including Suzanne Valadon and Erik Satie. Suzanne was often painting inside the café. The owner allowed artists who didn't have any money to hang their work, whilst waiting to pay their bill. The name 'Clou' refers to the fact that the café was decorated with nails where visitors could hang their coats and artists their art.

Similarly important was Le Mirliton in boulevard Rochechouart. It was considered by many to be the soul of Montmartre. Lautrec created a painting of the owner, Aristide Bruant, a French cabaret singer who also was a comedian. Most people know him as the man with the red scarf and black cape depicted on a famous poster by Lautrec. Some suggest that they became close friends. Le Mirliton was also known for the place where people sang popular songs that were all transgressive and very anti-bourgeois. Songs about freedom and the hypocrisy of the ruling classes.

Possibly the most famous of these cabaret-cafés was the Moulin Rouge about which we have already spoken earlier. Till today this is a well-visited tourist attraction."

Gosh, little did I know about the importance these cafés had in those days. During our talk we watched old photos taken during the period we are discussing and we have also looked at images of paintings, some of which are either in private collections or in museums abroad. Looking at these images brings everything to life for me. We order another drink and I am keen to learn more about the writers who were very much part of this café culture.

The importance of the word

Well, that's what writers believe and I'm delighted to get more knowledge about some of them. I write, I call myself a writer, or better said, a storyteller. I have published ten books so far, and I love telling stories. I also like to read. But the question is: when you read a book, will you actually get to know the writers? Their life stories? The reasons and inspirations for their work? Sometimes you might, but I must say that I'm intrigued to learn about the well-known writers and the women they met. Those individuals who once roamed the streets of Paris.

First a short introduction.

Paris, in the second half of the 19th century, was a city that, given its grandeur, still had many narrow streets and dubious neighbourhoods which were the perfect setting for police themed writings. A specialty of French literature is the *Polar*, short for roman policier in English crime fiction. At a later stage the French police stories will become popular in the entire world and turn into cinema and television series. Interesting to mention is the American writer, who had never set foot in Paris, who wrote a few stories, *The Paris Mysteries*, that take place in the streets of the city. One of which is called *The murders in the rue Morgue*. We are of course, talking about Edgar Alan Poe.

When we talk about the writers in Paris at that time, we must take into account that the majority of them were men, and many of them also frequented the brothels which we have already talked about. Apart from enjoying the 'services' offered, they also went there to get inspired and meet other men to talk about political affairs, literature and philosophy.

There are many writers who recounted stories of the great changes of Paris that turned a dirty and dangerous city into a beautiful imperial capital. They illustrated the proletarian areas and the neighbourhoods of the aristocrats, the grand boulevards and narrow streets with many mysteries. The impressive architecture and the splendour which go hand in hand with beauty created by magnificent artists, yet at the same time showing the ugliness of the lives of humble people.

But let's not forget that our trip, to a great extent, is to find out about women who inspired artists and writers. And about women who, despite the difficulties they were facing in a male-dominated society, created art or literature.

And although we are covering a rather specific period, from 1850 to 1940, we have to mention a ground-breaking, rather special lady who already became well known during the Romanticism era. She was born in 1804 and her name was Amantine Lucile Aurore Dupin de Francueil. Now that's a bit of a mouthful, however, she used a penname for her writings and her work was published under the name George Sand. Yes, a male name, but that shouldn't surprise us considering the era she lived in, with men being the rulers, the decision makers and presumed to be not only more important but also more intelligent than women. So, to me it's extra interesting to find out about this woman who was able to stand tall among these men. Who was she?

"George Sand was a French journalist and novelist and she wrote plays, political texts, tales and over seventy novels. During her lifetime she was among the most popular writers in Europe, even more famous than Honoré de Balzac and Victor Hugo, and she continued to be very popular as a writer throughout her lifetime and after her death.

She was born into a well-off family, but she fought against prejudices of women in a conservative society. What I find interesting is that she was one of quite a few women in the 19th century who would wear men's clothing in public. Women had to apply for a permit to do this. This could be for health or for example recreational reasons, think about horseback riding. George Sand, however, wore men's clothes without such a permit, which shows her rebellious character. It would have also given her access to venues that barred women.

She was only twenty-seven when she decided to use the pseudonym George Sand, which possibly had a lot to do with better chances of being published.

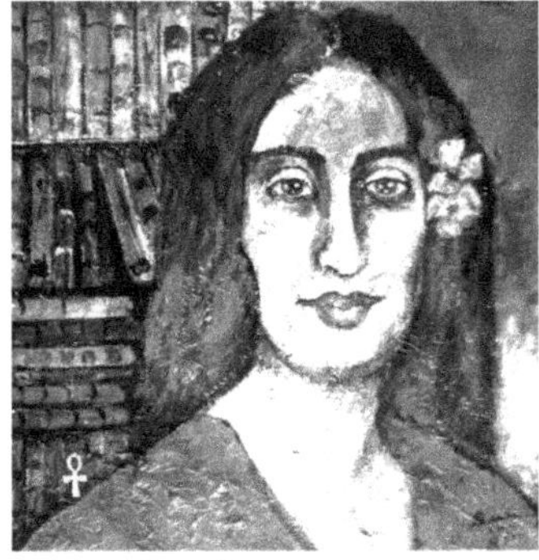

George Sand

She married and became a baroness when she was eighteen and had two children, Maurice and Solange, who both became writers. She ended up leaving her husband but did get custody of their children. She had quite a few romantic affairs among which was Frédéric Chopin. She actually wrote a novel which is presumed to be inspired by her relationship with the Polish musician. The novel is called *Lucrezia Floriani.* Later in her life she became close friends with Gustave Flaubert. She certainly had an interesting love life as she also was intimate with actress Marie Dorval. George Sand died at the age of seventy-one in Nohant-Vic in France. I cannot help thinking that she inspired other female writers and artists, but let's discuss some of the well-known male writers and find out what their relationship to women was.

I will start with Marcel Proust. He is considered one of the greatest writers in France and even in the entire world at the time. He too came from a wealthy family and he always frequented high society events. He is most famous for *À la recherche du temps perdu*, a novel which consists of seven volumes.

Proust started writing the novel in 1909 and continued to work on it until 1922. The theme is referred to as 'involuntary memory' as it is a recollection of experiences of the narrator, from childhood into adulthood, in high-society France. Proust was already suffering from asthma as a young boy and later in life he fell ill with pneumonia. A pulmonary abscess, from which he eventually died when he was fifty-one years old, meant that the last three of the seven volumes had unpolished passages, but his brother Robert made sure they were edited and published as well. When he was still alive, he had already published several volumes. He paid for the first one himself, as several publishers had rejected it.

The seven volumes are a reflection on love and life of the main character Marcel, learning about participating in society, while he is growing up. It is not thought to be an autobiography, but certainly to have been inspired by his own life. It is important to know that Proust was a homosexual and at that time he had to repress his sexuality as this was not widely accepted. Nevertheless, women were important in his life and work. All the women that appear in *À la recherche du temps perdu* are wonderful, beautiful, elegant, intelligent, and educated. His mother was very important to him too. She was overprotective, which you could argue is not necessarily healthy for the development of a child, but she always took care of him, including taking him to spas to treat his asthma.

Proust had a whole archive of photos of the women he knew and who were his friends. He was very sociable and cared about his reputation. He felt he had to hide his homosexuality in order to not compromise his life. Although he is not believed to have had a sexual relationship with a woman, he did have a male lover. I'm finding it interesting that the vast majority of the characters that appear in his books, whether they are men or women, will have had some homosexual experience.

Also worth mentioning, in his work he writes in the first person and the character appears to be a seducer of women. So you could say that he disguises himself in his work as a heterosexual, because for him his homosexuality was a disgrace and something to be ashamed of. We can only wonder what the life of this brilliant writer, and his books would have looked like had he lived in our times.

Let's talk about Victor Hugo now, he is someone we of course need to mention. Many are familiar with his work through musicals and films. He is considered one of the great writers of France and he is best known for his historical novels *Notre-Dame de Paris* and *Les Misérables*. He always defended the condition of women denouncing the injustice that was done to them in a society that did not recognise their rights, neither private nor socially. He married his childhood sweetheart, Adele Foucher and despite both having affairs, they lived together for nearly forty-six years.

He also had a very important lover, Juliette Drouet, who was in his life for fifty years. Victor Hugo was very sensitive to the condition of women at the time. He expressed that it was painful to see how women were treated as slaves and were victims, but to him they were sacred as a woman had given life to him.

He was one of the few men who fought for equality of the sexes. One day he saw how a man in the street beat a woman, a prostitute, and he went out to defend her and then acted as a witness at the police station. It was this experience that inspired him to create one of the characters in the play *Les Miserables*. He named her Fantine.

Despite his outspoken opinion on women rights, as was normal for men in his time, Victor Hugo also frequented prostitutes. He wrote romantic literature, which means that, on the one hand, he could be a feminist, but at the same time he considered women in love relationships as something that could make men suffer; it turned them into evil creatures. However, he has also said that the eighteenth century had proclaimed the rights of men but that the nineteenth century had to be that of women.

Till this day it is possible to visit the apartment that he rented from 1832 to 1848, on the 2nd floor of 6 place des Vosges. Here you can, among other things, see his very high desk, as he always wrote standing. Interestingly, there is also a Chinese room in the house. He died in 1885 in Paris.

We see that the nineteenth century was not a century of many advances for women rights; it was in fact a tremendously unfair and cruel century towards them. But it was also the decline of an era and the beginning of something new, both in art and literature.

Another interesting figure is Charles Baudelaire. But what was his relationship with and view of women? He is considered one of those great poets, revered because of his complex sensibility to reveal modern themes. Poetry changed thanks to his work, which was considered scandalous at the time. It was censored because of the strong sensual content marked by the women in his life. Who were those women?

Baudelaire's mother, a widow, was very important to him and he adored her, but when she married another man, their relationship deteriorated. His mother is well reflected in some of his poems. Another important woman in his life was Mariette, who was the servant who had a big heart for him and he always gave her his support. Then there was his relationship with Sarah, la Louchette, this was a nickname, because she was squint-eyed. Sarah was a prostitute, who presumably gave him syphilis. Not much is known about her and their relationship didn't last long but he did write at least three poems about her.

Baudelaire did not become a professional poet immediately and first worked as an art critic, writing reviews for exhibitions in the salons of 1845 and 1846. His first published and well-known bundle was *Les Fleurs du mal*. When Baudelaire received his inheritance, he became known for spending it freely on parties and luxury objects, but also on opium and hashish. He soon got into debt and later had to live off an allowance provided by his family. But there were several women who very much influenced his poetry, among which was Apollonie Sabatier, the courtesan we have already described in a previous chapter. This interesting lady became his muse. Baudelaire fell in love with her and has dedicated some quite sensual poems to her.

But the love of his life was Jeanne Duval. They met in 1842 when she worked in a theatre. She was a very tall mixed-race woman. At first, she was his mistress, but she was in his life for the next twenty years. He wrote sensual love poetry and *La Chevelure* translating into 'the head of hair' is a great example of this. It can be said that their relationship was quite stormy with breakups, reunions, and selfishness. They made a rather special couple in Paris and people insulted them. Although he protected her, they did not live together. We don't really know whether she was in love with him and it must be said that a lot of women at the time exploited their charms in order to survive.

According to the beauty standards of the time Jeanne wasn't considered very attractive with her thick black curly hair but Baudelaire fell for her. He frequently invented his poetry orally and Jeanne would then be there to take notes of what he said. He was a writer who would express what he saw, but with irony and often creating a magnificent world from where anything can happen, full of curiosities, mystery and beauty. In 1863 he went to Brussels to give some lectures, but sadly he suffered a number of strokes that left him partially paralysed. He died at the age of forty-six in Paris, but his terminal illness was believed to have been caused by syphilis.

As we can see, writers had an important role in society and many of them went to the brothels. In their writings they explained about the lives of the prostitutes, making their situation visible to society. They wrote about the difficult life of these poor women who were practically imprisoned in a brothel and when they got sick, they had to go to the hospitals which were like jails. These writers wrote about them, but at the same time they took advantage of these women.

The exception was Émile Zola, whom we have discussed before, who did go to brothels but who is not believed to have used the services of these women. He merely went to these places for inspiration and to show examples of the hypocrisy of society in his writings. He wrote about this injustice; however, he did not appreciate prostitutes very much. He denounced the servitude to the bourgeois, but at the same time he found these women vulgar.

Guy de Maupassant is one of those writers who denounced the hypocrisy of the wealthy classes as well. He is seen as a master of short stories depicting the lives, social situations and destinies in gloom-ridden wording.

He had a very pessimistic view of the human existence. Like Zola and Flaubert, he was a realist writer and became one of the most important writers of that movement. He was born in 1850 and his mother was passionate about literature. He had a happy childhood. He was twenty-five when he published his first story. Maupassant is above all a short-story writer and he published over three hundred stories. He only wrote six novels.

In his work he talks about the bourgeoisie and about the humble people such as peasants, but quite typical for Maupassant, both in his novels and short stories he also includes many esoteric themes and people who are about to go mad. We could say that madness, along with hypocrisy, are the important themes in his stories.

He describes a world in decline. His first novel called *Une vie* tells a realistic French 19th century story where the main character, Jane, who is an aristocrat, is going to leave the convent at the age of seventeen years old. She is allowed to live in a castle and meets a viscount who will become her husband. After the honeymoon they travel to Corsica where he is going to cheat on her, first with the maid and later with a friend of Jane's. They have a son named Paul who has health issues, which is also causing problems for her. Jane's life goes from boredom to suffering, not only because of the health of her son, but the husband of Jane's husband's mistress, is going to kill both his own wife and Jane's husband. Jane is left alone, sad, and the only consolation she will have in her life is that a man called Paul will come and live with her. His son joins them as well as the mother of this boy had died when he was born. Jane will raise the son and that's the only joy the woman will experience in her life.

Maupassant always creates disastrous situations for the female characters in his stories. He literally said about women *"I don't love them but they amuse me"*. He criticised courtesans saying that they were women who treated love as a pastime, but that their hearts could not be moved by anything, they were impotent, they could not love nor lead, and their emotional life was always a mess. He said that these women were narcissistic and the supposedly superior man would become a toy in the hands of those ruthless women, since they were only with men to get money and power. He also said that in their real love life they were having intimate relationships with other women.

We know that Maupassant never got married, but he had many lovers. One of them was Joséphine Litzelmann, the mother of his three children.

Maupassant's novels and pessimistic stories are presumed to come from the fact that he was ill, not just mentally ill, but he also had syphilis that led to his death. There is another famous short story called *Boule de suif*. It is a story about a prostitute. In this story he talks about the hypocrisy that some people feel towards a courtesan, but that at the end of the story the courtesan is going to save the lives of these people by having sex, for example, with Prussian military officers.

He could be quite cruel regarding women when he wrote about the fact that he had contracted a venereal disease, but it was almost as if he was proud to have it. He wasn't afraid of prostitutes and in fact felt superior. He was a brilliant writer, but he was also a very misogynistic man. He was forty-two years old when he died.

We couldn't possibly cover all writers from the Belle Époque but there are a few more worth mentioning. Starting with Gustave Flaubert who was a literary realist novelist. He wasn't born in Paris, but he lived there for a number of years. He is best known for his novel *'Madame Bovary.* At first, when it was published the novel was attacked by public prosecutors as they said it was full of obscenity. This resulted in a trial in 1857, but this in itself made the story notorious. He was subsequently acquitted and the novel became a bestseller. It is a two-volume novel and until this day considered to be Flaubert's masterpiece and seen as an influential literary work throughout history.

The main character is Emma Bovary who married a middle-class man, but after a while, she could not stand this life. She then spent her entire life trying to escape the boring lifestyle by having love affairs and financially ruining her husband who loved her.

But who was Flaubert and who were the women in his life? From letters that have survived we do know that he had a nine-year relationship with Louise Colet, who was a poet. He lived with her in Paris. He then left Paris and went back to Croisset, close to Rouen, where he was born and where he would spend the rest of his life. He did stay in touch and frequently visited both Paris and Great Britain, where he is presumed to have had a mistress, but we don't know anything about her. He referred to himself as a romantic and an enraged liberal. He was against authoritarianism and supported people who were fighting against monopolies and power.

He did travel quite a bit, among other places to the Middle East and is believed to have contracted syphilis in Beirut. Flaubert never married and didn't have, nor want any children. He was very open about his sexuality and wrote about his visits to prostitutes during his travels, also having sexual activities with male prostitutes in Beirut and Egypt. His biographer, a man called Émile Faguet wrote that Flaubert's only serious relationship was with Louise Colet. There were two more women who were important to him, his niece Caroline Commanville and George Sand.

As you will have understood by now, women were in a sense discriminated, but homosexuality wasn't accepted either and therefore I feel it is good to mention two great writers who were active in the late 1800s, who had a very intense love affair. We are talking about Arthur Rimbaud and Paul Verlaine.

They met when Rimbaud was only seventeen years old. Verlaine was married at the time and actually left his wife and child to be with Rimbaud. The relationship only lasted a few years until one day they had a fight and Verlaine fired a gun at his lover. He was sentenced two years in a Belgian prison for this. Verlaine was a French poet known for his symbolism, but he was also associated with the Decadent movement, a late-19th-century literary and art movement representing an aesthetic ideology of artificiality and excess. Both Rimbaud and Verlaine are considered some of the greatest poets, in France and internationally.

Rimbaud is best known for his influence on modern literature because of his surreal and transgressive themes. He was born in Charleville where he started writing when he was still a young boy. He also was a very good student, but when he was a teenager, he left his formal education and went to Paris. This was during the Franco-Prussian war. It must have been a hectic time for such a young man. When he was twenty years old, he had already created the biggest part of his total body of work.

To me it is rather surprising to find out that Rimbaud stopped writing literature after he had completed his best-known work *Illuminations* at the age of twenty.

Rimbaud was a restless soul, and a 'libertine'. When he stopped his writing career, he travelled three continents as an explorer and a merchant, until he died from cancer when he was just thirty-seven years old."

We can surely say that men felt superior to women, however, without them as inspiration, they wouldn't have written their masterpieces in literature. But there were also women who did stand up for their rights and I'm looking forward to hearing what Mario will tell me about two powerful women. Both rather special ladies. Colette and Louise Michel.

Colette and Louise Michel

Fighting for the right to exist

Not long ago, I watched an English spoken film about Colette, released in 2018. Mario had already mentioned her. What an intriguing woman she was! The movie is quite a romanticised portrayal of her life, but it's nevertheless fascinating to watch.

"I haven't seen that film, but I feel, much like many others, that she was ahead of her time. Her full name was Sidonie-Gabrielle Colette, born in 1873 into a bourgeois family in the countryside. Her parents were quite unique as they were libertarians and this was reflected in her upbringing and education.

She was only twenty when she married Henry Gauthier-Villars, fourteen years her senior, who was already a renowned author and editor, as well as a notable figure in Parisian society. He used to publish his work under the name Willy. He introduced Colette to artistic and intellectual circles and, recognising her talent for writing newspaper articles and stories, pushed her to write. He then published her writings under his name. It must be said that it was a consensual exploitation. She was deeply in love but also suffered greatly due to his infidelities. Later in her life, Colette mentioned that she wouldn't have become a writer without Willy.

A series of four books known as the Claudine stories were published. They were an immediate success. The first was titled *La Maison de Claudine*. They were based on, or perhaps it's better to say, inspired by her life as a girl and young woman in the countryside. She said, *"Claudine is me, and yet she isn't, but let's say she is."* They weren't autobiographical, but nonetheless, the Claudine books dealt with things that happened to Colette and things she wished had happened to her.

It's fair to say that Willy and Colette had a tumultuous relationship, and he wasn't always kind to her. In fact, he could be quite cruel. He would lock her in a room and tell her she couldn't leave until she finished writing something. And as I mentioned, he was unfaithful, but also encouraged Colette to have relationships with women.

In 1906, she decided to separate from him, but because the copyright to her work belonged to Willy, she had no access to the profits. Later, she went to court to regain ownership of her own work, which was granted. Initially this new life wasn't easy due to her financial situation, so she began performing on stages throughout France. This wasn't well-paid work, and she decided to start working as a journalist as well. Her novel *La Vagabonde*, published in 1910, recounts this experience. It also exposes the condition of women at that time and how difficult it was for them to be independent in a male-dominated society, a recurring theme in her later works.

She also had several relationships with women, the most notable was with Mathilde de Morny, known as Max, who often dressed as a man. They shared the stage multiple times, and in 1907, they kissed on stage in a pantomime at the Moulin Rouge called *Rêve d'Egypte*. The kiss practically caused a riot. After this, they couldn't be publicly together as a couple, but their relationship lasted for several years.

In 1912, Colette married Henry de Jouvenel, the editor of *Le Matin*. When Colette was forty, they had a daughter nicknamed Bel-Gazou, but the marriage ended after twelve years, partly due to her affair with her stepson, Jouvenel's son from a previous marriage, who was only sixteen at the time. Overall, we can say she led a truly free life and fully embraced her sexuality. She was considered a scandalous woman. She didn't care much about what others thought of her. She managed her life, the scandals, her relationships, and the more people talked about her, the more fascinating she became. She was also a nature lover, adoring the countryside and being surrounded by animals, especially cats.

Most of her journalistic writing was done between the nineteen-twenties and forties. She published over twelve hundred articles, but she also continued to write novels, including *Sido*, *Le Fanal Bleu*, *La naissance du jour* and *L'ingénue libertine*. In the English-speaking world, she is best known for her 1944 novel *Gigi*.

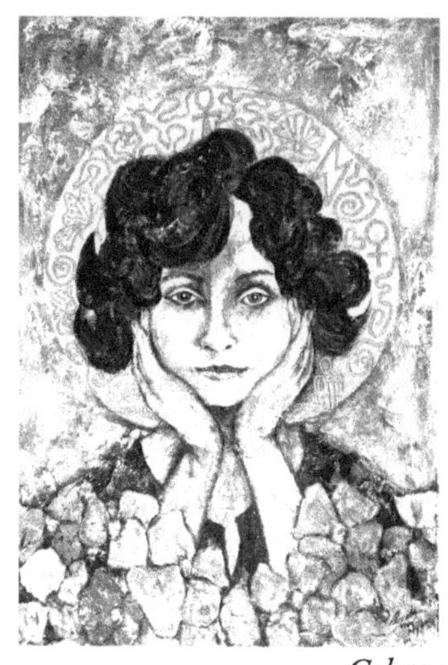

Colette

Her notable articles were published in a newspaper called *Le Journal de Colette*, articles about women. For example, about illegal abortions, how terrible they were, and other injustices towards women. Colette never claimed to be a feminist, which is quite curious considering her life and worldview. However, today she is an icon of feminism.

She passed away in 1954 in her apartment in Palais Royal and due to her lifestyle and divorces, she wasn't allowed to have a church funeral. Instead, she received a state funeral, something unprecedented for a writer in France."

I'm truly impressed. What a woman, what an inspiration, also for the younger women of our time. I believe it's important to be aware of these women who, in some way, paved the way for our freedom.

"The same can certainly be said about the next lady we will get to know, Louise Michel, who is known, among other things, for her significant role and her active participation in the Paris Commune, a very violent revolution which took place in 1871. At that time France was at war with Prussia and was defeated, but many Parisians didn't want to surrender to Prussia. Paris was in turmoil. The Paris Commune, which lasted for a short period, in fact, only three months, was quite brutal. We've already discussed previously how many artists and writers supported the Commune. Many women were involved as well.

Louise Michel stands out above all others as a feminist icon. She was called the Red Madonna because she fought for women's rights and was seen as an enemy of the bourgeoisie. She never married nor had children, and she endured much ridicule, also because she often dressed as a man. She was the illegitimate daughter of a woman who worked as a maid, and who became pregnant by the owner of the house. Possibly due to this, Louise received a good education and was able to go to school. She read a lot and started writing as well. One day, she reached out to the writer Victor Hugo and sent him some of her work. He responded and praised her writing. He recognised her talent, and one thing led to another.

Louise moved to Paris, to Montmartre. Here, she began working as a teacher, as she wanted to change the education of girls, who were mostly taught domestic tasks like sewing and embroidery. Louise wanted them to learn literature and mathematics. She truly fought for an egalitarian society.

Then she became involved in the Paris Commune, organising women's battalions, caring for the wounded, and even fighting on the front line. Many people were malnourished and sick, as there was nothing to eat, and numerous people died during the conflicts.

There came a point where Louise surrendered to the enemy because her mother was imprisoned, and she didn't want anything to happen to her. Her trial was on December 18, 1871. Apparently, two thousand spectators attended as it was a major event. She wore black, and one of the things she was accused of was setting fire to the Paris City Hall. She was forty years old at the time. She wasn't sentenced to death, but she had to spend almost two years in solitary confinement. Her imprisonment became a spectacle, as people from the town could go see her in her cell. It was like exhibiting an animal.

After being released from prison, she was deported to New Caledonia. Those who were part of the Commune were defeated by conservative forces, and the Third Republic would last until 1940, when they were beaten by the nazis. A new Vichy government, which collaborated with Germany, was installed. In 1958, Charles de Gaulle created a new constitution that established the current French Republic.

But let's return to Louise. Many of those who had fought during the Paris Commune were deported to New Caledonia, a group of islands off the coast of Australia. Louise lived in New Caledonia for eight years, but she always stood up for marginalised people. She befriended the indigenous Kanak people. She started teaching, but she also studied the Kanak culture and learned their language. In fact, she helped them rebel against French colonial power. Interestingly, in that same area where she was, there were others who had participated in the Commune but advocated for colonisation under the pretext of ending the savage state of these people. Louise was different and sided with the inhabitants.

In 1880, she was pardoned for what she had done during the Commune and was allowed to return to France, where she was welcomed triumphantly. Now recognised as a brave woman, she could travel throughout Europe but Louise was always fighting for change.

She died in 1905, and a huge crowd attended her funeral. There were many more women who fought during the Commune and did amazing things. But this isn't a political guidebook; it's about women with a major influence on art. Louise wasn't a writer of books, but she's important because she was part of the Commune, which also helped shape the city being part of the early feminist movement. To this day, she is remembered in Paris with, among other things, a park, a metro station and a square bearing her name."

The weather has cleared, and we're going to 14 boulevard des Capucines where Mario will explain the importance of photography and film in Paris of the time.

Photography

Images of a new world

My head is positively buzzing with so much information about the Paris Cafés and writers. I look at the passers-by and feel grateful for the experience of visiting and getting to know Paris in such a unique way.

"Look at that man Renate, he is the spitting image of the photographer Félix Nadar!"

We already spoke about him before didn't we?

"Yes, when we were talking about Impressionism."

Mario shows me a black-and-white photo and indeed, the man, drinking a glass of wine two tables away from us looks very much like him.

"Nadar was born in 1820 in Paris as Gaspard-Félix Tournachon, but he became known by the name Nadar, possibly given to him by his friends who called him Tournadar which then was abbreviated to Nadar. At first, he was known for creating caricatures, which were published in *Le Charivari*, a satirical periodical. He was also a novelist and a journalist, but best known for his photography. He began taking pictures of family and friends, but became a professional photographer in 1854 and opened his studio in 113 rue St. Lazare.

It was around that time that he married Ernestine Lefèvre, who was only eighteen years old. He was thirty-four at the time. Perhaps it was true love, this marriage between a young middle-class girl and the bohemian artist, as they stayed together for fifty-four years, until she died.

Nadar soon became a sought-after photographer and had gained fame for capturing portraits of prominent figures of his time such as George Sand, Courbet, Baudelaire, Delacroix, and Sarah Bernhardt. His early photographs of Sarah Bernhardt, in particular, exude a mysterious and seductive aura.

Portrait photography was booming at the time, but Nadar had his own style and preferred to portray his clients in natural daylight and without a lot of décor. At some point Nadar moved his studio to 35 boulevard des Capucines, where he hosted the first impressionist exhibition. It is also close to the café where the first cinema projections took place in 1895. Photography was of course the precursor of cinema, as the latter is photography in motion.

Although photography was invented by the Frenchman Joseph Nicéphore Niépce in 1824, it was Nadar who revolutionised this new art form by using electric lighting. Instead of relying on natural light in outdoor settings, he essentially invented the flash, enabling taking pictures in indoor locations with artificial lighting. Even in very dark places like the catacombs or sewers in Paris. He was also the first to take aerial photographs using a hot-air balloon in 1858.

Let's dive a little deeper into the importance of photography in general in Paris. There were two important periods. At the beginning it created significant changes in the arts and you could say that the birth of Impressionism can be attributed to photography. It hugely influenced art, as painters didn't have to ask people to come to their studios to sit for them for hours on end, in order to create their portrait. And they could work from pictures of landscapes to fine-tune their work. There was no longer a need to portray people in a traditional painting, which liberated artists to embark on new creative paths. You could say that it changed the way art represented life.

Not only that, it became a tool as well. For example, and we already talked about this before, courtesans could now get their picture taken and use them as calling cards to promote their services. The police also had photographs and personal information of these women, so they could have a register of their activities.

Photography greatly assisted painters in capturing movement realistically. Images of a running person or a galloping horse allowed painters to study movement in detail. Not only did it open up new possibilities for artists, photography also played an important role in science, especially in medicine. Figures like Jules Marey utilised photography to freeze images and study motion.

The arrival of photography also introduced a new way to portray the allure of women. Simultaneously with the birth of photography, a whole new phenomenon emerged, namely creating pictures of nude women for both commercial and pornographic reasons. These photographs were distributed clandestinely. They also served as references for painters and sculptors. It's pretty obvious that photography made a significant contribution to painting.

Another important photographer that I would like to tell you about is Eugène Atget who was best known for documenting the vanishing architecture of the 'Old Paris', a project that was the focus of his career from 1897 through to the 1920s. Atget started as a theatre actor but transitioned to photography because he suffered from vocal cord issues. He collaborated with painters who were interested in landscape photography, greatly aiding the development of contemporary painting. Architects also sought his services for commissions. Atget focused on capturing streets, usually with a hazy or retouched quality, and deserted urban scenes, often in sepia or violet tones.

Towards the end of the 19th century, he settled down in rue Campagne Première in Montparnasse, where he established his studio and eventually passed away in 1927. His work gained a resurgence thanks to surrealist artists like Man Ray, André Breton, and Bérénice Abbott, who found inspiration in the mysterious ambiance of his photos.

Also, thanks to photographers like Atget, photography became an invaluable witness to the profound changes in Paris, including Haussmann's urban renovations, the construction of the metro, demolitions of buildings, the creation of new bridges, and the Universal Exhibitions. They also documented curious incidents, such as the massive flooding of the river Seine in 1910, which submerged much of Paris. One can find photographs depicting people using boats to navigate the flooded streets and a memorable image of a locomotive that failed to stop and emerged from the window of the Montparnasse train station.

When photographers sought recognition as true artists, painters of the time refused to acknowledge it as art. Baudelaire argued that photography should serve the purpose of painting. However, Napoleon III, who recognised photography's success, established a salon for it alongside traditional painting, but this led to protests from painters and writers.

Later on, photography gained recognition as an art form, serving advertising and self-promotion purposes. It also became a medium for family photographs. And look Renate, isn't it intriguing to see that in the 19th century, it was uncommon, if not frowned upon, for people to smile in photographs? Today, it's completely normal to smile or laugh on photos. Photography of that era required individuals to hide their emotions."

Wow, what a waterfall of interesting facts about photography. It is so nice to learn about this art form. And all this inspired by a man who looks like Nadar! This is truly how art works isn't it? You observe, you get inspiration and out comes the creativity, whether this is an interesting story, an intriguing picture, a painting or a sculpture. It all starts with an observation, an image, an inspiration.

A big change in sculpture

We are in the Musée Rodin and quite frankly I'm really looking forward to this. Given the time and materials I would love to do some sculpture myself again. I did once go to a soap-stone workshop and thoroughly enjoyed it. The statue I created is still taking pride in my home. I've also created quite a few ceramic figures, but without a kiln it is something I'm not pursuing. At this time in my life, I focus on writing and painting. But who knows, I might get back into sculpting and today could be the day to inspire me.

I've heard about Rodin, but I would like to find out more about him, especially about the women in his life. In chapter one we mentioned passing the house of Rodin, now a museum. I would have thought I could get used to seeing these stately buildings, but I have to say it's rather impressive that this used to be his house. As expected, the museum houses a large collection of sculptures, around six thousand in fact, many by Rodin himself. He also used to collect work from other artists, including Van Gogh, Renoir and Monet and these works are still in the museum. One room in the museum is dedicated to the work of Camille Claudel, who was both his mistress and his student. And I'm delighted that Mario will tell me all about her. We enter the garden and take a look at the different sculptures.

"Renate, as you can see some of these works of art by Rodin seem slightly unfinished. It's as if the sculpture is emerging from a block of stone or other material, like it's coming to life. In Rodin's work you can still see the raw material from which it's made, this was actually very unusual at that time.

Let me tell you a bit more about the (r)evolution of sculpture from the end of the 1800s and the early 1900s. I will explain more about the work of Rodin, and in the context of our trip, more importantly, about Camille Claudel later. I also feel it's important to talk about Maillol. These three artists in my view are great examples of how sculpture as an art form, just like painting, went through a liberating phase.

The production of sculptures in France during the second half of the 19th century was enormous because Paris was undergoing changes. They had to beautify the city with avenues, boulevards, and urban furniture like the *colonnes Morris,* those cylindrical columns where they put up advertising posters. You can also find plenty of *Wallace* fountains, dotted around the city, typically featuring four women; they aren't just regular fountains, they are sculptures. Wallace fountains are public drinking fountains. Even the metro entrances, like the ones by Guimard, are somewhat like sculptures.

In a transforming city like Paris with new gardens, parks, and squares, not to mention the significance of Emperor Napoleon III, there was a high demand for sculpted art. The bourgeoisie also wanted impressive tombs, and it is easy to imagine the significance of funerary sculpture in a Parisian cemetery, some of which are breathtaking, especially in the enormous Père Lachaise Cemetery.

Palaces and residences within the bourgeois society, owned by wealthy people were also filled with sculptures. It's worth noting that before artists like Rodin and Camille Claudel came along, architecture and sculpture were quite academic, heavily influenced by classical Greek ideals of beauty. It's important to remember that the aim was to represent women in an idealised way, often drawing inspiration from mythology. Some sculptors specialised in animal sculpture as there was a demand for this as well, for example, artworks of horses to decorate gardens, squares and bridges. We can see these types of animal sculptures by Carlo Bugatti, Bruno Zupan, and others in the Musée d'Orsay.

And let's not forget Frédéric Auguste Bartholdi, who created the Statue of Liberty, It is thought that he based the image of the statue of liberty on his mother, it represents liberty and hope. There's also another monument in Montparnasse created by him, *Le lion de Belfort.*

Did you actually know that there are various copies of the Statue of Liberty in Paris? In the Musée d'Orsay there is a reduced size of the statue, and La Flamme de la Liberté on the Pont de l'Alma is a full-sized replica of the torch of the statue, in fact it has the same size as the original. It was gifted to the city in 1987 by the International Herald Tribune, an English-language daily newspaper in Paris, representing the celebration of its hundredth anniversary.

Come to think of it, isn't it fascinating that the allegories for homeland and freedom are represented by women? France is considered to be a woman, both the name of the country, La France and the statue of *la Marianne*, who represents la France symbolising the homeland that nurtures and protects her children. Another example can be seen in the painting by Delacroix, *La Liberté Guidant le Peuple.* In this painting the woman is painted with a bare chest. This, it is said, inspired women in our time who show their breasts to vindicate women's freedom. Even the Eiffel Tower is called *La dame de fer*, which translates to 'The iron lady.' Like in paintings, many statues were female figures.

But let me tell you about some great sculptors who moved away from classical sculpture towards a more expressive style; Auguste Rodin, Camille Claudel and Aristide Maillol.

Rodin is considered the father of modern sculpture. His first work, *Masque de 'l'homme au nez cassé*, created in 1864, also caused his first scandal, precisely because it seemed unfinished. It was rejected by the salons where it was presented. This work, known for its realism, sparked controversy because it was believed that Rodin had cast it from a corpse. However, he denied this.

Later, he made *L'Âge d'airain*, his first successful statue of a naked man inspired by the Italian renaissance. This also caused a scandal because of its extreme naturalism. It took him eighteen months to create it and it was based on a live model. One of Rodin's masterpieces is *La Porte de l'Enfer*, which is a monumental bronze sculptural piece of art, depicting a scene from Dante Alighieri's Divine Comedy, the *Inferno*. Camille Claudel played a significant role in creating this work. Rodin worked on this project for many years. A lot of people when they hear the name Rodin, they think about *Le Penseur* known as *The Thinker* and *Le Baiser*, which are two very famous sculptures of him. *Le Baiser*, also inspired by Dante's Divine Comedy, depicts a passionate kiss between a man and a woman, combining tenderness and eroticism.

By the end of the 19th century, Rodin was an acclaimed sculptor, but he was often surrounded by controversy. One notable scandal was his commission to create a sculpture of the writer Honoré de Balzac, which was rejected. The sculpture depicted Balzac in a somewhat grotesque manner and appeared unfinished. What truly characterises Rodin's work is its realism and expressiveness."

Most people have heard about Rodin, but do people also know about Camille Claudel?

"That's a good point and I indeed want to tell you about Camille. She was an apprentice in Rodin's workshop. He fell in love with her almost immediately, admiring her artistic talent. They had a passionate affair and she was his mistress, his model and his muse for ten years. But they never lived together as Rodin didn't want to break up his relationship of twenty years with Rose Beuret, a seamstress. His relationship with Rose started in 1864, and they had a child together. Two weeks before her death, in February 1917 he married Rose and he himself died later that year when he was seventy-seven years old.

Let's get back to Camille. She was born in 1884 and was the sister of writer and poet Paul Claudel. From a very young age, she had a passion for sculpture, but her mother opposed it. Still, she persevered and studied with the master sculptor Alfred Couche, who later created an artist community in Paris, where artists like Chagall and Modigliani would gather. Camille felt that her mother favoured her brother Louis over her in their childhood. In her family home, there were constant arguments and violence, which she couldn't express in words but found an outlet for through sculpting.

Camille initially settled on boulevard Montparnasse and later met Rodin, who then hired her as his apprentice. She became Rodin's best student and work companion. Rodin once said *"she came to learn from me but now I consult her for almost everything"*. She actively participated in significant works of Rodin.

He was fascinated by her face. There exist several sculptures that represent her, such as *Camille Claudel aux cheveux courts* and *L'Aurore* that were created in her image. Camille also created a bust of Rodin in 1897. Perhaps her mental state, and subsequently her way of life, led to her not receiving the acknowledgement that she deserves. But she was a truly amazing artist and skilful sculptor. When you look at her work it's almost as if you can sense her psychological input, such an intensity of expression. Camille loved to experiment and we can discover her interest in the dynamics of gatherings of people in her work, intrigued by the moods and behaviours when humans interact. I think we can safely say that she was an expressionist sculptor.

At some point, Camille felt that Rodin was distancing himself from her, and she sought her independence as an artist. She developed her own style and claimed it proudly. As her mental health deteriorated, she became very active but also feared that Rodin would steal her work. She burned the wax moulds and claimed it was to keep warm."

I feel a bit saddened by this story about this brilliant artist as we are looking at her photo. She looks rather sad...

"Yes, she had little tenderness in her life, only violence. Rodin must have been quite a difficult person as he didn't want rivals and at one point, he became envious of her talent. Camille fell pregnant with his child. Some say that Rodin forced her to have an abortion, but others say that she felt she had to choose her artistic career over having a child. But she was also jealous and couldn't bear the thought of Rodin being with other women. Her paranoia became a total delirium.

She surely had a difficult personality and lived in isolation after leaving Rodin. They broke up in 1892, when Camille ended the intimate part of her relationship with Rodin, but they continued to see each other with some regularity till 1898. Her sculptures became more expressive, passionate, and intimate. They became her autobiography, depicting life, death, and pain. One of her works, created in 1897, is called La Vague ou Les Baigneuses, made of onyx and bronze."

Mario points out this work of art, here, at the Musée Rodin. It's really beautiful, the colours of the wave and the three small female figures beneath the wave are intriguing. I can't decide whether I find it menacing or playful. Camille felt drawn to Japanese art because of its curves. I know she primarily worked with onyx marble, but was she actually considered an Art Nouveau sculptor?

"Yes she was, but she also was a realist. Building her career without the presence of Rodin was hard. She tried to find recognition from the public but wasn't very successful. She began speaking ill of Rodin to everyone, even though he was already a highly regarded artist. There is a lot of controversy about her mental state, her mother was very religious and ashamed of her rebellious daughter. Her father loved her and protected her, but when he died, Camille's mother and brother had her forcibly institutionalised in an asylum. This was in 1913. Apparently, doctors said that it wasn't necessary for her to be there, but her brother and mother insisted, saying that she was showing signs of schizophrenia. Camille's later writings also showed that her mental state was excellent. She was first institutionalised in Maison Blanche / Villévrard, but in 1915 she was moved to the Asile d'aliénés de Montdevergues, Montfavet, five kilometres from Avignon. She also died there. She stayed in these asylums for a total of thirty years. I believe that if she had been allowed to leave the asylum and given support to continue her work, she could have saved herself. In my opinion, her sculptures, while powerful and emotional, didn't reflect her true mental state. They portrayed an isolation, a forced withdrawal from and a rejection of the world. Camille Claudel died in 1943."

We've spent quite a few hours in the Rodin Museum and gardens and I have to say it was fascinating to see so many sculptures. Quite overwhelming actually and I think for the time being I will stick to painting and writing. This is such a wonderful 'learning' journey though. Before we continue our sculpture adventure, we decide to have a coffee break in the café in the museum's garden.

After our coffee we walk to the Jardin de Tuileries, which is close to the Louvre, where Mario will introduce another important sculptor and his muse to me. I must admit that I had never heard of them before, so I'm very keen to find out.

"Let's talk about a really important French sculptor, Aristide Maillol, who was born in 1861 and passed away in 1944. He's a big deal because he inspired other artists who did some amazing things in sculpture, like Picasso, Brâncuşi, and Henri Moore. We're discussing this sculptor because he was a specialist in the female nude. But he didn't start with sculpture. He began as a painter and ceramist.

When he was around forty years old, he turned to sculpture. What's interesting about him is that, besides being a bridge between older art and future avant-gardes, he had an artist-model relationship with a young girl when he was already seventy-three years old. I do want to clarify that, although he admired her, they were never lovers. There was admiration, inspiration, and friendship. Her name was Dina Vierny, but I will explain a bit more about her later.

Maillol, was part of the Nabis art movement when he started painting. His artworks were similar to the paintings of Pierre Bonnard. There's a famous painting by Maillol from 1892 called *La Femme à l'ombrelle* which we saw in the Musée d'Orsay, remember? When he discovered sculpture around the age of forty, Maillol found his true calling. He felt that sculpture was poetry and that he could express the verses of poetry through his sculptures.

He met Rodin and this encounter was crucial for him, as Rodin admired his work right away. Maillol's sculptures had pure forms without a narrative substance. He believed that a sculpture was like a house, with the legs as its pillars. He could create multiple versions of the same subject, make changes, or even destroy it and start all over again. One day when he was on the beach, he saw his sister playing with the water, and that later inspired him for years to express these movements in his sculptures. He always kept this image alive in his head. That moment was transformative for him, and he spent his life trying to capture it in his sculptures. He needed models, so he drew from the female nude.

Maillol mostly painted and sculpted naked women. Even when George Clemenceau, a politician of the time, asked him to create a sculpture in honour of the revolutionary Auguste Blanqui, Maillol made it in the form of a woman.

Meeting Dina Vierny was pivotal for Maillol. For the last ten years of his life, she was his inspiration, representing nature, like the mountains and rivers. She became his muse. Dina also posed for Matisse and Bonnard. She was born in 1919 as Dina Aibinder. Her parents were Jews from the east of Europe and they moved to Paris in 1926. She soon became friends with people in the art and music scene and met Jean-Claude Dondel, who was a good friend of Maillol. Dondel would later become the founder of Musée d'Art Moderne de la Ville de Paris. He introduced Maillol to Dina. She agreed to pose for him, initially only for simple portraits.

In 1938, she married Sacha Vierny, who became the director of photography for Alain Resnais, a famous film director. She was already married for two years when she visited Maillol and Clotilde, his wife, in Banyuls. This is when she started posing for him regularly and we can see her in several of his paintings and many of his sculptures. Apparently, she had a significant intellectual background and engaged in long and interesting conversations with Maillol. She also posed for his masterpiece L'Harmonie, which he sadly didn't finish, as he passed away before that.

Dina was an artist's model, but later she also became a singer, an art collector, an art dealer and even a museum director. She was popular as a model but she was picky. For example, Picasso wanted her to pose for him, but she declined because he had a reputation for chasing after any woman.

During World War II, as France was occupied by the Germans, Maillol moved to the Catalan Pyrenees. Dina stayed in Paris and worked for the Resistance, helping refugees escape to Spain. She was known as 'the girl in the red dress' who guided people to safety. Maillol helped her devise a shorter route across the border, but disaster struck. In 1943 there was a big raid in Montmartre and Dina was arrested by the nazis.

Maillol tried to help her, even finding a lawyer. Something rather special then happened. A German sculptor who admired Maillol's work and who worked for Hitler intervened. Thanks to this Dina was released after six months of imprisonment and torture.

In 1944 Maillol was involved in a car accident at the age of eighty-three and passed away shortly after. Dina felt like an orphan as she had now lost her spiritual father, Maillol, and also found out that her real father had died in the concentration camp of Auschwitz.

She took on the responsibility of preserving Maillol's work, which she had inherited. Dina became a specialist in Maillol's art and opened an art gallery in Paris in rue Jacob. The small gallery, which still exists, became an important place for artists. She exhibited Picasso's and, above all, Maillol's artworks. Sadly, after World War II, the interest in Maillol's art started to decline. Dina fought hard to ensure his legacy would not die.

She took his work to the United States, where he was already known, and promoted it extensively. She also approached the French Minister of Culture, André Malraux, for help. Malraux agreed to place eighteen Maillol sculptures, including those with Dina as the model, in Jardin des Tuileries near the Louvre. In return for this help, Dina donated these sculptures to the French state. Thanks to this we can see these beautiful works of art here today.

Later, with the money she had earned from selling his works, she established the Maillol Museum, which you can visit as well. She was quite a remarkable lady I feel. Dina passed away in 2009. Her death wasn't given much attention, which I believe was a mistake as she has done so many important things in her life".

You can say that again , that's incredible, what a woman. Saving the lives of many and then 'saving' the art and recognition of Maillol. I would have loved to have known her.

"Yes, me too. But she will live on, also because we are talking about her now, sharing her story, which will help people to get to know her. Dina died in Paris, five days before her 90th birthday, leaving behind two sons who continued her work. Olivier Lorquin became the director of Musée Maillol and her other son, Bertrand Lorquin, became an art historian and the curator of the museum."

It's been a very special day and of course, as with all the people we are discussing, we cannot possibly mention all the incredible sculptors who've left their mark on Paris. But talking about leaving a 'mark'... How about the Eiffel Tower Mario, isn't that a sculpture? To me it looks like one!

"That's an interesting observation. We have briefly mentioned the Eiffel tower before, how it was part of the universal exhibition in 1889 to showcase the amazing strength of iron. And if it wasn't for the communication antenna, first radio and later television, it would quite possibly have been taken down. It certainly gives the impression of a sculpture. But can we call it that? Should we consider the engineer, Gustave Eiffel both an engineer and a sculptor? Of course, the tower is a landmark, you can see it from many locations in Paris and it's a must-go-and-see for most tourists.

But let's dive a little deeper into this. It is a great architectural piece but now that you mention it, to me it's also a sculpture, so Mr. Eiffel is also a sculptor. At the time it was built there certainly was a lot of controversy. The original colour was red, to showcase the industrial strength of iron. But later they painted the tower in ochre to allow it to blend in with the Haussmann buildings. And, for example, the interior structure of the Statue of Liberty, was made by Eiffel. I think that, from now on, I will refer to the Eiffel tower as a sculpture! A lady even, and as we already said before, people refer to the tower as '*The iron lady*'. Surely interesting don't you think, for such a masculine monument?"

Moving images

A new phenomenon

*I*n this chapter we are going to discuss the film industry. But depending on where you live, words can have different meanings. As a writer, I'm choosing British spelling for my description of this journey in Paris, but first let's clarify some of the words as this can be somewhat confusing.

When we talk about a movie or a film, we are literally talking about the story told in pictures that we watch in a cinema, television or a device. Movie is used in the United States and film is used in the UK and Ireland. Now a cinema refers to the building where you go to watch a film, but in the US, they call it a theater (movie theater). In the UK a theatre, which is spelled slightly different, is known as a building to watch plays. Both film and cinema can refer to the film-making industry in general. The French refer to it as 'cinéma'.

We are in the Paris of grand boulevards, on the boulevard des Capucines, which was painted by Monet in 1873 from the window of Nadar's studio. We stop in front of Hotel Scribe at number 14 and Mario points out a commemorative plaque on the door of the hotel. It reads *"Ici le 28 décembre 1895 eurent lieu les premières projections publique de photographie animée a l'aide du cinematographe appareil inventé par les frères Lumière"* (Here on December 28, 1895, the first public showing of animated photography took place using the cinematograph device invented by the Lumière brothers). We are looking at the plaque and Mario explains...

"There used to be a café here and in one of its salons, called Salon Indien, about ten short films were projected on this day in December. The event was attended by around thirty people, not that many. The press was invited but they didn't show up, which suggests that it wasn't seen as an event of major importance. How wrong they were. As it was here, in the basement of the old café, that cinema was born, or to be more precise, it was where the first public screening took place with an audience that had to pay an admission fee to get in.

Now we know how significant cinema has been in the history of the 20th century, and its inventors, the Lumière brothers, never imagined the fabulous business it would become. The first film of this 1895 screening showed women leaving a factory in the city of Lyon. The invention began to gain success, and the Lumière brothers started filming all over the world, capturing images that introduced the diversity of the planet to the public.

Later, a magician named Méliès, who had attended the first screening at that café, was enthralled by the invention and began making films as well. Méliès is known for his tricks, what we would now call special effects, where he could make objects or people appear and disappear in images. Méliès's short films were less than a minute long, and each had its magic trick. He played a fundamental role in the development of cinema. A few years ago, the American film director Martin Scorsese paid tribute to him in the movie *Hugo Cabret*. As a curiosity fact, at the end of his life Méliès was selling toys in a small shop at the Montparnasse train station."

But what role did women occupy in this new type of art that had just been born?

"In this emerging art form the role of women was complex. Alice Guy-Blaché, considered to be the first female film director in the history of cinema, created many short films and knew that she would never be recognised in a male-dominated world. When people discuss the beginnings of cinema, they mention the Lumière brothers, the inventors, and Méliès, but Alice Guy is hardly ever mentioned.

One of the films she directed in 1906 is *Les Résultats du Féminisme*, where she reversed gender roles, showing men doing household chores whilst women were drinking alcohol. Alice Guy was an entrepreneurial woman who built a film production factory with studios for shooting, a laboratory, workshops for making costumes and constructing sets. She certainly was an exception as in the film industry, women could not hold significant roles; they primarily appeared on screen, with actresses featured on posters and in magazines. Out of the around seven thousand five hundred films made between 1898 and 1918 in French cinema, few were directed by women.

Some women, like Sonia Delaunay, a cubist style painter, worked as set decorators. But the reality was that women mainly served as secretaries on set, script supervisors, or stylists who dressed the actors. On screen, men were portrayed as strong protectors, while women were depicted as weak, dependant and sometimes hysterical.

Alice truly was a pioneer filmmaker and one of the first to use narrative fiction in films. She enjoyed experimenting with sound, colour-tinting and special effects. She was also in favour of interracial casting.

She was born in Paris, but in her early life she travelled a lot throughout the world with her parents. Back in France, in 1894, Alice started working as a secretary for a camera and photography supply company. This, I imagine, was the start of her interest in film-making. She learned about this new artistic phenomenon and met early film engineers such as Louis and Aguste Lumière. Alice's pioneering career in filmmaking lasted over twenty-five years. She was writing, producing, directing, and overseeing more than seven hundred films.

Another important director was Germaine Dulac, closely associated with the avant-garde movements of her time. She directed over forty films, with the most notable being *La Coquille et le Clergyman* from 1927. She was a French journalist, critic and filmmaker. Later in her career she became the president of the 'Fédération des ciné-clubs', an organisation which presented and promoted work of new young filmmakers, such as Jean Vigo and Joris Ivens. She also taught at the École Technique de Photographie et de Cinématographie in Paris in 85 rue de Vaugirard.

Let me tell you a bit more about Germaine as she was an interesting lady. She was born in Amiens, but her family moved to Paris when she was still a child. In 1905 she married Louis-Albert Dulac, an agricultural engineer. She was increasingly interested in socialism and feminism and started her career as a journalist. She wrote for a feminist magazine called *La Française* and got a job working as an editor for *La Fronde*, which at the time was a radical feminist journal. It was around this time that she became interested in photography and later in filmmaking.

Her husband and a friend helped her to start a film company, at first directing some commercial films. It didn't take long for her to move into surrealist and impressionist filmmaking. Her best-known impressionist silent film is *La Souriante Madame Beudet*, created in 1923, starring Germain Dermoz and Alexandre Arquillière. I believe this is one of the first real feminist films.

We are now strolling through the Latin Quarter, an area where students used to come in the 1950s, '60s, and '70s to watch art-house films. Many have closed down; I remember one called *Accatone*, which had the charm of being highly alternative. Everything was independent, from the films to the cinephile audience. The theatre was small, accommodating thirty to fifty people, and the ticket counter resembled a bar top. The program was written on a blackboard with chalk.

It was at this cinema that I saw *La Passion de Jeanne d'Arc*, directed by Carl Theodor Dreyer, with Renée Jeanne Falconetti in the role of Joan of Arc. Renée Jeanne was a silent film actress. She appeared in four hundred out of the fifteen hundred shots in the film. Her expression of suffering, her shaved head, and the suffocating harassment in a male-dominated court left a lasting impression both on the audience and herself. She made few films and eventually moved to Argentina, where she ended her life by suicide. Dreyer's film is a masterpiece, and Renée Jeanne's image is immortal."

We've now reached the Seine River and Mario shows me a picture of her in the movie, I remain silent for a moment. It is such an emotional image, and we also see an image of a poster for a film being sold by the booksellers or 'bouquinistes' to tourists. It's the poster for the film *Les Vampires*, featuring a woman in a tight black outfit sleeping in a chair and a man's head peeking out from behind a curtain.

"This film, made in 1915, was part of a series of episodes created by Louis Feuillade. The actress who plays Irma Vep, an anagram of 'vampires', is Musidora, whose real name was Jeanne Roques. She had previously worked as a sculptor, a theatre actress, a music hall performer but also as a writer.

Her father Jaques Roques was a painter and music composer and her mother, Adèle Clémence Porchez, was a feminist. Jeanne adopted the name 'Musidora' which is Greek for gift of the muses. She was very young when her career started and she wrote her first novel when she was only fifteen years old. She went on to become an actress and worked with Colette, who became a close friend. She acted alongside Colette in cabarets like Sala Bataclan and later adapted Colette's works, *L'Ingénue Libertine* and *La Vagabonde*, for the cinema.

In the early stages of French cinema, Musidora started working with film director Louis Feuillade who was already very successful and she made her debut in *Les misères de l'aiguille* in 1914. It was directed by Raphael Clamour. Interestingly this film talks about the difficult life of French working-class women in the early twentieth century.

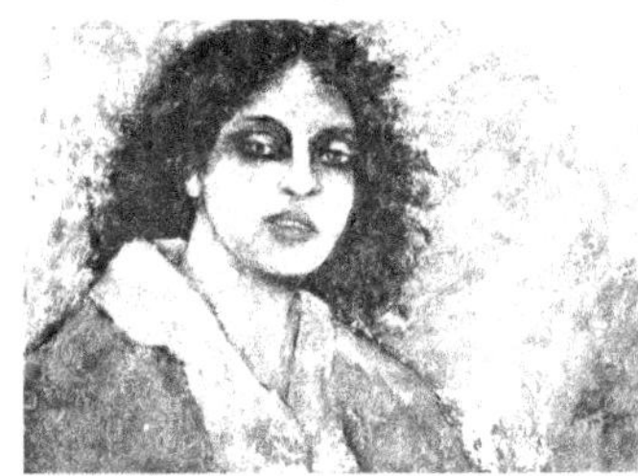

Musidora

Musidora became famous for her role as Irma Vep in *Les Vampires*. Soon she turned to directing and adapted two novels by Colette into films. She was much more than an actress; she was the muse of the surrealists and played a significant role in both theatre and music halls, already before her film career. She collaborated with the Dadaist and Surrealist movements and worked with poet and writer André Breton, who was one of the co-founders of Surrealism. One of his writings was the first *Surrealist Manifesto* of 1924.

During that time, theatre actresses began to venture into filmmaking, with the most famous being Sarah Bernhardt, who adapted theatrical works like *La Tosca* (1909) and *La Dame aux Camélias*

(1912) for the screen. Sarah actually lamented that cinema had not been invented earlier which shows her love for this medium.

In the male-dominated world of cinema, the stories of the women we've described highlight the struggles faced by women and in particular Musidora who, despite her many achievements in the film industry, is known by few. Her legacy isn't common place and I feel that this is a real shame, even a mistake.

Cinema was becoming a major industry, with France already boasting great directors like Abel Gance and René Clair. However, shortly after its invention, cinema nearly disappeared due to a tragedy that shook society. At a fair, the Bazar de la Charité, where films were being shown, the celluloid of a projector caught fire, causing a terrible blaze. Of the twelve hundred people present, a hundred and twenty-five died, of which only five were men.

This led to the belief that the men used their strength to push some women into the flames to escape more quickly. The press sensationalised the tragedy, and cinema was demonised. Soon after, the Lumière brothers modified the projector's lamp to prevent such fires. Till this day you can visit a chapel that was built at 23 rue Goujon in honour of the victims."

Post-Impressionism

Searching for free expression

I'm excited, again I should say, as I feel like a sponge soaking up the most amazing knowledge about art and artists and that makes me happy. Today we will talk about several post-impressionist artistic movements, one of which is called Les Nabis.

"Impressionism had broken away from academic art, and not so long after this a new art movement appeared called Post-Impressionism. There was a specific group that is also referred to as Les Nabis. It started in the 1880s and lasted roughly till 1900. Les Nabis was a group of artists in Paris, who played an important role in the transition from Impressionism to less figurative forms where colour was given more importance, something we also see in Fauvism which I will explain to you later.

Let me tell you about some of these Nabis artists, starting with Gauguin. He is not really considered a Nabis painter, but he certainly was the artist who played a significant role in this movement. Gauguin's story is quite intriguing, but it's essential to consider the context of his time. Back then, things were quite different, and cultural norms varied widely.

Gauguin was born in Paris but spent his childhood in Peru. He later returned to France. At some point he visited Copenhagen in Denmark and fell in love with a Danish woman called Mette Sophie Gad. They got married and had five children. To get an income, Gauguin tried to sell tarpaulins, but because he didn't speak Danish, he didn't sell many. He struggled financially. His passion lay with his painting, but he couldn't make a living from his art. His wife's family didn't support him, and they eventually kicked him out of their home. He had to return to Paris and became friends with Vincent van Gogh. During this time Gauguin referred to himself as a 'cursed' artist.

In 1888 Vincent invited him to come to live with him in Arles. Both Gauguin and van Gogh led rather solitary lives, especially artistically. While it was a rich artistic period, in the sense that he created a lot of paintings, Gauguin found himself accumulating debts as his income wasn't substantial.

He was fascinated by Polynesia and in 1891, he decided to move to Tahiti, escaping France. When he arrived, he initially tried to assimilate with the French colonists on the island, creating paintings for them. It didn't work out as he expected. Gauguin found this colonial society in Polynesia to be rather closed, with limited real contact with the indigenous people.

So, he decided to live with the Tahitians, and there he found one of his muses, a young girl named Teha'amana, who he renamed Tehura. Her name was later Europeanised as 'Teodora'. She was around thirteen years old at the time, and Gauguin was captivated by her. It's important to remember that the customs and norms of that era were quite different from today's standards. In those times, girls were often married at a young age, and it was not uncommon for French colonists to have relationships with underage women. It was a self-sufficient culture with an abundance of fish, wild boars and fruits to be gathered by the wives and their families. And Tahitian families often arranged marriages for their young daughters for reasons of financial advantage or status. Tehura's family had arranged their marriage.

Gauguin began studying the Tahitian language and culture with the help of Tehura, and she became his inspiration. He painted her frequently, portraying femininity and maternity, which were central themes in his work. This period marked a creative and relatively happy time in Gauguin's life, as he had someone to love and paint, and for him, the two were equally important. His art during this period was sensual, and it was a departure from painting reality, an exploration of emotions.

In his paintings from this time, you can see supernatural elements and spirits blending Polynesian culture with Western themes, sometimes giving his female subjects a halo, reminiscent of saints or the Virgin Mary in Western art. Despite being on the island and deeply in love with Tehura, Gauguin still held onto a photograph of his wife in Denmark. This occasionally caused tension and jealousy between him and his young wife.

Gauguin's time in Tahiti lasted for about two years, during which he created around seventy paintings, some of these became highly successful. When he returned to France, Tehura, who was pregnant, knew he wouldn't come back. Later, he travelled to the Marquesas Islands, where he became increasingly ill and turned to alcohol, morphine, and arsenic. He also suffered from advanced syphilis, which no doubt contributed to his death. The last months of his life he sold paintings to buy morphine, marking a tragic and challenging end, at the age of fifty-four, to a complex and remarkable life in art. He left a great legacy and inspired many painters, in particular Les Nabis.

One of the most famous and colourful artists of Les Nabis was Pierre Bonnard. He was renowned for his intimate nude paintings, particularly of his wife, Marthe. I'll tell you a bit more about him later. The Nabis movement started when Paul Sérusier created a painting manifesto known as *The Talisman*. It was a landscape with bold, vibrant colours, where forms were barely distinguishable and there was a pronounced emphasis on contrasts. The name Nabis was invented by the painters Maurice Denis, Paul Sérusier and Paul Ranson. In Eastern traditions the term loosely translates to prophets or initiates. It's interesting to see that their art was heavily influenced by Japanese art.

Maurice Denis, along with Pierre Bonnard, Eduard Vuillard and Felix Vallotton were great representatives of this new form of painting. Vallotton believed that before choosing a subject, whether it be a woman or a horse, the surface of the canvas had to be covered in colours. Colour was of utmost importance."

How interesting! This is something I always do: I start with a random, colourful background and then create the artwork that I have in mind. For me it's a very intuitive process, it just happens. I don't even think much about the colours of the background. So, do I have some

Nabis in me or is my art best described as Fauvism? I don't know, but I'm now more intrigued about these artists.

"One day, Paul Sérusier met Bonnard and Vallotton and introduced them to Gauguin, who as we already said, would become the great inspiration and precursor to this movement, which wasn't exactly a formal movement nor a school of art. These were artists who shared a mutual admiration. It all revolved around a publication called *La Revue Blanche*, which also involved musicians and poets. You could say that the Nabis movement was a reaction against Realism, such as the paintings of Courbet and Manet. While Impressionism was all about capturing different colours and changing light, the Nabis, and especially Bonnard, were more influenced by Japanese artists. Bonnard painted in fragments, much like in Japanese art. The viewer had to imagine the whole scene; it wasn't presented in its entirety.

The Nabis aimed to reinvent the visual language through colour. They contributed to the evolution of Impressionism and paved the way for other important movements like Fauvism, Art Nouveau, and even Expressionism. Their art glorified nature and had a mystical quality. Maurice Denis and Paul Sérusier were also influenced by Egyptian, Medieval, and Byzantine art. They simplified forms and had a spiritual interest, which is why they can also be called symbolist painters.

There was another trend within the Nabis as well. The more modern and perhaps less spiritual artists like Bonnard and Vallotton drew inspiration from Degas' artworks. They abandoned traditional perspectives in favour of pure colour and arabesque shapes. Their art was all about simple forms in rhythmic harmony. They didn't so much observe nature as they were more about expressing the emotions their art would arouse within them.

A good example of Nabis art is the work created by Edouard Vuillard. In his works, he blended characters with their surroundings. There's a striking painting called *Deux ouvrières dans l'atelier de couture*, where you see two women in a sewing workshop. It's quite challenging to distinguish their forms as they blend into the surrounding colours.

I'd like to tell you a bit more about Pierre Bonnard now. He was a real lover of playing with light and colour. At one point in his life, he headed to the Mediterranean with his wife, Marthe. By 1927, he was already highly regarded in the art world. He painted around three hundred pieces during his time in their Mediterranean home, and I mean, he painted everything, from furniture to objects, but mostly his wife. You could say that he was utterly obsessed with her and he painted her in the most intimate moments, for example, when she was bathing in a tub. It is said that she had a beautiful body but her face wasn't all that attractive, hence why he mostly painted her face in the shade.

Bonnard's work was about capturing the magic of colours as they changed in the smallest of details. He had this almost religious connection to nature and said that art couldn't exist without it. He often sketched on paper before painting. He wasn't the type to go out into nature to paint; he did it from memory. He'd go back to his studio and bring his memories to life on the canvas. He used to say *"one must sacrifice form for colour"*. And let me tell you, Bonnard's work is always so vibrant and joyful, you could say he lived in the happiness sector of art.

Like many artists of his time, Bonnard had a keen interest in photography, and it greatly influenced his work. He took lots of photos to capture spontaneous moments. Marthe, his partner and muse, was a special woman. When they met, she was selling flowers, and he invited her to come to his studio. In one of his paintings called *l'Homme et la Femme* you can see her sitting on the bed and him standing with a screen in between them. Marthe looks sensually perfect in that painting. She also inspired symbolist poets like Verlaine, and Bonnard even illustrated a poetry book for Verlaine, using Marthe as the model. He always painted Marthe as a beautiful and young woman, even when she was older, depicting her with a perfect body and radiance.

Around 1918, Bonnard met Renée Monchaty, who also became his muse. He painted around twenty works featuring her and they became lovers. Despite this, Bonnard ended up marrying Marthe, after having lived together for many years. Renée tragically took her own life not long after. Marthe, passed away in 1942, and Bonnard closed off the room where she used to stay; he never entered it again. He continued painting after her death, but focusing mainly on landscapes and objects he found in nature, like almond trees, and flowers. Bonnard passed away in 1947 but his legacy continues.

The Nabis held their last joined exhibition in 1900 and then all the artists took different directions in their art journeys.

I'm going to talk about Georges Seurat now, who died quite young. He is mostly famous for an art style that he has created, or at least claimed as being his own. It is called Neo-Impressionism or Pointillism. Up close, you only see dots, but from afar, the scene emerges.   Félix Fénéon, a friend and important art critic, invented the term Neo-Impressionism to distinguish it from Impressionism. Pointillism aims to create an optical effect using pure colours placed in dots, which produce an optical effect for the viewer.

For his painting *Un dimanche après-midi à l'Île de la Grande Jatte*, Seurat made numerous sketches and studies, meticulously planning his work. He then worked on the large painting for two years. He was a solitary painter who spent long hours in his studio, dedicated to studying light and the scenery.

When the painting was exhibited at an impressionist salon, it received mockery and incomprehension from critics who found the figures in the painting lifeless. Seurat faced challenges when it came to depicting the human figure in a different way. His forte lay in landscapes, and his self-portraits were not as successful. He was often criticised for creating emotionally detached works. However, Félix Fénéon, explained Seurat's technique in his articles and books.

The neo-impressionist artists were defended by symbolist writers and poets. Neo-Impressionism was quite different from Impressionism; it had its own theories and scientific foundations, similar to later art movements. Seurat always claimed to be the leader of this movement. A major art dealer, Julien Tanguy, exhibited the works of these artists in the United States, where they gained popularity. Seurat did feel somewhat resentful that other artists were copying his technique as he was a rather stoic man.

An interesting fact is that in response to all the criticism he received, Seurat created a fascinating large-format painting titled *Les Poseuses*, painted between 1886 and 1888. In this artwork we see the same woman in three different poses: standing, sitting, and with her back turned. He incorporated a partial reproduction of *La Grande Jatte* on the left side of the canvas.

Later in his life, Seurat had a secret affair with a woman named Madeleine Knobloch, who he depicted in the painting *Jeune femme se poudrant*.

Towards the end of his life, he ventured into a movement that some would consider the precursor to Futurism in art. Unfortunately, he died at the young age of thirty-two while visiting his family. He seemingly contracted tonsillitis, which complicated into hysteria and led to his untimely death."

Fascinating all this. Is there a specific museum that we can visit to see the works of these artists in Paris?

"Yes, you can find several of these artworks in the Musée d'Orsay."

Fauvism

A colourful movement

It was you Mario who told me, even before we decided to go on this art-journey in Paris, that my work would be best described as Fauvism. Now, I must admit, even though I've been a professional artist for over thirty-five years, I had never heard of this painting style, but I'm fascinated by everything that I'm learning. I know that today we will dive into Fauvism and I'm exceptionally curious of course. So where are we going?

"Yes, I do think your work is falling well into the Fauvism range, although you also use Symbolism in your art and even Surrealism. You do have your own recognisable style, which I feel is important for artists these days. Too many are copying styles and even though promoted as the best new thing by some art curators, you only have to go back in history, like we are doing right now, to see that the true innovators were people like Monet and later Matisse and Picasso to name some of the great artists that we are discussing. Shall we go to the 8th Arrondissement and find a pavement café on the Champs-Élysées where we can talk about an important event which, you could argue, created a shift in the art world?

So far, we've seen that, especially artists such as Manet with his impressive painting *Olympia*, and the works of Courbet, marked the end of Realism. There was a significant break from Academic art. As you know this was then followed by Impressionism, which was truly a revolution, then came Post-Impressionism and other artist movements, some of which formed groups like the Nabis. Finally, within this era of modernism, Fauvism emerged and it again created quite an upheaval within the established art world of that era.

We will go to the Grand Palais. We've already been in this area when we paid a visit to the Petit Palais, but I now specifically want to talk about a significant scandal which unfolded during the 1905 Salon d'Automne exhibition in Le Grand Palais. The first Salon d'Automne or Société du Salon d'Automne exhibition was in 1903 and it has grown into an annual art exhibition still existing today. It was the brainchild of, among others, Hector Guimard and Félix Vallotton who was a painter himself. We've already discussed Hector Guimard, but just so you understand who he was, Vallotton was born in Switzerland but he persuaded his parents to allow him to study art in Paris, where he also died.

The goal for the Salon was to showcase what was new, especially the works of impressionists, who had finally gained acceptance despite having faced quite a bit of resistance. Various forms of art had been exhibited, including painting, drawing, sculpture, and photography, which had struggled to find its place, but by 1903 and 1904, it was considered a serious art form.

Initially works by artists such as Rodin, Cézanne and Bonnard were displayed during the 1905 Salon d'Automne. Artists who had by then been accepted by the established art world. Some exhibition rooms were reserved for the works of Henri Matisse, André Derain and Maurice de Vlaminck. This is where the problems began. This new style of art was not accepted by the art critics, the bourgeoisie, and the general public and it took time for them to become accustomed to the change.

The reaction from the critics was harsh. The term 'Fauves', which freely translates to 'wild beasts', arose when art critic Louis Vauxcelles saw these strikingly colourful paintings and felt that it was like putting Donatello, the sculptor, in a cage with fierce animals like tigers or lions. The paintings were seen as untamed and wild, and the impact it had was akin to throwing pots of paint at the audience. People felt that the works appeared to be unfinished. In reality it was a similar criticism faced by Impressionism earlier, suggesting they lacked skill or craftsmanship. Some even called it a form of naivety, like what a child would do if handed a box of crayons.

Fauvism is seen as an early 20th-century art movement that emerged in France, particularly in Paris, around 1905-1908. While there were various factors and influences that contributed to the development of this new movement, it was characterised by bold and vibrant use of colour, often applied in a non-naturalistic way. Fauvism was a result of artistic exploration. The artists themselves were influenced by various sources, including the works of post-impressionists like Paul Cézanne, as well as African and Oceanic art."

Were there any female fauvist painters?

"Yes, and there also were a few women who were associated with, or supportive of, the fauvist artists, and some of them had indirect roles in the movement. I would like to mention one of them specifically. Her name was Gertrude Stein. She was an American novelist, poet, playwright, and art collector. She moved to Paris in 1903 and then made it her home for the rest of her life. She hosted a salon at her home at 27 rue de Fleurus, which became a famous gathering place for artists and writers. It was here that the likes of Pablo Picasso, Georges Braque, Henri Matisse, André Derain and many others came together. While she was not a painter herself, Gertrude Stein played a crucial role in supporting and promoting the work of avant-garde painters and writers. She became friends with many of these artists and collected their works. She is perhaps best known for her patronage of Picasso, who, in fact, painted her portrait.

Gertrude's own literary works are also noteworthy as she became famous for her experimental and challenging writing, particularly her prose poetry and her book *Tender Buttons*, which she wrote in 1914. The short book consists of multiple poems talking about mundane subjects with an experimental, abstract use of language. Her work had a significant influence on the development of modern literature and was admired by many fellow writers, including Ernest Hemingway and F. Scott Fitzgerald.

Another important figure in the promotion of the work of many fauvist artists was Ambroise Vollard, one of the most influential art dealers, an art collector and a gallery owner. Vollard was born in 1866, in La Réunion, which is a French overseas territory in the Indian Ocean. He moved to Paris when he was still a young man and opened an art gallery in the late 19th century. He organised exhibitions and his support and patronage contributed significantly to the recognition and success of Fauvism and its artists. Supporting and showcasing the artworks of, for example, Matisse and Derain was instrumental in bringing this art movement to a broader audience.

Vollard was not limited to Fauvism alone; he also worked with other prominent artists, including Pablo Picasso and Paul Cézanne, and had a profound impact on the art scene of his time. His gallery served as a hub for avant-garde artists and played a crucial role in the development of modern art in the early 20th century.

It was difficult for women to become established or even live and work as an artist, but some of them were influential through promoting art in salons, gatherings, galleries or as patrons. I've already mentioned Gertrude Stein, but now I'd like to talk about Berthe Weill. She was a French art dealer who also played a significant role in the early 20th-century art scene in Paris and particularly in promoting and supporting emerging Fauvism artists. Esther Berthe Weill was born in Paris into a lower/middle class family and was one of seven children. She worked as an apprentice in an antique shop where she met collectors and art dealers. Thanks to Roger Marx, a renowned art critic, she became interested in the art of new young painters. She started buying, exhibiting and selling work by Pablo Picasso even before he moved to Paris, becoming his first dealer."

Picasso is, of course, someone we extensively need to discuss, don't we? Since we both live near Malaga where he comes from, but also because he's a brilliant artist. Not so sure about his character, but I'm sure you will tell me all about him?

"Yes, I will absolutely talk about Picasso. He's mostly become famous thanks to his Cubism art. We will also talk about Henri Matisse, a painter who had a long and influential career and was also part of the

Fauvism movement. Matisse and Picasso were both friends and rivals. They are considered the great artists of the early 20th century. Personally, I find that the inception of Picasso's Cubism was a revolutionary act in painting, but Matisse was an innovator in his own right.

However, let me tell you more about Berthe Weill. On December 1, 1901, she opened Galerie B. Weill at 25 rue Victor Massé. It was here where she bought and sold modernist works of art, mostly from the fauvist and cubist movements. The list of artists that exhibited in her gallery is truly impressive and includes André Derain, Georges Braque, Maurice de Vlaminck, Diego Rivera, Kees van Dongen, Maurice Utrillo, Jean Metzinger and of course, Pablo Picasso and Henri Matisse. But she also had an important role in the early exposure of artworks by female painters such as Suzanne Valadon, Emilie Charmy and Jacueline Marval. Berthe Weill continued to be a prominent art dealer and promoter of modern art until her death in 1951.

By the way, in 2012, the City of Paris placed a memorial plaque at 25 rue Victor Massé, where her gallery used to be, and Pablo Picasso's portrait of Berthe Weill, painted in 1920, was designated a French national treasure."

What a woman. I would very much like to find a 'Berthe Weill', as self-promotion as an artist is, to say it mildly, challenging. But can you tell me a bit more about the Fauvism artists and in particular the female artists Emilie Charmy and Jacqueline Marval? We've already discussed Suzanne Valadon.

"Emilie Charmy is a very interesting fauvist artist. She worked closely with artists like Matisse and often exhibited her work in Paris, in particular in Berthe Weill's gallery. She came from a bourgeois family and what makes her choice of painting even more interesting is the fact that her grandfather was the Bishop of Toulouse. She became an orphan when she was fifteen, and she and her older brother went to live with relatives in Lyon. Her artistic abilities already became apparent when she was a child. Most women at the time regarded painting as a hobby, but for Emilie painting became an obsession. She initially mostly painted women in domestic or bourgeois settings, as well as portrait, still life and flower paintings, possibly because they were decorative and sought after by the middle class. Her style could best be described as Impressionism, but she also painted nudes in which she clearly tries to restrict the intimate parts. Roland Dorgeles, a French novelist describes her as *"a great free painter; beyond influences and without method, she creates her own separate kingdom where the flights of her sensibility rule alone."*

Works a bit further on in her career can be described as quite abstract, considering her rough brushstrokes and bold use of colour. The latter makes her fit into the Fauvism movement. She became a respected artist, despite the fact that her paintings of nude women were very unusual for women artists of the time. As we've already seen, female artists were often banned from sessions with live models. But Emilie Charmy's work shows an interest in painting female models, often prostitutes, also including an expression of women's sexuality, which was rare for women artists, but common for male artists such as Degas. Female artists usually chose a domestic scene and especially mother and child paintings were popular.

The count of Jouvencel, who had seen Emilie Charmy's work at Berthe Weill's gallery, organised a solo exhibition of her work in 1921 at Galerie d'Oeuvres d'Art. It was criticised and created discussions about what feminine art should look like. Around that time Emilie met Colette and they became friends. Colette, who was by then very popular, wrote an introduction for the catalogue of a large exhibition of Emilie's work in 1922.

After the war, Charmy held fewer exhibitions of her work than she had done during the height of her artistic career, but she continued to paint into her 90s.

Jacqueline Marval was also a fauvist painter; her real name was Marie Josephine Vallet. She was both a painter and a sculptor. She was born in Quaix-en-Chartreuse, got married and became a mother. But her son died when he was six months old. It was a turning point for her and she divorced her husband. To make a living she became a seamstress. Then, in 1894 she met François Joseph Girot, a painter and came to Paris to live with him. She was then introduced to the group we spoke about earlier. Les Nabis. Subsequently she was introduced to another painter called Jules Flandrin, and they fell in love. She left Griot and moved in with Flandrin in Montparnasse. They lived together for many years. She became an accomplished artist, working on paintings, engravings, sculptures but also tapestry designs.

During Jacqueline's first participation at the Salon des Indépendants in Paris, the art dealer Ambroise Vollard bought ten of her paintings, including a nude self-portrait *Odalisque au Guépard* painted in 1900. This is seen by some as the first female nude self-portrait in art history. Vollard continued to buy and sell Jacqueline's works for ten more years. Between 1901 and 1905 she also became friends with Matisse and he often worked alongside her and Flandrin, it is said that they also influenced each other. Berthe Weill, who was interested in promoting artworks of female artists in Paris, also exhibited her work.

In 1913, Jacqueline Marval was involved in a protest against the removal of *The Spanish Shawl* from the Salon d'Automne. *The Spanish Shawl* was a painting by Kees van Dongen and he and Jacqueline became friends. She even set up her studio near his. In fact, Jacqueline and Flandrin moved into 40 rue Denfert Rochereau, which was next door to the studio of Van Dongen in 1914. Her artworks began to be recognised across Europe, exhibiting among others in Barcelona, Venice, Zurich, London, Kyoto and even in the United States. Guillaume Apollinaire referred to her as "*One of the most remarkable artists of our time*". Jacqueline Marval died in Paris in 1932. During her artistic career, she never wanted to exhibit in all-female exhibitions and didn't see herself as a feminist; however, after she died her work was celebrated in the Société des Femmes Artistes Modernes (FAM) a female artists' collective in Paris. Many feel that she did live a feminist life."

It's very nice to hear that these female artists were able to be accepted and established as professional artists in Paris during a time when art made such an important shift. You mentioned quite a few male Fauvist artists and I would love to hear a bit more about them too.

"Yes, I think it's important to name these artists as well. Henri Matisse was considered one of the leading figures in this movement and we know that he drew a great deal of inspiration from the work of Van Gogh. This connection is understandable as he had a very expressive use of vibrant colours. You could even say saturated, filled with light and optimism. In the early stages of his career, Matisse used photography extensively, unlike many painters. He used it for framing his compositions. He would take a photograph, then paint a near copy with vibrant colours. This created a significant change in his art. He also discovered Oceanic and African art, and he introduced this to his friend Picasso, and others. Matisse dabbled in some primitive art, and his sculptures and some of his paintings certainly show this influence. In Matisse's work, you can see his personal optimism and joy. His life appeared complicated, with moments of suffering and happiness, like everyone else, but Matisse's art embodies the dynamism and energy that characterised his personality.

Henri Matisse, still seen as one of the most influential artists of the 20th century, was a key figure in the development of modern art. The scandal surrounding his work during the first Salon d'Automne exhibition in 1905 is a notable episode in the history of modern art. Matisse's painting, *La femme au chapeau*, was one of his works displayed. This particular painting, which is now considered a masterpiece, depicts his wife, Amélie, wearing a vibrant, colourful hat. Matisse's use of intense, non-representational colours and bold brushstrokes was seen as radical and shocked both visitors and the art establishment. The painting became the focus of much controversy during the exhibition. Critics and viewers were appalled by the painting's unconventional use of colour and its disregard for classical representation.

Interestingly, the scandal surrounding *La femme au chapeau* did help to bring the emerging fauvist movement to attention, and it played an important role in the development of modern art, marking a significant step toward the acceptance of modern art.

Artists within the Fauvism movement included André Derain and Maurice Vlaminck, Albert Marque, and Georges Rouault. They were inspired by earlier artists who had worked extensively with colour, such as Van Gogh, Cézanne, Gauguin, and Seurat, as well as the earlier mentioned Matisse.

I would like to highlight two more of the artists who, to me, were pivotal for the birth of modern art. André Derain was a French painter, sculptor, and co-founder of the fauvist art movement in the early 20th century. His work during this period was marked by his bold and expressive use of colour in a way that departed from the realistic representation of the subject. While Derain's work and life were primarily focused on his artistic pursuits, there was a special woman in his life, Alice Princet. She posed for Derain, but also for other artists. She was fairly recently married when she met Derain. Apparently, it was love at first sight between the two, they went off together and never separated since. In fact, they stayed together till Derain died.

They were close friends with Picasso and spent quite a bit of time together. Derain's art was also influenced by the work of Paul Cézanne and you can see the interest in African sculpture in his work. According to Gertrude Stein, Derain was influenced by African sculpture before Picasso was.

In 1907 Daniel-Henry Kahnweiler, an art dealer, purchased Derain's entire body of work which gave him financial stability. He also worked together with Matisse through the summer of 1905. Later that year their paintings were exhibited at the Salon d'Automne. In March 1906, Ambroise Vollard commissioned Derain to produce a series of paintings in London. This resulted in a series of thirty paintings and remain among the most popular works of his entire career.

We can certainly come to the conclusion that André Derain had an important role in the development of two significant artistic movements in the avant-garde art scene in early 20th-century Paris, which made a lasting impact on the art world. Together with Henri Matisse and Maurice de Vlaminck the totally new Fauvism movement was born and his collaboration with Georges Braque and Pablo Picasso was crucial to early Cubism.

I've also mentioned Maurice de Vlaminck. He was a French painter also known for his association with the Fauvism movement. He started painting when he was still a teenager. But a turning point in his artistic career occurred when he came back from his time in the army when he was twenty-three years old. He met André Derain on the train and they started their lifelong friendship. When Vlaminck had completed his time in the army in 1900, he and Derain rented a studio together. There isn't much known about specific women in his life. He was married and most probably he had muses that inspired his art, but this is not as well documented as is the case with other artists."

Before we finish our lunch, Mario is showing me various examples of the artworks that we have discussed. I really like looking at these paintings, but also at existing photos of these great artists. It just brings them to life.

We now go towards Montmartre where we will pay a visit to the Bateau Lavoir in 13 rue Ravignan. It's promising to become an interesting visit!

Bohemia

Picasso, and the women in his life

After a ride on the subway, we get out at the Abbesses stop, from which it is a three to five-minute walk to 13 rue Ravignan on place Emile Goudeau in Montmartre. We've been here before but today we are diving into Picasso's life! I continue to be impressed by the metro network in Paris. It's rather interesting isn't it, that what you see inside the metro was constructed in Hausmann's time? It's like an underground city with its 309 stations, long corridors, many lines, and people in a hurry!

Mario, you also keep talking about the bohemia, so how exactly can you best describe that?

"Well, it's best described as a way of life which doesn't comply with conventional norms and expectations of a society. *La Bohème*, was a term especially used during the mid19th century to describe writers, journalists, artists, musicians and actors who often lived in a state of poverty, even hunger, in major cities throughout Europe. They often were associated with anti-establishment social or political views. Some refer to the wealthier, or aristocratic bohemian circle as *haute bohème*."

Thanks, and I must say that now that we are standing in front of Le Bateau Lavoir I think back to what I've learned about Picasso's life, from a really interesting documentary series that I saw recently. I presume you could say that he was both part of la bohème and la haute bohème. Of course, many books and documentaries have been created around this rather amazing figure, but for me personally it has made me view Picasso in a different way. He was incredibly talented, but quite frankly a horrible guy to fall in love with. Apart from his *Blue period* I never felt attracted to his work, but now, with so much more knowledge, I do very much admire him as an artist as he certainly was one of the greatest artists having roamed the streets of Paris. I'm interested in what you think about him.

"I agree with you. Already from a very young age he was extremely gifted. His father was actually a painter and an art teacher. Picasso was born in Malaga in southern Spain, but when he was still a young boy his family moved to Barcelona where his father got a job in a college as an art teacher. Picasso joined his classes from the age of fourteen. There are portrait drawings and paintings he made of his father and other people from this time that are remarkably good. His self-portrait also created when he was fourteen shows his amazing talent. He was a far better painter than his father which quite possibly created a sense of superiority in him.

In the Museo Picasso in Barcelona they have a series of erotic drawings by him, which were clearly made in a brothel at a very young age. He used prostitutes as his models and some suggest that at that early age this might have created a deep-rooted disrespect for women.

Throughout his artist career you can also see his love for bullfighting. He felt attracted to the drama, the show, but also the cruelty, machoism and death. He almost certainly picked this up from his father who loved bullfighting as well. When he was fourteen, tragedy struck. His young sister Conchita died of diphtheria. Paloma, Picasso's daughter, stated in an interview that he prayed and said "*dear Lord, if you keep her alive, I promise I will stop painting*", but he couldn't stop drawing and painting and she did die. This must have been very traumatic for him.

In 1900, after having spent his teenage years between Barcelona and Madrid, Picasso, at nineteen, went to Paris, the centre of the art world of that time. He didn't have a lot of money and ended up in Montmartre, which was the poorest part of the city, with a lot of crime and despair. But soon he began making friends, initially with Spanish artists, among which his close friend, Catalan painter Carles Casagemas. They met Germaine Gargallo and she and Carles started a relationship. It didn't last and Carles was rejected. In a dramatic moment he tried to shoot her, but ended up shooting himself. This was in February 1901. Picasso was devastated, and this prompted his *Blue period*. A series of paintings with mostly blue tones, showing figures that seem to suffer. I feel there is a sadness in all these paintings. A few months after his friend's death Picasso started a relationship with Germaine, but she went on to marry Picasso's friend, Ramon Pichot, in 1906.

It was clear that Picasso had a lot of talent and in 1901 he was invited for an exhibition in Gallery Vollard. He produced sixty-four commercial paintings which he thought and hoped would sell. Critics wondered who this guy was. An artist so clearly influenced by Van Gogh, Degas and Lautrec, but still looking for his own style. Most artists copied other artists to get more skilful, but Picasso once said *"Bad artists copy, but great artists steal!"*

You could say that if you would like to get to know Picasso you have to study his work as he so clearly expresses his emotions in his art.

At the beginning of his time in Paris Picasso started mingling with other artists, primarily poets. Among whom Max Jacob, a fairly humble French poet who also was a painter, writer, and art critic. He became one of Picasso's best friends. It's curious how they met. One day, Max discovers a work from Picasso's blue period in a gallery and asks the art dealer to introduce him to the artist. The dealer told him that this artist sold very poorly but was named Picasso. Jacob finds out the address, goes to see him, and they become friends. Picasso was not yet established in Montmartre. The meeting between Jacob and Picasso was challenging because they didn't speak each other's languages.

Soon Picasso also became friends with Guillaume Apollinaire, a restless person who created poems and revolutionised the world of poetry with his calligrams. At that time Picasso had just found a place that would be important in his creation. It's where we are now, Le Bateau Lavoir, a name Apollinaire thought up because 'lavoir' means laundry, like those washhouses on the riverside where women used to wash clothes. It was a building with several artists' studios, but it was damp, hot in the summer and cold in the winter. There was only one sink and one toilet to share among the residents. When you entered you could go down to a basement which was practically empty apart from mice, a cat, and a small stove. However, this is where Picasso and his friends began to create, where they painted and inspired each other.

During this time he meets Fernande Olivier, a beautiful and much-loved artist's model, who posed among others for Dutch artist Kees van Dongen. Picasso adored her, but he was very jealous. They started a relationship and moved in together. Picasso asked her to stop modelling for other artists, but Picasso himself created many paintings of her. After a while he didn't even want her to go out. But they did have an amazing social life as many interesting people were living in or around the area. They liked drinking and smoking together and also consumed opium; Fernande did as well as we now know from her memoirs. Picasso and his friends spent many nights at the Lapin Agile, and occasionally they went to the Medrano circus on boulevard Rochechouart. At the time many artists felt attracted to the world of circus with its acrobats and clowns. But when he went out, he locked the door of the studio keeping Fernande there, like a prisoner. It must have been difficult for a woman who had such an independent life before they got together, but in those times women were treated like that, so it wasn't necessarily seen as bad.

Fernande wasn't able to have children, so they adopted a thirteen-year-old girl called Raymonde from an orphanage. At first, the girl was well received, also by Picasso's friends. Some say that after a short time, Picasso started using her as a nude model and even created some explicit erotic images of her. When Fernande found out they returned her to the orphanage, saying that the Bateau Lavoir was not a place to raise a child."

Oh dear, that all sounds pretty wrong, doesn't it? I know those times were different, but I admire Fernande for having taken that decision.

"Indeed, I agree with you. What is interesting in Picasso's work is that almost every time he has a serious relationship with a woman, his art changes. The period with Fernande is marked by his pink period, more joyful than his rather depressive blue period.

Le Bateau Lavoir had become a meeting place for many artists and by now Picasso also had become friends with Andre Derain and Georges Braque who both would play a significant role in his life. He also met the Stein brothers, Leo and Michael, and their sister Gertrude, who visited the place in 1906. The Steins were American Jews who fell in love with Paris, and began collecting art. In their house, they already had paintings by Matisse and of some impressionists. They were pivotal in the development of the artistic world of Montmartre at that time. Later on, they helped their American compatriots like Hemingway, in what became known as the *Lost Generation*.

Meeting Gertrude Stein was special. Picasso was fascinated by her robust appearance and wanted to paint her. It was a challenge for him but he did finish the painting. Gertrude also started to invite Picasso to her art gatherings in her house together with Braque, Derain, Vlaminck, and of course, Matisse. It is supposed that this is where Picasso and Matisse met for the first time. In a sense it's a really special, even historic meeting, because they became both rivals and mutual admirers. Matisse already had his big scandal at the Salon d'Automne with his fauvist artworks, and they considered each other the great masters of art at the beginning of the 20th century and I think this is certainly true.

In 1907, Picasso began to change his way of painting. He was working on a new piece that would be a decisive work in the history of modern art. We're talking about *Demoiselles d'Avignon*, which was actually inspired by a brothel in Barcelona. It depicts five women, and two of them, especially the central figures, resemble Iberian statues that Picasso was enchanted by. The ones on the sides have faces inspired by African masks with large feet, thick hands, and twisted noses. With this painting, Picasso is showing a new way of expression. The influence of primitive art, especially from Africa is evident. During that time, many houses had African figures and masks. Art from Oceania and South America also had an important role in the development of modern art, just as Japonisme had in its time."

You know Mario, I read something fascinating. There are people who say that he was inspired to create *Demoiselles d'Avignon* by *Les Odalisques*, an artwork by fauvist artist Jacqueline Marval.

"Well artists did copy from other artists, so it's not impossible. It is curious that practically everybody has heard of Picasso, but few have heard of Jacqueline Marval even though she was important in the history of art. Anyway, Picasso invites Apollinaire, Georges Braque, with whom he had become friends, and the Steins to show his just-finished painting. But no one understood the artwork. Even Apollinaire, the most open to innovative changes, didn't get it. Gertrude Stein was the only one who defended Picasso's work. Sometime later Kahnweiler, the art dealer who purchased Derain's entire body of work, wanted to buy it, but Picasso refused. But I believe he did end up buying the drawings Picasso used to create the work. Picasso kept the painting in his studio and it wasn't publicly exhibited until 1916.

Picasso was an interesting character, aware of his creative genius. His friends all adored him, but more than once, he betrayed them. Picasso started making money and, after five years in Montmartre, he moved to Clichy. He moved there with Fernande. It was a much more comfortable place, and he spent his days drawing and painting. His friends did feel somewhat abandoned. It wasn't like Le Bateau Lavoir but once a week, Picasso, who had become known for his difficult character, invited his friends to his house for dinner.

Picasso's encounter with Gertrude Stein also marks a crucial moment, leading to the birth of Cubism. Picasso and Braque developed this new style of painting, breaking away from traditional perspectives and reducing their paintings to just a few colours. The cubist movement evolves, introducing Analytical Cubism, where recognisable subjects disappear, and Synthetic Cubism, which incorporates elements like text and musical notes.

Of all his friends, perhaps the one he connected with the most on a creative level was Georges Braque. With him, he started this wonderful Cubism adventure. Cubism is decisive for the evolution of modern art. At first, their art was inspired by Cezanne who we can see as a precursor of Cubism, as he had already simplified forms and made them more geometric.

When we view Picasso's and Braque's artworks, we can see that the subject of the painting begins to disappear and becomes unrecognisable. It's difficult to distinguish the person who had posed for the artworks, painted in all those angles and geometric shapes. In 1911 the figurative side of the works gradually disappears, and Picasso and Braque start putting words in the paintings and also numbers and musical notes in shades of grey and ochre. During this time, they didn't sign their work, so it's quite difficult to see which artwork was created by Picasso and which by Braque. The next step was to introduce fabrics or pieces of paper onto the painting, which was never done before and this changed modern art completely.

Friendships among artists were important at the time, but there was an incident that marked the friendship of Picasso with his friends. It's the famous Louvre theft case. The *Mona Lisa* was painted in France when Leonardo da Vinci visited the country, and the *Mona Lisa*, and other art objects, were stolen from the Louvre. This was in 1911 and this iconic painting was found again two years later. Apollinaire, who had bought some of the stolen objects knew that Picasso also had some stolen Iberian figures in his workshop.

The Louvre Museum didn't have a good security system at the time. People jokingly said, "*I'm going to the Louvre, do you want me to bring you something?*" Apollinaire and Picasso panicked because with the theft of the *Mona Lisa*, they knew that at some point, someone would come after them. They decided to get rid of the Iberian figures, but they didn't succeed. Picasso then distanced himself from his friend during the investigation and Apollinaire is eventually accused of theft and taken to jail. Picasso is also called to testify, but he denies knowing Apollinaire, which shows his character. He's very scared, knowing that if they find out he had some of the figurines, he could be expelled from France and end up in jail. After some time, Apollinaire was released. In 1912, he publishes his work *Alcool*, a significant work reflecting on women and his time in prison. It's a poetic work which doesn't have any punctuations.

While Matisse and Picasso were rivals, Marcel Duchamp appears on the scene, becoming a significant step for the evolution of modern art. He was part of a new cubist group. Some of the artists of this group were Duchamp, Delaunay, and Picabia. They exhibited their work at the Salon des Independants causing tensions with Picasso and Braque who did not share the same aesthetic ideas.

Marcel Duchamp's painting, *Nu descendant un escalier n° 2* is a 1912 painting and now a well-known work which has contributed to the evolution of modern art. Duchamp, the future Dadaist artist, even went to New York with this painting. This period of artistic innovation and interpersonal dynamics shapes Picasso's journey, setting the stage for further developments in the world of modern art."

For me, it's this kind of information that makes Picasso so interesting. However, we are talking about the women who were important in the development of modern art in Paris. It is well-known that Picasso was a womaniser and had mistresses outside his longer-lasting relationships. It is also well-documented that most of his paintings are inspired by the women in his life. I would love to know more about who these women were. Why were they so fascinated by Picasso? How was he able to attract these women even, in some of these relationships, when he was many years their senior?

"You are certainly right there. He often had romantic relationships with several women at the same time. This is also quite clear in his art which has a lot of sexual references. You can see many of these women in his paintings. Let's discuss the most important ones.

Although there are several paintings of a woman called Madeleine towards the end of his blue paintings from 1904, but not much is known about her. Apparently, she was important to him as she was pregnant with his baby and then lost it. This affected him greatly, and he started creating drawings of women with babies. In 1968 one of these drawings was discovered and Picasso, who was still alive, said that he would have had a sixty-four-year-old child if she hadn't lost it.

But his first important love was Fernande Olivier who we've already talked about. Their relationship actually lasted for seven years and ended in 1911. About twenty years later she started publishing a series of memoirs about her years with Picasso. He was already famous by then and paid her money to stop publishing them until they both had died.

Eva Gouel and Gabrielle Depeyre Lespinasse were also lovers of Picasso. Eva died young of tuberculosis, but his affair with Gabrielle stretched over many years in secret. Gabrielle ended up marrying Lespinasse, an American artist who lived most of his life in France. The affair between Picasso and her was only discovered in 1972 after her husband had died and a niece decided to sell all Picasso's artworks from her collection, which now belong to the Musée Picasso in Paris.

There were more lovers, but I'd like to talk about Olga Khokhlova now, with whom he was married for ten years and who was the mother of his first son. She was a dancer in the Russian ballet, but originally from the Ukraine. They met when Picasso was working on the set of a ballet show, which he had designed. They fell in love and Olga even left the ballet company and moved to Paris. They got married in 1918 when Picasso was thirty-six and she was twenty-six. Their marriage lasted for ten years, but it is fair to say that it changed after Olga had given birth to their son Paulo, in 1921. Picasso fell back into his old habits and started having affairs with other women."

I do love his paintings of her. In particular the painting called *Portrait d'Olga dans un fauteuil* from 1918. It has a Spanish feel to it, because of the chair and the fan, but she looks serene, yet somewhat sad to me. It shows Picasso's skill to paint realistic, but the contrast with the unfinished background brings it into modern times. I'm showing Mario an image of the painting.

"Yes, it's special, although I prefer all the different portraits he created of her, in slightly different styles. In a sense he moved on from Cubism and went back to more traditional art. He used to say that he didn't want to be expected to create art in a certain way. I think this was typical for Picasso, becoming obsessed with the women in his life and depicting that in his art.

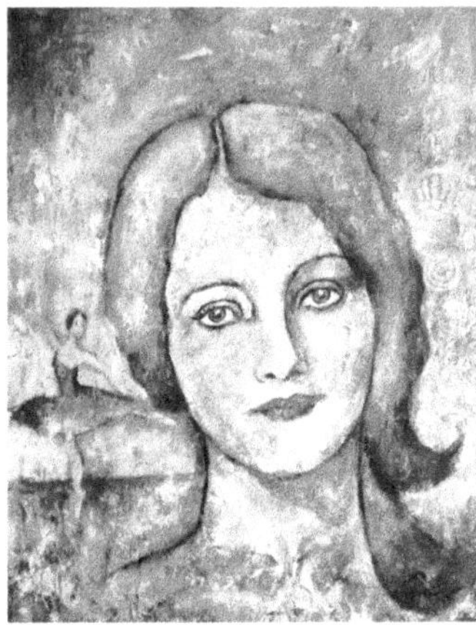

Olga Khokhlova

In 1927, when the marriage with Olga was already unstable, Picasso met seventeen-year-old Marie-Thérèse Walter. He was forty-six years old at the time. She became his model and lover and also gave birth to their daughter Maya in 1935. Marie-Thérèse was called Picasso's 'golden muse' as she inspired numerous of his sculptures and artworks created during their relationship. These are interesting paintings showing Picasso's typical signature. They look rather abstract and yet you can clearly see Marie-Thérèse Walter's face. Some of these paintings, even though painted fairly abstract, are sexually quite explicit.

Marie-Thérèse was a very athletic young blonde woman with striking facial features. It is said that she was the illegitimate daughter of a Swedish businessman and a French woman. She met Picasso in Paris, in front of Galeries Lafayette. He approached her and asked her if he could paint her portrait. She had never heard of him, although Picasso already was quite well known by then, but she was flattered and she went to his studio every day. After a week they already started an intimate relationship. Olga was unaware of this.

Marie-Thérèse later said *"My life with him was always secret, calm and peaceful. We said nothing to anyone. We were happy like that, and we did not ask for anything more"*. Picasso's first retrospective exhibition was in 1932 in Galeries George Petit. He curated it himself as he didn't want to stick to any rules. He didn't respect the chronological order of his works and it was a total mix of his artworks. There were many nude portraits of Marie-Thérèse revealing the nature of their relationship. His artworks had become increasingly erotic, but he was able to do so because of the position he had in the French art world. The retrospective showed the strength of his history and the innovation of his work."

I've seen a few of these artworks and in particular *Le Rêve* from 1932. It's quite cubist and it clearly shows Marie-Thérèse's profile, but you also cannot miss the phallic symbol in her face.

"Yes, some say that the brutalisation of women is part of his imagery. It can either be tender or cruel. In 1935 Marie-Thérèse gave birth to their daughter Maya. But even by the time she was born Picasso had been seeing several other women. Some say that Olga Khokhlova was told by a friend that Picasso had a long-term relationship with Marie-Thérèse and that she was expecting a child. Others say she found out he was seeing someone else when she saw the paintings during Picasso's retrospective but accepted this for a while. It must have been hard for her. Whichever way it was, when she found out Marie-Thérèse was pregnant she left Picasso and moved to the South of France, with their son Paulo. Picasso wanted to divorce Olga, but she didn't allow that, so she and Picasso continued to be legally married until Olga died of cancer in 1955.

You could say Picasso had a mid-life crisis and even though it was normal to have a mistress, people frowned upon a relationship of a forty-five-year-old man with a seventeen-year-old girl. In an interview, years later, Marie-Thérèse claimed he was very kind to her, and she loved spending time with him. But she did say he introduced her to sadomasochistic sex. He also got an etching machine and created a series of over one hundred etchings of Marie-Thérèse called the Suite Vollard. They are highly erotic and often quite violent. It feels like they are marked by the pleasure of looking at women in pain. Interestingly the paintings of Marie-Thérèse after Maya was born are no longer erotic.

It was only a few months after Maya's birth that Picasso started a relationship with a surrealist photographer, Dora Maar. Dora also started modelling for him. Maya, Picasso's daughter, later said that she believed that the painting *Femme au béret rouge à pompon* from 1937 was a combined portrait of her mother Marie-Thérèse and Dora Maar, as he was maintaining a relationship with both women."

I've heard about Dora Maar, she sounds so interesting, can you tell me a bit more about her?

"Yes, she was a French surrealist photographer, but also a painter and a poet. The story goes that he saw her one day at the café Les Deux Magots, wearing white gloves and playing with a knife flicking it between her splayed fingers, now and then hitting a finger which made some blood appear. Picasso introduced himself and asked her whether he could have the gloves. Dora had a masochist personality and Picasso was cruel, sadistic. Somehow, they complemented each other. Dora was already part of a Surrealism scene and was friends with people like Frida Kahlo and Salvador Dali. She was a very talented surrealist photographer, exploring the dream world and other forms of reality.

She actually took pictures of Picasso working in his studio on his famous anti-war painting *Guernica*, in 1937. He apparently was abusive to her. He created a series of paintings called *La Femme qui pleure*, which means weeping woman and the paintings depict Dora Maar. The series is about universal suffering, about grief and pain. Some thought that it was because Dora Maar was suffering a lot during the relationship, but in an interview shortly before she died, she stated that this wasn't the case. The series was because of the state of the world, the upcoming war.

Dora was only living two hundred metres from Picasso's studio in Paris, in rue des Grands Augustins, but she could only visit him on his terms. He wanted to be in control of his women and that must have been hard for a highly talented and independent woman like Dora.

When the war broke out Picasso was invited to go to the United States, but he refused and stayed in Paris, where he cleverly stayed away from the parties that the nazis organised, and where people like Coco Chanel could be seen. He is said to have donated money to the Resistance and helped hiding people.

Dora and Picasso stayed together for much of the war, but her mother died and Dora's mental state started to deteriorate. She had a nervous breakdown. Some friends blame Picasso, but Picasso blames the surrealists who, according to him, put these strange ideas into her head.

After her treatment she almost withdrew from life, she became very religious. Picasso had made many paintings of her, but one day he just stopped seeing her. He never really ended his relationships, just stopped seeing the women, like was the case with Dora. She wanted to be with him, but he just cut her off. In a sense like he had done with Fernande and Olga. He had such emotional power over these women. Marie-Thérèse even committed suicide after Picasso had died.

In 1943 Picasso met Françoise Gilot at a café in Paris. She was twenty-one. He was sixty-one. He said to her *"you must come and see some of my paintings"*. Françoise and Picasso at first had an intellectual attraction as she was an artist herself. She came from a well-off family and was supposed to study law, but she wanted to become an artist. They started a relationship, but she wasn't naïve, she knew what she was getting into. After the war they bought a house together. La Gallaise in Vallauris. During the war his paintings were very dark, but now colour came back into his paintings. They had two children, Claude and Paloma. But he went away a lot, especially to bullfights which he loved and he met other women and had affairs. This was hard for Françoise.

In 1954 he saw a nineteen-year-old girl with a ponytail outside his studio. Her name was Sylvette Davis. She becomes his model, but he never was intimate with her. In an interview she claims that he never touched her and she never posed without clothes. Picasso created more than sixty portraits of her, drawings, sculptures and paintings. This series is described as his *Ponytail Period*.

Françoise knew about the model and was OK with that, but she did grow tired of his abuse and affairs. She left him in 1953 and was the only woman who had ever left Picasso. Eleven years later, she wrote a book called *Life with Picasso*. He tried to offer her a lot of money to not publish it, he and Jacqueline, his new partner, tried everything they could, but it didn't work. After the book was published Picasso disinherited Françoise and didn't want to see his children again. This was very tough on the children who used to visit their father every summer holiday. Françoise ended up marrying Jonas Salk in 1970. He was an American physician and medical researcher who is well known for having created and developed the first successful vaccine against polio.

Picasso met Jacqueline Roque in 1953 at the Madoura Pottery studio. This was in a period when he created his ceramics. Jacqueline had recently divorced her first husband with whom she had a six-year-old daughter named Catherine. Jaqueline and Picasso started a relationship, and she became totally devoted to him. She became his second wife in 1961. She was thirty-four and he was seventy-nine. Picasso was greatly inspired by Jacqueline, creating more works based on her than on any of the other women in his life.

When Picasso died on April 8, 1973, Jacqueline prevented his children, Paloma and Claude and his grandsons, from attending the funeral. One of his grandsons, Pablito, killed himself after he was refused entry to the house. In 1986, Jacqueline Roque took her own life on the eve of a major Picasso exhibition in Spain. She shot herself.

As far as Picasso's work is concerned, he never stopped creating art. He was afraid of dying and obsessed with working. He created many prints, almost as if he wanted to recapture his life. But there was also a lot of erotic and even rather pornographic work. If you wanted to see the works in the gallery where they were exhibited you had to be over eighteen years old. He was an old man, but it was almost as if he was trying to show his potency. He also created self-portraits as he had done throughout his entire life, but his last self-portrait is almost like a mirror to death. He died of a heart attack when he was ninety-one years old."

Gosh, what a man. Again, I don't like him, but I do love to see how his art developed. I don't like all of his work but I can certainly admire it. I feel a bit of unease after watching the images of his prints from those last years of his life and a bit sad about the tragedies of those suicides related to who he was. I would like to shake that feeling off me, so what shall we do next?

"Well, we can have a little stroll through Montmartre if you like and then go back to our hotel. Tomorrow I would like to talk to you about Orphism."

That is a new term for me! I'm looking forward to that and yes, let's have a walk through Montmartre as after all this information it feels as if the energy, specifically of the women in Picasso's life, is still here, impregnating my skin and my soul. I wonder if it will affect my future artwork.

Orphism

And the colourful world of a woman

Mario is in his element. This is the part of Paris where he was born. The part where he spent his childhood and teenage years. We are in Montparnasse. When he was a young boy Montparnasse was still popular with artists and he, possibly unknowingly, saw Giacometti and other artists in the streets near his home. Nowadays Montparnasse is not really a popular tourist destination. In a sense that's a shame as its artistic history comes to life through the memories collected in books, films, artworks and photographs, if you know where to look for them. I feel it's certainly worth a visit.

We are in rue Daguerre, close to the Denfert Rochereau metro exit. It's also close to the Montparnasse cemetery, which, if you have sufficient time, is worth a visit. The atmosphere is buzzing and it's pleasant to be in a pedestrian area. It's actually a really lively market street and after a short stroll we decide to go for a coffee in Café Daguerre, which is on the corner of rue Daguerre.

We talk about Orphism, which is sometimes referred to as Orphic Cubism. This is not a surprise as Orphism can be seen as the key chain between Cubism and Abstract art. The name was actually thought up by Apollinaire in 1912, referring to his 1908 poem *Orphée*, Mario shows me the poem and explains what Orphism actually is…

"It was certainly influenced by Fauvism, but focusing more on the abstract representation of objects. The main pioneers of Orphism were František Kupka, from Opočno in Austria-Hungary, who settled in Paris in 1894, and Sonia and Robert Delaunay. They reintroduced colours during the mostly one colour phase of Cubism and tried to express sensations, depicting subjects in abstract shapes, but concentrating on bright colours and form. The simultaneous contrasts of two colours created optical effects, going beyond Seurat's Pointillism.

Apollinaire described Orphism as *"the art of painting new totalities with elements that the artist does not take from visual reality, but creates entirely by himself. An Orphic painter's works should convey an 'untroubled aesthetic pleasure', a meaningful structure and sublime significance."*

I'm especially interested in Sonia Delaunay, so who was she Mario?

"Sonia was an artist who spent most of her working life in Paris. She was born in the Russian Empire, in the area which is now Ukraine, as Sarah Elievna Stern. Her parents were poor and at the age of five she was orphaned and went to live with her uncle Henri Terk, a successful lawyer, and his wife Anna. They adopted Sarah in 1890 and she became Sonia Terk. She was well educated and when she was eighteen years old, she went to an art school in Germany where she studied until 1905. She then moved to Paris and settled in the Latin Quarter and enrolled for art classes at the Académie de La Palette in Montparnasse. She didn't very much like their strict way of teaching and was only there for a short period.

She admired Fauvist artists, especially Bonnard, but they say that she disliked Matisse, finding his art too bourgeois. She met the art dealer and gallery owner Wilhelm Uhde, whom she later married in a sham arrangement to conceal his homosexuality from his family. Sonia enjoyed the deception. Thanks to exhibitions at Wilhelm's gallery Sonia could benefit from his connections. She also met Picasso, who she admired, but regarded as a malevolent genius.

A regular visitor to the gallery was Comtesse de Rose, who was the mother of Robert Delaunay. When Sonia and Robert met, they fell in love and became lovers. They decided that she had to divorce Wilhelm. In 1910 Robert and Sonia, who was by then pregnant with Robert's child, married. They were financially supported by Sonia's aunt in St.

Petersburg. Sonia said about Robert: "*In Robert Delaunay I found a poet. A poet who wrote not with words but with colours*".

Sonia Delaunay was a woman who supported her husband. She certainly didn't consider herself a feminist. Despite having as much talent as her husband as a painter, she prioritised his work over her own. Robert, though egocentric and ill-tempered, considered Sonia a great painter. Together, they formed an almost perfect union of love and art. Sonia admired her husband as a poet who painted, praising Robert's dominance over her. Over time, Sonia's combination of figurative and abstract elements in her paintings proved more intriguing than Robert's static abstraction."

Mario shows me the painting *Le Bal Bullier* which depicts a lively café with brightly coloured backgrounds, capturing the tango dances of the time. You can clearly recognise the dancers, yet it's a very abstract work of art.

"Yes, Sonia's intuition guided her. She must have led a full and exciting life, meeting a variety of interesting people of that time. One of the people she met was writer Blaise Cendrars, a one-armed poet and novelist, who she greatly admired. Sonia considered him a great friend, collaborating on an illustrated poem which is worth mentioning: *La prose du Transsibérien*. This poem unfolds like a two-meter accordion.

With the Russian Revolution and the disruption of funds from Russia during World War I, Sonia and Robert faced financial ruin. They travelled to Spain where they settled in Madrid.

Sonia certainly was a woman with a vision and with very good commercial and marketing knowledge. She developed her skills as a seamstress. Sewing fabrics printed with her own designs, she started designing clothes and accessories but also offered interior design, and staging. In a sense Madrid was a time of experimenting and she also gradually started earning money. This was very needed as Robert wasn't making much money from his artwork and they also had a child to support. It is said that Sonia's dresses, with vibrant colours and inspired by abstraction, were made from fabric scraps which she had found.

She dared to wear these unique dresses herself, becoming her own mannequin, this way bringing art and abstraction into everyday life.

She did face some disdain from the art world because textile artists were seen more as craftsmen than as true artists. Nevertheless, she managed to create a small business where she not only sewed but also designed clothes for artists and aristocrats of the time. She was an artist, breaking the mould. Sonia then established Casa Sonia, a fashion house in Madrid, near the elegant Calle de Serrano. Her work became fashionable and she even designed for Spanish marquises. She also decorated the interior of Le Petit Casino in Madrid, which later became a prominent theatre named Teatro Benavente.

Although successful, Robert and Sonia eventually decided to return to Paris. Back in France she continued her multidiscipline art business. Painting, but also creating her art accessories and dresses. Each dress she made was unique; she didn't mass-produce them. In wartime Europe, she was oblivious to politics and conflicts, even questioning why artists had to leave due to terrible conflicts. Her husband fell ill in 1941, and Sonia, who was of Jewish decent, took a considerable risk moving through occupied France to the free zone in the south east of France to save him.

Unfortunately, Robert died on October 25, 1941 in Montpellier, due to pulmonary problems.

After the war Sonia fought for her husband's artistic recognition. However, in 1953, Sonia had an exhibition of her own work at the Museum of Modern Art in Paris, which influenced many artists. She supported young abstract artists, but was not interested in figurative painters. She really was an icon, and even French politicians like De Gaulle and Pompidou recognised her. I like the fact that we are giving her some extra attention now during our journey in Paris. Towards the end of her ninety-four-year life, she was able to enjoy a comfortable lifestyle.

She had lived a colourful and intense life which included various lovers, among which was gallery owner Jacques Damas, who helped revive her career. Sonia, seemingly in her husband's shadow, was perhaps the first female artist working in multiple disciplines. She stands as one of the first great female artists of the 20th century, surpassing many male artists. She was in fact the first female artist to have a retrospective exhibition, during her lifetime, at the Louvre in 1964. She left a colourful legacy with her paintings, but also her books, umbrellas, coats, dresses and more and was certainly pushing boundaries and influencing later generations. In 1975 she was awarded the Légion d'honneur, the highest French decoration. For two centuries, this decoration has been presented on behalf of the Head of State to reward the most deserving citizens in all fields of activity."

As an artist myself I'm finding it interesting how she evolved from her, in my opinion, fauvist series of Finnish girls, into the abstract world of Orphism. I must say I very much like that series of colourful, but recognisable portraits of these young Finnish girls. They look sunny and also surreal to me, but you can already see that her art is going in a more abstract direction.

So, what happened to Orphism, as I know it didn't last long did it?

"You are right, Orphism kind of became Dadaism and the increasingly abstract paintings of dadaist artists Fernand Léger and Marcel Duchamp were also considered to be Orphism art by Apollinaire. And there was an interesting link. The dadaists from Cabaret Voltaire in Switzerland, found out about the works of Robert and Sonia Delaunay. They asked Sonia to illustrate the magazine they had created, called *Dada*'."

Dadaism

A provocation in the art world

It's really nice sitting here in Café Daguerre enjoying our coffee and a very interesting chat about Orphism and now about Dadaism. I must admit I had not heard of either of these terms but it's great to learn more about art and the artists who created it.

"OK Renate, let me explain. Dada or Dadaism was a movement that emerged during the First World War in neutral Switzerland. It all happened in a club or café called Cabaret Voltaire in Zurich. The establishment closed shortly after due to scandals and noise, but it was here where painters, artists, and writers gathered and where arguably one of the most revolutionary movements in the history of art was born.

There were all kinds of characters who later became important figures in history. For example, Lenin was there, playing chess with Tristan Tzara, a Romanian avant-garde poet and essayist, who was also a performance artist and active as a literary and art critic, playwright and journalist. Tzara is thought to be the creator of the Dada movement. German refugees like Hugo Ball were also present during the meetings in the café. One day, these intellectuals decided to give a name to this new movement. The story goes that they told Tristan Tzara to open the dictionary, and the first word he found would be the name. The word turned out to be 'dada,' which doesn't really mean anything, but could refer to a toy horse. Others say it comes from the Rumanian word 'da', which means 'yes'. Essentially, such a simple name, but it is clear that the intention of Dadaism was to shake up the world of art first and in turn, the entire society."

Mario shows me an interesting portrait of Tristan Tzara, painted by Robert Delaunay, the orphist artist. It is a fairly realistic painting, and Tzara is wearing a scarf which looks as if it is made by Sonia Delaunay with those so recognisable colours and patterns she used in her work.

"We know that the First World War from 1914 to 1918 was truly a massacre. Millions of young people died for nothing, due to alliances and the absurdity of war. Dada proposed to break with all of that. The dadaists were horrified by the war and denounced the society of their time, a society that gave great importance to science, progress, the destructive power of weaponry, machinery, speed. You could say they were against the trend of the time and of a society dominated by the bourgeoisie, manipulating and leading people to destruction. Dada rebelled against all of that.

In 1916 the first public performance took place at Cabaret Voltaire. A Dada magazine was published, featuring intellectuals we've mentioned before, such as Apollinaire and Picabia. The Dada movement expressed itself in all arts: literature, poetry, theatre, music, and painting. It was a movement meant to provoke, playing with the absurd and the satirical. Dada was bigger as a movement in Germany, where it had become more political, although there were dadaists in Paris and later in New York, thanks to the Frenchman Marcel Duchamp.

Dada lasted a short time but was decisive; it gave rise to Surrealism. When Dadaism reached Paris in 1918, Surrealism did not yet exist, as Surrealism is somewhat a consequence of Dada.

Tristan Tzara arrived in Paris from Zurich in 1920, organising a show that, as almost always, ended in a scandal. Dada was a very provocative movement; it even provoked the audience, and participants often ended up in the police station for public scandal. The difference between Dadaism in France and in Germany is that in France it didn't have a social tendency; it did not want changes, unlike on the German side.

Dadaism in Paris ignored society and did not want to commit socially because they wanted to end everything that had been done before. Their weapon was irony and provocation. Their actions started to shake society, as the press would focus on them. At the time all avant-garde movements were seen as a threat. They were accused of unpatriotic behaviour, safely staying in Switzerland, protected from the war, while thousands of young French people were dying in the battlefields. They also considered these young people, who were creating a new revolution in art, as bourgeois children and saw them as a danger.

The dadaists mocked everything sacred in society, such as religion and power. This could alienate the people from patriotic feelings. They were also criticised for having money to publish their newspapers and pamphlets during inflation and crisis due to the war. And of course, they thought that the dadaists were Jews, protestants, outcasts, parasites, and even Germans in the worst sense of the word... enemies in the war, and also Bolsheviks because there had been a revolution in Russia. The ruling class feared that Dada could encourage the workers to rebel against power. Still, Dada had no ideology in itself. It was merely a denunciation of a destructive inhuman society.

Even the left would see it as a threat. Initially, it was thought that Dada would be useful because it was against the bourgeoisie, but the dadaists felt more liberated than that and did not want to support the workers' struggle for fear of history repeating itself. They were against all types of power and simply wanted to revolutionise and demystify all art. Dada did not want to be used for any cause."

In Paris dadaist artists often met in the cafés in Montparnasse and it is interesting that we are discussing them now, here in one of those cafés. But I would like to know what the role of the women was. This was such an important and seemingly modern movement that you would think that women were seen as equals, but sadly this was not necessarily the case, was it Mario?

"As revolutionary as Dada may be, it follows the same pattern as other earlier movements, sidelining women to some extent. It's true that there are quite a few women involved in Dada, perhaps more than in previous movements. But, the majority of dadaist artists were men, and women also experienced misogyny. For example, Hans Richter, a German Dada painter, avant-garde film producer, and art historian, said about Hanna Höch's Dada art that she was a woman who made magnificent collages but excelled even more at making sandwiches. Very unjustified, but typical for that time.

In fact, Hanna was an interesting woman and one of the most well-known Dada artists. She participated in many events, but they mostly saw her as Raoul Hausmann's wife. Raoul was an Austrian artist and writer and a key figure of Dada in Berlin. Hanna used collage and photomontage with a characteristic sense of Dada humour, cutting and pasting from press photos related to the domestic world and sewing patterns. Women in Dada manifested their art through dance, painting, sculpture, collage, puppetry, and even activities traditionally considered for women, like tapestry and embroidery.

Even in that era of great changes, women were still merely seen as muses and mothers. Some women, like Hanna Höch, attended dadaist events as wives, including Gabrièle Buffet and Sophie Taeuber. Sophie was the wife of Hans Arp, better known as Jean Arp, a German-French dadaist and abstract artist. Sophie, who was Swiss born, studied textile art in Paris, using wool, silk, and paper, and was valued for her work on fabrics. She really was an all-round artist working as a sculptor, painter, textile, furniture and interior designer, as well as an architect and a dancer. She and Jean Arp met during an exhibition in 1915 and they both became associated with the Dada movement. One of Sophie's most famous works, created during this period, is *Tête Dada*, a wooden sculpture painted with oil and metallic paint. It is on exhibition in the Centre Pompidou, Musée national d'Art moderne in Paris.

Sophie and Jean moved to France in 1926 till the beginning of the Second World War, when they returned to Switzerland. Sadly, Sophie died before her time. The story goes that she missed a tram one evening in 1943 and stayed the night in a summer house, which was covered by snow. She died from carbon monoxide poisoning, due to a leaking gas stove.

This important artist has not been given much attention since her death, yet she should be considered one of the most important artists of the twentieth century, and more precisely of concrete art and geometric abstraction. She certainly left a legacy, and an interesting fact is that the face of Sophie Taeuber was the only female portrait on a series of Swiss fifty-franc banknotes; this was from 1995 to 2016.

But I'd like to tell you about a woman, Gabrièle Buffet-Picabia, an important French art critic and writer affiliated with Dadaism. She also was a composer and musicologist and the first wife of artist Francis Picabia, the famous Dada surrealist artist who was a great master of the avant-garde of that time. He was a painter, a writer, a poet and filmmaker. Picabia the artist and Apollinaire the poet, were spiritually advanced for their time, and like many artists of that era, they were heavy consumers of drugs, especially opium.

Gabrièle was admired by many, and Jean Arp, referred to her as a queen, a chess tower, signifying her importance in the game of art. Gabrièle also inspired many artists, including Picabia himself. Her husband used to say that Gabrièle had a spirit, a place where everyone came to find inspiration and ideas. She also played a crucial role in introducing Varese, the Italian musician, to new rhythms, in particular to jazz, a genre that was emerging in New York and which would significantly influence European art and music.

She participated in opium-fuelled discussions where groundbreaking ideas for art surfaced. Gabrièle was a driving force behind the new sounds that were about to change the world of music. She is credited with creating a new spirit in the art world, bridging the gap between art, music, and the modern world that was emerging alongside machinery and engines. She played a significant role in the artistic partnership of Francis Picabia and Marcel Duchamp, two quite distinct personalities, with Gabrièle in the middle. Duchamp was discreet, while Picabia was flamboyant.

Some say that Gabrièle was behind every artist of the time, changing their ideas, as a promoter of the avant-garde and this certainly was the case with Duchamp. He, Picabia and Gabrièle formed a trio, both in an artistic sense and sentimentally. They were inseparable in their creations. Duchamp, a dadaist and surrealist, is seen as the artist who changed the history of modern art. In a sense he owes everything to Gabrièle because she allowed him to meet Picabia.

Thanks to Gabrièle, Duchamp broke free from his provincial life, entering Parisian society in 1913. It was in that same year that they presented artists, showcasing twelve hundred paintings, many from Europe, at the International Exhibition of Modern Art in New York, referred to as *The Armory Show*. This had a profound effect on American art. The event, also featuring Duchamp's works, caused a scandal but marked the entry of United States art into modernity.

Duchamp's famous painting, *Nu descendant un escalier*, is said to represent Gabrièle. Duchamp was in love with her and after separating from Picabia, Gabrièle started a relationship with Duchamp. She inspired Duchamp's famous work, *La mariée mise à nu par ses célibataires, même* often called *Le Grand Verre* which is considered one of his masterpieces. She suggested to Duchamp to use everyday objects in his art.

Gabrièle also had romances with significant figures such as the Russian composer Stravinski, Calder, Brâncuşi, Samuel Beckett, and she even played a crucial role as a resistance fighter against nazism during World War II. We can certainly say that she lived a full and interesting life and I feel it's important to remember that. She died at the age of one hundred and four!

There were of course more women involved in the Dada movement, for example Celine Arnold, a French-Romanian woman who studied at the Sorbonne and was part of Apollinaire's circle. Celine wrote experimental novels like *Tournevire*, and performed poetry and theatre. And Suzanne Duchamp, sister of Marcel Duchamp and part of an artistic family, shifted through different styles and settled in Montparnasse. These women, expressing their art in various ways, were not feminists as we understand them today. They were women trying to find their place and express their art in a world dominated by male artists.

It's been a hundred years from then, now, sitting here in Paris in 2023, and women no longer face the same difficulties to create and be recognised as in that era. But these were the pioneers in the avant-garde movements of the first part of the twentieth century. Dadaist women were the ones who, within the limitations imposed by men, truly expressed their creations."

Orphism and Dadaism, what interesting movements they were. I'm delighted that we have been able to give a voice to some of the women in these movements. So, what happened after these periods?

"Well, we are in Montparnasse, so I feel that we should talk about *L'école de Paris.*"

L'école de Paris

A creative hotspot for foreigners

We are still in Montparnasse. The name of this district is actually quite interesting. It is thought by many to have come from the Greek 'Mount Parnassus', considered the home of the Muses in Greek mythology, and referring to the nine daughters of Zeus; each representing a different type of art. They often accompanied Apollo, God of the arts. These muses inspired artists.

The name of Montparnasse in Paris was given to it long before it became a popular area for artists and their muses. I am thinking of the best-known muse of that era, her name was Kiki, La Reina de Montparnasse. Kiki was the muse of many artists from the *L'école de Paris*, for example, of painter Kees van Dongen, photographer and painter Man Ray and sculptor Alexander Calder.

Mario shows me a picture, *Le Violon d'Ingres*, that I immediately recognise as it's a famous black-and-white surreal photograph of Kiki, created in 1924 by Man Ray. Funny how I know of the photo, but I didn't remember the name of the artist or his model.

Mario explains that in the 1920s Montparnasse had become the centre of the avant-garde. It confuses me a little as I remember him talking about *Les années folles* during this time. Mario, what is the difference between *L'école de Paris* and *Les années folles*?

"They overlap, *L'école de Paris* starts before *Les années folles*. *L'école de Paris* isn't an artistic movement; it's more of a gathering of artists in the Montparnasse district in the twenties. It especially refers to foreign artists who immigrated to and worked in Paris in the first half of the twentieth century, but this also includes French artists who taught art in art schools like l'Académie de la Grande Chaumière. This was more or less from 1914 to 1930.

Les années folles relates to the decade of cultural, artistic and social collaborations in the 1920s only, and is also referred to as the *Roaring Twenties*. It was like one long 'party' which ended in 1929 with the great crisis and shortly after, when populism and the Second World War arrived.

But let me explain more about *L'école de Paris* and Montparnasse as they are closely intertwined. We talked about the importance of the Parisian cafés in the lives of the artists we discuss during our journey. This is where they met, ate and drank, laughed and perhaps argued, discovering new ways of looking at things. Especially as Paris was such a hotspot for international artists. This mixture of different cultures must have been invaluable for young artists.

We also know that the cafés were very important in Montparnasse. Artists and writers who came from all over the world frequented cafés such as Le Dôme, La Rotonde, La Coupole, but also in salons, such as the one of Gertrude Stein in rue de Fleurus. Montparnasse is the part of Paris where most of these international artists lived, gathered and shared studios. For example, in La Ruche in 2 Passage Dantzig, was an iconic building with studio apartments. It was built by Alfred Boucher, a successful French sculptor, who wanted to create this artistic hub where artists that were struggling could interact, work and also live.

Boucher was also a friend of Auguste Rodin and a mentor to Camille Claudel. He built this studio in 1902 with the remains of the Medoc Wine Pavilion from the World's Fair. He created around fifty studios with large windows to allow light to flow in. He also created fifty more studios in nearby buildings and often referred to La Ruche as a beehive. There was even a large room where the artists who had little money could draw from a live model, which Boucher paid for. He also created a small theatre space for concerts and performances.

La Ruche was often the first place where foreign artists came to, in order to find a place to live and work. Long-lasting friendships were forged, and they inspired each other. Great artists like Marc Chagall and Chaïm Soutine from Russia, Italians like Amedeo Modigliani, Japanese like Tsuguharu Foujita met here. Also Constantin Brâncuși, a Romanian sculptor, painter and photographer, Blais Cendrars a Swiss-born novelist and poet who became a naturalised French citizen in 1916, Kees van Dongen a Dutch-French painter, and many more came to the area. *Les années folles* was indeed a time of intense artistic activity. I'll explain a bit more about some of the above artists as they left such an important stamp on the evolution of art!"

Wow, if only I had lived in that time! I would have loved to be part of that, although I doubt that as a female artist, I would have had equal access to these facilities as those male artists had back then.

"Actually Renate, you know I really rate and like your work, your unique style. I have studied the work of many artists as from a very young age and even worked with artists throughout my life, and to be honest, I have no doubt that if you had lived and worked in the way you are working now, in this period in Paris, you would have been discovered and received patronage and you would have gained fame all over the world. Well, that's my opinion."

Thank you! But who was Kees van Dongen? Since I'm Dutch myself I'm curious as I had never heard of him before this trip, I'd love to find out more.

"He was born in 1877 in the Netherlands, but is considered to be a Dutch-French painter. He studied art at the Royal Academy of Fine Arts in Rotterdam, where he also met Augusta (Guus) Preitinger, a painter herself. They married in 1901 and had two children together, a boy and a girl, but their son died a few days after he was born. You can see the influence of the *Haagse School* in Van Dongen's artwork but he went through an interesting evolution in his art. We can see a significant change in his work after he had come to Paris. He was considered one of the leading figures of the Fauvism movement and participated in the controversial 1905 Salon d'Automne exhibition of which we spoke before. His artworks made between 1905 and 1910 were more radical in both form and use of colour. This is considered his most important period.

His paintings were about the Paris nightlife and are colourful scenes of dancers, theatre, singers and more. His models were also his lovers. He met people from the nightlife and artistic life of that time, including the famous fashion designer Paul Poirret and Picasso's former wife, Fernande Olivier. In fact, when Van Dongen arrived in Paris, Fernande had introduced him to the artistic world of the city. Kees van Dongen and Guus Preitinger also lived in Le Bateau Lavoir in Montmartre for a period, becoming friends with Picasso and Fernande, this was in 1906.

In his Montparnasse studio, he received a diverse crowd - anarchists, bohemians, but also very wealthy women. In a way, he anticipated Andy Warhol, who, in the sixties, also hosted a varied and creative crowd in his studio.

Van Dongen was, in a sense, a mirror of the society of his time. He soon got a reputation of painting sensuous portraits of mainly women. In 1921 Van Dongen and Guus divorced, but he was already involved with fashion director Léa Alvin, better known as Jasmy Jacob and this relationship lasted till 1927.

During the 1920s, a time of elegant women's parties, Kees van Dongen was a quite attractive, silent man. He was very elegant, more or less the prototype of a man from that time, with a car and living surrounded by women. Van Dongen became a kind of illustrator of the Art Deco era, where there was a close relationship between art, fashion, and the world of decoration. Paul Poiret, the man who had liberated women from the corset, introduced him to the world of luxury and this meant that Van Dongen attended numerous parties. But his main love was art in its different forms as, apart from painting, he was passionate about sculpture, theatre, and cinema.

At the beginning of the twenties in Paris, as we mentioned, he frequented the avant-garde artists of Montmartre. Van Dongen did enter the world of luxury, the world of nightlife, and high society, but he had an anarchist spirit. Therefore, his works should be seen with a bit of irony and distance from what they represent.

Although he became associated with Fauvism, he did not consider himself a fauvist. Unlike Matisse, who loved the light of the Mediterranean, Van Dongen was more interested in electric light than natural light. He loved the night and in particular circuses, as in a circus there was electric lighting that created a unique reality. He began to frequent places where acrobats and tightrope walkers were, whom he painted in scandalous paintings. He also made paintings of half-naked women with coats, creating even more scandal. He brought modernity to his paintings, reflecting the changing times, the liberation of women.

He left Montmartre for Montparnasse, near Denfert Rochereau, where he had his studio. Van Dongen enjoyed a mix of a snobbish dandy and bohemian life. He painted women with very long, almost endless legs, dressed in the designs of the fashion designers of the time, and with considerable sensuality. He himself remarked on his work as a portraitist of high society women, *"The essential thing is to elongate the women and especially to make them slim. After that it just remains to enlarge their jewels. They are ravished."* He also used to say *"Painting is the most beautiful of lies"*.

He found himself somewhat trapped in this world of luxury, participating in the madness of the *Roaring Twenties* in Paris. Always mingling with affluent people living in luxury in an Art Deco setting, and at the same time, associating with creators like Poiret and Matisse. He expressed everything through his artwork. Although he depicted the luxury of parties, he always did it from a somewhat anarchist perspective, almost caricaturing that era. He emphasised through his use of acidic colours. It was an era full of appearances and very artificial. In 1959, Kees van Dongen moved to Monaco where he died in 1968."

Very interesting and I have to say I do love his work from that period. Did you see his portrait of his wife Guus, *The blue dress*, from 1911? I guess those are my kind of colours. Shame I cannot find much information about her on her own. She's constantly linked to Kees. I did find an auction of floral paintings by her, but they weren't sold for high prices. I have to admit that I don't very much like floral paintings, but still. She was a professional artist who continued working as a painter in

Paris after she divorced Van Dongen. It feels unjust that she hasn't been given any recognition. I'd like to look up photos of the people we discuss, but I cannot find any of her either. Only paintings of her by Van Dongen. I guess this is why our journey is important isn't it? Giving these women a voice.

"Yes you are right. There is so much more information to be found about male artists. It's a dilemma, isn't it? We want to talk about the importance of women, but we cannot ignore the importance of the work of these male artists. For example, the works of Alexander Calder, Chaïm Soutine and Tsuguharu Foujita. I've said it before and I'm going to say it again. We cannot possibly cover all the artists that have been important for the evolution of art. I guess our selection is to a great extent based on artists that we personally admire and I'm sure we will miss a few.

Let me just briefly explain a bit more about some of those artists who worked in La Ruche. Let's start with Soutine and Foujita. Chaïm Soutine was a Belarusian born French painter who made a major contribution to the expressionist movement, while living and working in Paris. He was born in a large, very poor family and wasn't allowed to study art. However, his mother managed to send him to an art school in Minsk, where the then illiterate Chaïm started his education.

In 1913 he had saved up some money and took a train to Paris. He somehow ended up in La Ruche where he would have met many now world-famous artists, among them Amedeo Modigliani who was twenty-nine when he met the then twenty-year-old Soutine. Apparently, Modigliani became like an older brother to him. In fact, Léopold Zborowski, who was Modigliani's art dealer, started to support Soutine through the First World War and in 1923, he showed Soutine's work to Albert Barnes who bought many paintings from him in one purchase, which changed his fortune. Other collectors also starting buying his work.

He became famous for painting carcasses of meat, which is somehow ironic as he couldn't eat meat himself, as due to the deprivation of healthy food in the beginning of his life, he suffered from stomach ulcers. In 1937, when he was forty-four, he met a German refugee,

Gerda Michaelis Groth, who was twenty-seven at the time. They had a three-year relationship but Gerda, who was Jewish, was deported to Germany. She survived the war, but they never saw each other again.

In 1943, Soutine, who was also Jewish, managed to get to the countryside where he was hiding with help from friends. Sadly, he died during the war of a perforated ulcer when he was fifty years old.

Tsuguharu Foujita is an interesting figure during the *L'école de Paris* period. He had studied Western-style painting at Tokyo's School of Fine Arts and really wanted to go to Paris. He arrived in 1913 and became friends with Soutine and Modigliani. He soon divorced from his Japanese wife, Tokita Tomiko. In 1917 he met Fernande Barrey in Café de la Rotonde in Montparnasse and he fell head-over-heals in love with her. They married thirteen days later. Fernande was an artist's model and a liberated artist herself."

I'm curious about her, she looks beautiful and fascinating and you now tell me that she was also the model of Modigliani and Soutine?

"Yes, Fernande actually was a child prostitute in Paris and became a model. Modigliani and Soutine told her to go to art school, which she did. But her art did not become much sought after. However, there exist many images of her. She and Foujita had an open relationship, and they both were interested in same-sex relationships.

In 1928 they divorced after Fernande had started a relationship with Foujita's cousin, Koyanagi, also a painter. After his cousin and Fernande split up Foujita supported her financially till her death in 1960.

Although Foujita was born in Japan, he received the French nationality in 1955. He developed a really eclectic art style with influences from both Japanese and European art. He became very successful during the 1920s creating watercolour and oil nudes, self-portraits and still-life paintings. His self-portraits are interesting I feel. He also painted cats in many of his artworks. He did go back to Japan during the war and became an official war artist, but then moved back to France in 1950 and lived there till he died in 1968."

Gosh, so many new impressions for me! I feel we need a short break though. Shall we pay and go for a walk Mario? Then you can tell me more about *Les années folles*.

Les années folles

Modigliani and the importance of women

We spoke about the name Montparnasse, how this relates to the Greek muses. Muses are women who have inspired and continue to inspire artists till this day. As we are walking through the streets of Montparnasse, I wonder how the muses in those times would have felt. Those models for the great artists we are discussing during this trip to Paris. Is there any documentation about that Mario?

"Yes, there is. Generally speaking, we can come to the conclusion that these women who posed for artists came from working-class families and it was a necessity for them to make a living. Models used to say that they felt uncomfortable the first time they had to get undressed in front of a male artist, but then they got used to it. Some went from studio to studio wearing nothing but a coat, to get undressed rapidly.

In the middle of the 19th century, it wasn't all that easy to find models. In fact, there were only male models in art academies. It was said that a woman who posed naked could upset male students. Only in some private academies did they have women posing for the artists. Some, for example Van Gogh, complained that they could only paint naked statues. For female artists it was even more difficult to create from live posing sessions. Some academies had workshops for men and others for women. They could perhaps paint or draw nudes in anatomy classes, but many artists had to go to the Louvre Museum to copy art and learn through that. It must have been challenging for female artists. For example, Camille Claudel made a sculpture of a naked couple and was forced to cover the woman's lower part. I think it is fair to say though that these women didn't want to fight for women's rights, they just wanted to create.

It was also said that many male artists got married to have a model at home. It was common for the wives of artists to serve as a model for their husbands and sometimes for their friends. Of course, as we've already seen throughout our journey, there were also many prostitutes and courtesans who posed. One day the writer Émile Zola told Cézanne..."*They draw them during the day and caress them during the night*". But not all artists were the same. Van Gogh did say that the artist who has too many sexual relations loses creative energy."

You said that these artists were going to the Louvre to copy the old masters. However, there were many images of naked women in those academic artworks weren't there? So how did these painters and sculptors find their models?

"That's a good question. They worked from ancient sculptures or paid for models, possibly prostitutes. The academic painter, that is, before Impressionism, painted nudes to idealise beauty, but let's not forget that they were men and, in my opinion, there was always something perverse in the relationship between the model and the artist. Just look at the violence in Delacroix's paintings, for example. Scenes of naked women suffering or murdered all in the name of creating historical mythology. When I was a kid myself, I was upset to see such violence in paintings at the Louvre. Also, another example, images of women in oriental baths could easily be seen as an excuse to show nudity.

This was not questioned by anyone, not by women either. The 'bad woman' idea can be seen throughout history, think of Salome, Eva, etc. Also worth mentioning, around 1850, there was a model market in place Pigalle. Not far from the Nouvelle Athene district. The women were almost all of Italian origin. They were looking for dark-haired and blond women who were beautiful and well-built and above all, young. There also were male models of any age and children with curly hair to depict angels in paintings. Women were paid one franc per hour (currently equivalent to three Euros). Due to the lack of hygiene at the time, they were asked to clean themselves before posing. The naked woman was normalised, but the large number of paintings and sculptures of naked women in parks and museums is questioned in our time.

Some critics said that when a vulgar man paints a nude, that nude will be indecent. In paintings it was indecent to paint a naked woman surrounded by dressed men. I'm thinking about Manet's *Dejeuner sur l'herbe*. I read the words of an art expert somewhere though I don't recall his name. He said that when you go to a museum, you see naked people everywhere and it can make you feel uncomfortable. You can also feel like seeing yourself in that vulnerability."

I hear you, but I kind of think that not much has changed... Well, something, but look at music videos in our times. Men dressed, women dancing in a sensual way, scarcely dressed. And in many mainstream movies the women are often shown in their full 'birthday suit' and men seem to only have a backside. Don't get me wrong. I don't believe there is anything wrong with nudity. I have created many paintings of nude women throughout the years, the shape of a female body with its curves is just beautiful, and enhancing that with surreal colours or some abstraction is what has always appealed to me. So, there are quite a few nudes in our house, but my husband luckily likes my art.

"Ha ha, but yes there is still a lot of inequality in the world, also in the art world. And in some cultures, women have no rights at all. I am a man, but I can understand this must be difficult for women. Something that I realised recently, doing my research for our Paris trip, is that the avant-garde of the beginning of the 20th century were transgressive, against the ruling system and they achieved all these different, important movements in art. All going against the bourgeois society. They defended these new expressions of art, but women have never been defended. Women were always just used. Actually, I know that when Frida Kahlo visited Paris with her husband Diego Rivera, a Mexican painter, she met quite a few artists, in particular surrealist intellectuals. However, they were very unpleasant to her and very misogynistic. It was the reason why Frida, with her Mexican temperament, didn't like Paris very much.

But back to the art models. In Montparnasse there also was a model market where artists came to search and choose their muses. This was at the Académie des beaux-arts where many artists were taught for over three hundred and fifty years. When the models arrived, they were asked to undress themselves and the students meticulously examined them one by one, like in a slave market in Ancient Rome.

Artists were also showing intimate moments of women in the brothels, sick women, vomiting in the toilet, etc. To me this feels like an abuse and not only in art but also in literature. Stories told by men about indecent women. As we've already said, many women posed naked to earn their living. If we talk about the muse as an inspiration, in my opinion, we have to keep in mind that it was usually an abuse of women. But there are of course exceptions. I would like to think that Bonnard was more dignified. He has painted his wife in the privacy of their home, with modesty and tenderness, but Degas and Manet painted women as they were, with their imperfections, including hair on their body."

Mmmmm... I wouldn't really say that having hair on a body is an imperfection, Mario. It's natural. The fact that someone decided that it was not attractive for women to have hairs under their arms, on legs and in our times also in private areas, in my opinion only means that it's a fashion idea that can change over time. But this fashion idea is so strong that we all seem to be brainwashed by it. I must say that I do wonder whether it was a man who decided that women shouldn't have hair apart from on their heads!

"I like the way your brain works. Furthermore, when they showed hair, they sexualised the woman because it brings it closer to what is natural, to what is animal. Academic art prefers to paint women as something pure or as a goddess, something that is paradoxical. There is a perversion in the display of naked women, in order to enable the men of that era to enjoy seeing nudes.

Also, I would go as far as to say that academic painting was hypocritical just like Picasso later. Using history and eroticising it. Picasso used his women to show his own suffering moods. His abusive side was not really recognised or noticed during his lifetime, because people saw Picasso as the man who painted freedom through the symbol of the dove and denounced war like in *Guernica*.

Anyway, we can come to the conclusion that the avant-gardes were both about progress and transgression, but they were also very misogynistic. Of course, we must view it with a mentality of those times, but we have to mention it nevertheless. What 19th century art showed as normal is now not acceptable. And I'm glad to say that in our time talented female artists of those times, such as Sonia Delaunay, Berthe Morisot and Suzanne Valadon are rediscovered. And that's what we are doing as well."

Yes, I'm really happy about that. I did find this model story really interesting; you know, I had not thought about that before. Anyway, are we still in Montparnasse now? It feels less touristy than Montmartre. Am I right to think this?

"Indeed, the vast majority of tourists prefer the monumental centre of Paris. They tend to go to Montmartre to check out the bohemian cabarets and artists. Montmartre is the place where souvenir merchandise is sold; products that are reminiscent of Lautrec and others that we have discussed. Montparnasse, on the other hand is not a tourist hotspot, and this is a mistake in my view. Here you can discover Paris almost as a non-tourist. It's an incredible neighbourhood and for more than twenty years, it was considered to be the centre of creativity in all the Western world. And specifically in the 1920s, it was an area full of artists, models, art dealers, buyers, and later, curious people who had to be seen in Montparnasse.

Of course, there were the numerous cafés as I've already explained, where the artists met. Many of these cafés have disappeared, but in some streets that artistic atmosphere is preserved. There still are many cafés and theatres, for example in rue de la Gaité. People visiting cafés in Montparnasse might be unaware of what happened here during the twenties, but they can experience a taste of it during its lively nightlife."

Is it possible to go to 3 rue Campagne-Première, as I believe this is where Italian born Rosalie Tobia later opened her Crèmerie/restaurant Chez Rosalie? I would like to see where that was. We've spoken about this already briefly when describing the cafés in Paris. But when you talked about these model markets, often being Italian women, she came to mind as I can imagine that this is where she went. Although from what I've read it was a friend who suggested she start modelling.

Look, I just found two pictures of her as a young model for academic artist Bouguereau, *Rêverie sur le seuil* and *Jeunesse* both painted in 1893. *Jeunesse* depicts her with curly-haired child angels. It says here that when she was around fifty years old, Rosalie stopped working as a model and opened her restaurant. This was in 1912, curiously the same year that Modigliani came to Paris. Chez Rosalie was very small but she still could seat twenty-four people. Perhaps due to her many years as a model, Rosalie became very protective of visiting artists.

Those with little money, which often happened to Modigliani, were allowed to pay for their meals with some artwork, like a drawing, that she then would hang on the walls of the establishment. It was a favourite place for many artists and writers, including Guillaume Apollinaire, Max Jacob and Maurice Utrillo, and Rosalie had an almost maternal affection for Modigliani, who of course also was an Italian. Apparently in 1924, Rosalie sold two paintings she had from Maurice Utrillo, who was by then a well sought after artist. She sold the business in 1932 and retired to the south of France where she died that same year. She was buried in Cagnes-sur-Mer. Having lived in Italy for five years I have a soft spot for everything Italian. I'm definitively going to paint her!

"I believe she must have been a strong, independent and beautiful woman. You mentioned Amedeo Modigliani and I feel we have to talk about him as he was an important figure in Montparnasse in the 1920s.

Modigliani came from a Sephardic Jewish family from Livorno in Italy. The family of his mother were authorities on sacred

Jewish texts and she even had traced back her family lineage to the seventeenth-century Dutch philosopher Baruch Spinoza."

Oh wow, how fascinating. I know that Einstein was a fan of Spinoza and his teachings and findings. And this is right up my street as well. I really like this quote by Einstein *"The most beautiful emotion we can experience is the mystical. It is the power of all true art and science. He to whom this emotion is a stranger, who can no longer wonder and stand rapt in awe, is as good as dead."* I'm just mentioning this because I do feel that creating art has a mystical quality to it. Well, at least it has for me.

"Yes, that's interesting. Modigliani's mother was rather special, actually. She spoke four languages including French and she educated Amedeo till the age of ten. He was troubled by illnesses already at a young age and he was only sixteen when he contracted tuberculosis. I'm not sure when he started to alleviate the pain with drugs and alcohol, probably trying to hide the fact that he had tuberculosis. The pain must have been a constant reminder that he could die young.

When Modigliani came to Paris, he already spoke French. Probably not that long after his arrival he met Romanian sculptor Constantin Brâncuşi, and he created quite a few sculptures spending a year working with Brâncuşi. But by 1914, he was devoting his time to drawing and painting. It is said that he could no longer sculpt because of his illness.

Modigliani must have been an interesting figure in Paris as he was a sophisticated, educated and rather good-looking man. It is easy to understand how he became like an older brother to Chaïm Soutine as they both had these underlying illnesses to deal with. Soutine suffering from his ulcers and Modigliani from his tuberculosis, which he had to hide from most of his friends as it is a contagious disease and he could not tolerate being isolated.

Artistically they were very different though. Soutine was more into the style of Rembrandt and Modigliani's fascination for African sculpture was not his thing. You can clearly see the African influence in Modigliani's work, both in his sculptures and his paintings, with images of elongated elegance. He painted several dozens of nudes between 1916 and 1919 in Leopold Zborowski's apartment, his art dealer, who paid for his models and then for his work.

How to best describe Modigliani's work? When you look at a portrait by Modigliani, you see oval faces, elongated necks and slanted eyes that seem to be closed, somewhat melancholic, and they have very rusty colours, such as light browns. I get the impression that he always painted a similar type of woman. You could say it's a bit of a fusion of what was happening in his life. Modigliani was Italian, and he was inspired by classical Italian art, which you can see in the postures of his paintings. He then mixes it with an African influenced style. He often went to Le musée d'Ethnographie du Trocadéro, which at the time, exhibited a lot of African masks. It is obvious to me that this is where he got inspired.

Talking about the style of Modigliani, he belongs to that period in Montparnasse, when various artists from different parts of the world gathered, Russian, Italian, Swiss, American, Dutch... all contributing to the art scene. It wasn't a cohesive artistic movement. Each artist had a distinct style, and what characterises that period in the École de Paris especially is the shared struggle they went through initially. For instance, Chagall, Soutine and Brâncuşi were all friends who frequented the same cafés. At this time, revolutionary artistic movements emerged as we have already discussed. Also worth mentioning is that Swiss born sculptor and painter, Alberto Giacometti, settled in Montparnasse although he was not exactly part of the Roaring Twenties.

Modigliani very much represented the bohemian lifestyle of living solely for art and being misunderstood in his time. Initially, everything seemed fine, but he ran into trouble with not paying the rent, and in 1904, he was evicted from his apartment in Montmartre. Like many artists, he moved to Montparnasse on the left bank of the River Seine. There, as mentioned, he frequented cafés with Chagall and other artists friends. He worked in La Ruche.

He started making drawings of people, the customers in the cafés of Montparnasse. These drawings were, so to speak, a way for him to get a drink. He also painted models, often women he encountered in a café or on the street. Modigliani was actually quite seductive, despite his humble clothing. He had great charisma. As we already mentioned before, he became close friends with Rosalie from the creamery/restaurant in rue Campagne-Première, where Modigliani also lived. The relationship between Rosalie and him was quite difficult and interesting, because both of them had strong Italian characters, but they were very fond of each other. One day she would kick him out and the next day everything would be settled as she also was very protective of him.

There were of course several women in his life, for example, an English woman called Beatriz Austin. She was a very wild, eccentric woman, a 'femme fatal'. She consumed a lot of alcohol and drugs and they had a passionate and wild affair. Modigliani's life was intense, it was about art and about alcohol and drugs.

He didn't sell many of his artworks, but luckily, like quite a few other artists, he met Berthe Weill and in the autumn of 1905 she put on Modigliani's first exhibition in her gallery. The exhibition immediately was perceived as a scandal, because Berthe had placed two of his nude paintings in the window of the gallery. Even the police were involved. Especially because you could see the model's pubic hair. Not many paintings were sold during the exhibition, but his friends later bought some paintings.

Look Renate, here are two examples of Modigliani's work. This painting is called *Nu allongé* and was probably exhibited in Berthe Weill's gallery. It is quite large, sixty by ninety centimetres and it is part of his series of nudes that I told you about. I think it is rather special as a part of her body is not in the painting, like her legs and part of her arm are missing and the woman looks at the viewer. A bit like Manet's painting *Olympia*. The eyes look at us, but as in many of his paintings, there is a certain melancholy. The background feels quite warm, with a blue cushion and a red sheet in contrast to her white body, which has some coldness to it. This coldness also appeared in his stone sculptures.

The other painting is of a woman with a black coat and blue eyes. Perhaps this is Jeanne Hébuterne. Part of her, like the hand and the face, look like a sculpture, strongly identifying with African sculptures. But you can still sense that mixture of Italian Renaissance with African influences, so typical for his work.

Also interesting, there is an art academy in Montparnasse called the Académie de la Grande Chaumière, which you can visit and pay around twenty euros for a session with a model, in the same setting where Modigliani met his last companion, Jeanne Hébuterne, so there's a true connection to the past. This is where Modigliani and Jeanne saw each other for the first time and fell in love. She was an aspiring artist herself, just like her brother André who introduced her to the art-scene in Montparnasse. She met many of the artists and even posed for Tsuguharu Foujita. Fernande Barrey, Foujita's wife, and Jeanne became close friends. Jeanne came from a middle-class catholic family.

When Modigliani met Jeanne, he tried to hide his reputation as an alcoholic troublemaker. He was a peaceful person, but alcohol abuse transformed him and it cannot have been easy for Jeanne. Her family disapproved of their relationship and allegedly, they even went so far as to kidnap her to keep her away from him. But their love was too strong, and they moved in together in Montparnasse and even got married by common-law. Sadly, he started drinking increasingly more and, it seems, he was also getting sicker, probably with lung issues. But Jeanne was special to him as he called her *"Ma femme"."*

I can relate to the fact that it cannot have been easy for Jeanne. I have spent twelve years of my life living with an alcoholic, I even wrote a book about that. Not just my story, but a collection of stories of people who were in some shape or form affected by the irrational effect of alcohol abuse. So I can vividly imagine how torn she must have been, perhaps trying to save him, not understanding why her love wasn't enough, why their precious daughter wasn't enough to help him stop drinking...

"They indeed had a daughter together, born as Giovanna Hébuterne in 1918, but she changed her name to Jeanne Modigliani. She became a historian of mostly Jewish art, but is better known for her biographical research on her father. She died in 1984.

In 1919 her mother Jeanne Hébuterne fell pregnant with her second child, fathered by Modigliani. In 1920 he started consuming a lot of rum. He was still painting from models at the Académie de la

Grande Chaumière. He didn't sell many paintings, and he was often in the company of his friend Maurice Utrillo, who also had an alcohol problem.

Modigliani's health got worse, but he didn't accept much help from those around him. In January 1920, after spending some time with friends at the Rotonde in Montparnasse, he was feeling very tired. It was raining but he and Jeanne went to his studio. As he was climbing the steep stairs, he collapsed and started vomiting blood. In his final moments, apparently, he yearned for his beloved Italy. Two days later he died from tuberculous meningitis. The news spread rapidly.

Of course Jeanne, who was eight months pregnant, was inconsolable even though her friend Fernande Barrey tried in vain to console the young widow. But Jeanne, who was slender, pale and small couldn't handle her loss. In despair, in the middle of the night, she got up from her bed, opened the window and jumped from a height of five floors. The next day someone discovered her. She was no longer alive.

In mourning, all their friends collected money and started bringing flowers. When Jeanne had passed away, some of her paintings survived. She had a style somewhat similar to Modigliani and I find them quite interesting. In particular a painting titled *Le suicide*. They were buried side by side, which is appropriate as apparently, Modigliani's last words before he fell into a coma in the hospital, were *"My wife and I are assured of eternal happiness."*

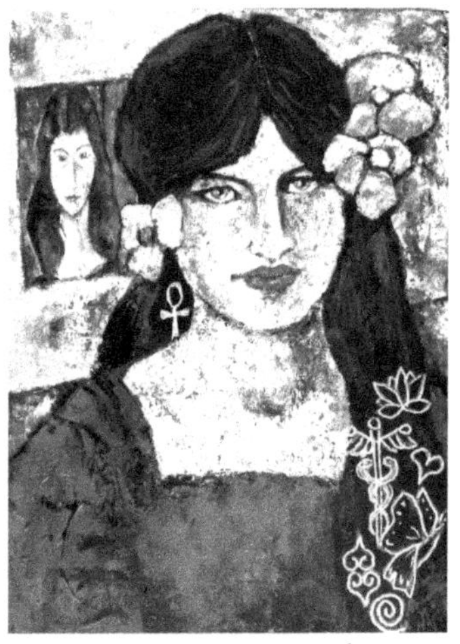

Jeanne Hébuterne

After his death, the misunderstood painter's work started selling, like we so often see when an artist dies. Art dealers rubbed their hands as his work would increase considerably in value, as had happened previously with Van Gogh."

That's a very sad story, isn't it?

Montparnasse

And 'La Génération Perdue'

After a long day full of emotions, walking through the streets of Montparnasse, we decide to go to Café Select. It's early evening, and it's already full of people who are here to have fun and meet up with friends. There are a lot of nice places to get a drink or something to eat in this neighbourhood but Mario suggests we go to this café which was one of Ernest Hemingway's favourites. I've of course heard of Hemingway, but I'm keen to hear what Mario has to say about him. The idea that he was in this café, not all that many years ago, makes the ambience rather special.

We are lucky to get a seat inside, close by the window, and I look around me. The interior is welcoming with tables and long benches fairly close together, which entices you to interact with other people. There are some artworks on the walls and I recognise the face of Hemingway. I'm not sure whether this is a continuing or temporary exhibition. I do wonder whether the people who are now in the café realise what happened in the 1920s when American writers, referred to as *La Génération Perdue* (The Lost Generation), came here to catch up with like-minded souls. I certainly become more and more aware of the history created in these wonderful places that we are visiting. Mario says a lot of writers from *The Lost Generation* frequented Café Select. Can you tell me more about this Mario?

"Absolutely! Let me tell you what I know about Hemingway first. Before more or less settling in Paris, Hemingway had travelled throughout France with his friend F. Scott Fitzgerald. But once arrived in Montparnasse he, like many other artists, frequented cafés like Le Dome,

La Rotonde, La Coupole and Café Select. For sure they mingled with other artists and both Hemingway and Fitzgerald were also invited to the home of Gertrude Stein. It was Gertrude who came up with the name *The Lost Generation* referring especially to these American artists coming to Paris. She said to them *"you are young, you have participated in the First World War but now you seem to only fill your time drinking alcohol"*.

Some of the other artists who were part of this *Lost Generation* were John Dos Passos, Henry Miller and George Gershwin, the composer. Hemingway wrote about his time in France during the Roaring Twenties in his memoirs, stating *"Paris was a party"*. And we can certainly come to the conclusion that the Montparnasse of the twenties was indeed a place of endless get-togethers and parties.

In this nightlife setting we can get a feel of what it must have been like for these American writers who had travelled around the world, covered wars in far-away-countries and who had more or less fled from American puritanism of the time, in order to experience a more liberated ambience. It started somewhere in the beginning of the century when there was still plenty of misery going on.

Montparnasse soon started to attract artists from all over the world as we've already discussed. Many of them frequented La Closerie des Lilas, which, back then, was a favourite place for artists and had been for a long time as Renoir, Monet and Pissarro also frequented the café long before Hemingway did. The maison close le Sphinx, which was actually a luxury brothel, but also a cultural hotspot and a favourite of many American artists and their spouses is also worth mentioning. It is not difficult to see how it must have been fairly easy to find kindred spirits and forge great friendships.

Café Select, where we are now, was like a headquarter for the Americans. I sometimes call it 'the second bohemia' which would last until the middle of the thirties and ended with the start of the upcoming Second World War.

Hemingway in my opinion was the most charismatic of these American writers. He was a traveller, adventurer and a journalist, but he also was a novelist and short-story writer. He received money from a Canadian newspaper called *The Toronto Star* who had hired him as a foreign correspondent. He worked for them during his first twenty months in Paris.

However, he was a gambler and lived beyond his means. As soon as he earned some money, he would spend it, betting on horses or taking his wife, Hadley Richardson, out for a copious dinner and then the next day he might have had no money left. He was known for having asked friends to invite him for a cup of coffee. Luckily, his wife had inherited enough money to support them financially throughout their years of marriage.

They first met when Hadley was visiting an old friend, Kate Smith, whose brother was sharing a house with Hadley's brother. Kate later married John Dos Passos. He too was a writer who frequented Paris. Hadley was eight years older than Hemingway, but they fell in love and within a year they were married and moved to Paris. Hemingway wrote "*I knew she was the girl I was going to marry.*"

They had a son together, but the marriage didn't last. When Hadley found out he had an affair with Pauline Pfeiffer, who was her best friend, and had been accompanying her and Hemingway during their travels, she filed for divorce."

I heard Hemingway got married several times. Is this correct?

"Yes indeed. He ended up marrying three more women, all extraordinary women, and we can certainly say that his marriages were full of passion, but also of deceit. Pauline Pfeiffer was a fashion journalist and she married Hemingway in 1927, only a few months after his divorce from Hadley. Pauline came from a wealthy catholic background and before their marriage Hemingway converted to Catholicism. She soon fell pregnant and wanted to return to America, which they did in 1928. Hemingway and Pauline had two children together.

It is widely known that Hemingway had a love for Spain, both for the culture and its people. He decided to go there in 1936 to cover the Spanish Civil War. It was there, on one of his trips that he met Martha Gellhorn. By then he was already a famous writer. Martha was an established journalist and later honoured for her war correspondence in several countries. She is considered one of the best war correspondents of the 20th century. They ended up living in Cuba where they lived an active life; hunting, mingling with high society figures and working on their books."

Wow, part of me thinks Martha deserves a lot more attention, but I guess she is not really related to our Paris art journey, just to Hemingway.

"You are right, she was a fascinating woman. But there are so many more. I do want to mention Hemingway's fourth wife, just to create the full picture. Her name was Mary Welsh and she was working as a journalist as well, but she was also an author. When they met, she was in London working for the *Chicago Daily News* and for the *Daily Express*. Both Hemingway and Mary were married at the time, but they fell in love, divorced their spouses and then Mary moved to Cuba to live with him. Hemingway led an intense life for sure.

You could say that he was always surrounded by death as he went to wars as a correspondent, he loved bullfighting and was a hunter himself. In fact, his father gave him his first rifle when he was still a child. He lost friends and family, among which was his father who committed suicide in 1928.

He was also involved in two near fatal plane crashes on successive days when he was visiting Africa. He was with his wife Mary when they went on a sightseeing tour by plane over the Belgian Congo, but their plane crashed. He survived with a head wound and Mary had some broken ribs. The next day they took a plane to reach medical care in Entebbe, but the second plane exploded at take-off. He suffered from yet another concussion and burns. When they finally arrived in Entebbe, they found out that reporters had written about his death and for a period he was reading his obituaries.

He did have a self-destructing nature as well and he certainly drank a lot. We can only imagine what those get-togethers with his friends in places like Café Select must have been like in the 1920s. He was a prolific writer and wrote most of his work from mid-1920s to the mid-1950s. His works explore love, war, wilderness, and loss. The theme of emasculation is also prevalent in his works, most notably in *The Sun Also Rises*. He was even present as a journalist with the allied forces during the Normandy landings and during the liberation of Paris in June 1944, and in 1954 he received the Nobel Prize for his book *The Old Man and the Sea*. Pretty impressive don't you think?

More or less between 1931 until late 1939 Hemingway lived in Key West in the United States, during which he wrote some of his literary classics like *To Have and Have Not* and *For Whom the Bell Tolls*. Then, from 1939 to 1959 he lived in Finca Vigía, a house in Havana in Cuba. In 1959 he returned to the United States and bought a house in Idaho. It is here where he ended his own life in 1961. Both houses have now been turned into museums."

Well, you are certainly right that Hemingway was an interesting character. I would have loved to have met him in one of those cafés and have a chat with him. You've got me curious about some of these other American writers as well. What about them?

"I guess one of the most recognisable names for most people is F.Scott Fitzgerald. But I personally am more interested in his wife Zelda. Fitzgerald was an American short story writer and novelist and mostly known for writing about the Roaring Twenties, or as it is called in the US, the Jazz Age. He actually wrote about this in his short story bundle *Tales of the Jazz Age*. He had some success as a writer during the twenties, but only received real success after his death and is now seen as one of the greatest American writers of the twentieth century.

Around 1917 he met Zelda Sayre, she was a novelist, painter but also a playwright and socialite from an upper-class family. She initially didn't want to marry Fitzgerald, but after he successfully published his novel *This side of Paradise* in 1920, she accepted his proposal. His second book also became a cultural hit. They lived an affluent life and to pay for this he wrote many stories for magazines such as *The Esquire* and *The Saturday Evening Post*.

The young couple soon acquired the reputation in the national press as the 'enfants terribles' of the Jazz Age as they were always partying. Zelda was called the first American 'flapper', referring to women in the

Jazz Age, who cut their hair into a bob, wore knee high skirts, which was considered short at the time. They listened to jazz music, wore a lot of makeup, and were known for smoking and drinking alcohol in public. They also drove cars and treated sex in a casual way. Flappers are actually seen as icons of the Roaring Twenties.

In 1924 Zelda and Fitzgerald came to Paris with their daughter, Frances Scott 'Scottie', who also became a writer and a journalist. At the time Fitzgerald was working on his novel *The Great Gatsby*. In that same year Zelda had an affair and asked her husband for a divorce. But he wouldn't grant her this and some say he locked her in their house till she stopped asking. They never divorced. After his book was published, Fitzgerald's drinking became quite excessive. During his years in Paris Fitzgerald and Hemingway became close friends. They had met in the Dingo bar at 10 rue Delambre in Montparnasse which was one of the bars that was open all night and was frequented by many artists. You can still see a plaque in honour of Hemingway on the façade.

Although these days *The Great Gatsby* is considered by many as one of the greatest American novels, it wasn't all that successful at the time. Meanwhile Zelda suffered from mental health issues and was suicidal.

She was placed in an institute to be treated for her schizophrenia. She ended up staying there for a year. After her release, they returned to the United States. This was in 1931, but only a year later she had another mental breakdown. She did, however, publish her first novel, called *Save Me the Waltz* which describes their troubled marriage.

By that time Fitzgerald's work received less interest, especially during the Great Depression which started in 1929. He was struggling financially. For many years he suffered from alcoholism, and although he did get sober, he died of a heart attack in 1940 at the age of forty-four.

After her husband's death, Zelda started working on *Caesar's Things*, her second novel, but her mental illness meant she never completed the work. She actually had been receiving electroshock therapy for over ten years and was suffering from memory loss as a result. Sadly, in 1948 she was sedated and locked in the room of the hospital she was staying in and the building caught fire. She died in that fire when she was only forty-seven."

Oh, that is so sad, but I like the fact that their daughter also became a writer and a journalist. I guess she inherited the love for writing from her parents. So what happened to these other *Lost Generation* writers?

"We also have to talk a bit more about another fascinating figure from the Roaring Twenties period, a woman who we can assume, must have met these writers. She was known as Kiki, La Reine de Montparnasse. I've already talked about her briefly when I explained about models, but she was an enchanting woman and I feel we need to talk about her as this Café reminds me of her. I'm sure she was here often at the time.

But I will first tell you about two other important writers, John Dos Passos and Henry Miller. John Dos Passos was mostly known for his books, but he was also an artist and you might find this curious. He used his own art for the cover of his books, like you do as well.

Although he never gained recognition as an artist, he never stopped painting. His art was clearly inspired by his travels in countries like Spain and Mexico, but also reflecting the streets and cafés of Montparnasse.

As a young man he travelled a lot and during the First World War he worked as a volunteer ambulance driver both in Paris and in Italy. One of his novels called *Three Soldiers* actually talks about his experiences through his main character. John was interesting because of his political views which he changed based on his life experience during his travels.

Personally, I find Henry Miller more interesting. He was a controversial figure who lived in Paris for around ten years. He was an American novelist and short story writer. He developed a new style of novel, semi-autobiographical, which was, at the same time, a blend of social criticism, philosophical thoughts, but most of all very explicit language, also sexual. In fact, his most famous books, among which *The Rosy Crucifixion* were banned in the United States till 1961. Interestingly he also was a watercolourist."

It's just a personal observation, but how you describe this man, doesn't sound like someone who would do watercolours. But I do like his quote *"One's destination is never a place, but a new way of seeing things"*. You could take that literally, but also spiritually, although not sure whether he intended it that way. It sort of ties in with something I believe: "*Wherever you go, you always take yourself with you and if you don't like what you see, then it's best to have a good soul search and try to look at it in a different way".*"

"Miller was a prolific writer and an interesting figure. He lived in Paris from 1930 to 1939 but upon his arrival he was homeless and had to sleep in the streets. Luckily a friend let him stay in his house and helped him survive. His life in Paris was marked by an excess of alcohol. At some point he lived in the Seurat villa near Montparnasse. This is a street where many artists and writers lived.

This is where he wrote his first autobiographical novel called *Tropic of Cancer*, which was a huge scandal for the North American society. This was because of its considered pornographic content. He was asked why he used this title and he explained that to him cancer symbolised the disease of civilisation, the endpoint of the wrong path, the necessity to change course radically and to start completely over from scratch. They say that Anaïs Nin helped to edit this book.

Miller had a great influence on the writers of the *Beat Generation* because his work was anti-conformist, transgressive and would liberate American literature."

What is the *Beat Generation* Mario?

"*The Beat Generation* was a literary movement of authors who explored and also influenced both American culture and politics after the Second World War, for example William Burroughs, and Jack Kerouac, who wrote *On the road*."

OK, but you mentioned Anaïs Nin, was this his wife?

"No, she was a friend. Henry Miller was married five times, but, in my view, the most interesting woman in his life was Anaïs Nin. She was born in France to Cuban parents but after her parents separated, her mother moved with her and two brothers first to Barcelona in Spain and then to New York City. When she was twenty, Anaïs married Hugh Parker Guiler who was a banker and an artist and later became an experimental filmmaker.

A year later they moved to Paris where Anaïs began to start writing. She is mostly known from her diaries and journals over a period of six decades. These diaries give an intimate insight into her personal life and especially her relationships, among which were famous artists and writers including Henry Miller. She lived in Paris till 1940 and then returned to the United States.

In Volume One of her diaries, she explains how she first came across erotic French paperbacks when she was in Paris. Fascinating, isn't it that a series of books can inspire a style of writing and how that, later on, led to her being hailed by many critics as one of the finest writers of female erotica. We can only wonder whether it was these books or the desperate need for money that led Anaïs, but also Henry Miller and some of their friends to write erotic and even pornographic stories for an anonymous collector. Although it is not a hundred percent clear whether Miller actually was the author of these stories or merely allowed her to use his name, but they saw it as a bit of a joke.

Anaïs and Henry Miller were friends but also had a passionate love affair, which strongly influenced her as an author. Anaís was bisexual and had an affair with Henry's second wife June. This becomes clear from her journal *Henry and June*. June was a femme fatale and irresistible both to Anaïs and Henry and they formed a love triangle, which would later cause June and Henry to break up. We mustn't forget that Anaïs was also married at the time.

She did what few women had done until then, write erotic stories and reveal her bisexuality.

I would now really like to talk to you about Kiki The Queen of Montparnasse. She was such an icon at the time. She was born in 1902 as Alice Ernestine Prin. Her father abandoned her mother and her mum left her with her grandparents, who were very poor, and went to Paris to work as a linotypist. When Alice was twelve her grandparents sent her to

Paris by train to live with her mother in rue de Lac, close to Montparnasse and to find work to support the family.

She had all sorts of jobs like working in a bakery, at a flower shop, a laundry and also as a maid. But she was already eccentric from a very young age and experimented with putting on make-up with a burnt matchstick. She soon found out that she could earn money posing naked for artists. When her mother found out she kicked Alice out of the house.

She was homeless, but determined to only make money posing for artists. She was very pretty, dark-haired and soon became the artist's favourite model. One night the painter Chaïm Soutine welcomed her into his house and allowed her to sleep in a bed whilst he slept in a chair. Still a young girl she sometimes painted some extra pubes with charcoal on her own body before posing. She posed literally for dozens of artists, quite a few of whom we already talked about like Van Dongen, Foujita and Romanian sculptor Brâncuşi. She also posed for Moïse Kisling, a French-Polish painter. He created some interesting portraits, almost unsettling, look, let me show you a few pictures..."

Oh yes you are right, quite intriguing.

"Kisling actually gave her the name Kiki. She soon became one of the most sought-after models and referred to as Kiki de Montparnasse. You could say that she helped liberate Parisian culture during Les années folles'. She became famous, almost like a celebrity, in the Montparnasse's social scene. She turned into a cabaret star, and Queen of the parties in the cafés of Montparnasse, like La Rotonde, Le Dôme and La Coupole. She had a strong character and said that she was only interested in men who were painters, actors or poets; other 'mortals' did not interest her.

In 1921 she met Man Ray, an American artist who actually spent most of his career in Paris. He's probably best described as a dadaist and surrealist. Although he was best known for his photography, he himself felt he was a painter first and foremost.

They had an intense relationship that lasted for around eight years. Kiki moved in with him in his studio in rue Campagne-Première until

1929. He literally made hundreds of portraits of her and she was clearly his muse.

What is interesting is that Man Ray was obsessed with Kiki's make-up and the way she dressed. He would put on her make-up and helped her choose what to wear. Her make-up was almost a work of art, changing colour that matched her clothes for example.

Kiki also had appeared in no less than nine short, often experimental films, such as Fernand Léger's *Ballet Mécanique* made in 1923. When she was twenty-eight, she was given the name *Queen of Montparnasse.*"

She sounds rather amazing actually, but did I hear it correctly that she also was a painter?

"Yes she was. And she had an exhibition of her work in Galerie au Sacre du Printemps in 1927 which was apparently sold out. She received very good feedback. She did mainly paintings and drawings of social activities, self-portraits and dreamy landscapes in quite an expressionist style. They say it was a reflection of her carefree way of life, but also of her optimism.

Two years later she published her memoirs in her book *Les souvenirs de Kiki.* Hemingway wrote an introduction and Foujita wrote a preface. You certainly can say that she led a full life. She even opened a cabaret in Montparnasse called Chez Kiki and moved in with André Laroque a musician. When the Second World War started and the Germans occupied the city in 1940, she left Paris to return after the war.

She died when she was only fifty-one years old when she collapsed, outside her house in Montparnasse, due to excessive alcohol and drug abuse. She was buried at the Cimetière parisien de Thiais. On her tomb stone it says "*Kiki, singer, actress, painter, Queen of Montparnasse*". She was loved and missed by many. Tsuguharu Foujita remarked: "*with Kiki's death, the glorious days of Montparnasse are buried forever.*"

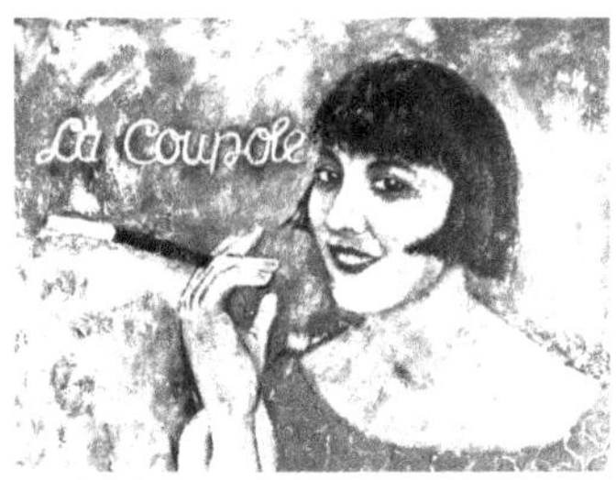

Kiki de Montparnasse

Now we've spoken about The Queen of Montparnasse but there was also someone nicknamed The Prince of Montparnasse. His name was Jules Pascin an artist from Bulgaria who later became an American citizen. He painted mainly casually posing women either partly dressed or naked and he did also use Kiki as a model. He had moved to Paris in 1905 and became one of the many foreign artists settling in Montparnasse.

Although he lived in Paris, he had his first solo exhibition at the Paul Cassirer Gallery in Berlin in 1907. In that same year, on one of his regular visits to Café Le Dôme, he was introduced to Hermine David. She also was a painter, and the two became lovers. Hermine David, who was born in Paris was already a successful young painter. When Pascin went to the United States she came with him, this was in 1915 and three years later they got married. She continued working as an artist and had an exhibition in New York as well. After returning to Paris in 1920 she had several solo exhibitions in galleries in Paris, but also exhibited in London.

When they lived in the States Pascin too had his work exhibited in New York and he was clearly influenced by Fauvism and Cezanne. In 1920 Pascin and Hermine returned to Paris even though he had just received US citizenship. Soon afterwards he started having an affair with Lucy Vidil Krohg, who was a model, and later opened a gallery in Paris. Lucy went on playing a very important role in the art scene of Montparnasse, inspiring and working with important artists of the time. Lucy had been Pascin's lover before, but she got married to Per Krohg during the time Pascin lived in the United States. Per Krohg was a Norwegian artist who grew up in Paris and studied arts with impressive artists like Henri Matisse. He is best known for his mural in the United Nations headquarters in New York City.

Lucy was actually born in Paris and already as a young teenager she became part of the Paris art scene working as a model. This is also how she met both Per, her future husband, and Jules Pascin. When she opened her own art gallery in 1932 at 10bis place Saint-Augustin, she sold Paskin's work, but also the work of his wife Hermine and many other artists, including Suzanne Valadon. At the time she was one of very few female gallerists in Paris.

After Pascin had returned to France, he became a symbol of the art community in Montparnasse. He always wore a bowler hat and was an interesting figure. He was mostly inspired in his work by his immediate surroundings and would paint both males and females as a subject.

He especially liked to paint almost fragile looking women, for example prostitutes waiting for clients. His art sold well, but he was a big spender and became well-known for the many parties in his flat. Whenever he was invited to a party, he would bring as many bottles of wine as he could carry. Hemingway was one of those who frequented these parties and wrote about it in his memoir, *A Moveable Feast*, in a chapter called *With Pascin at the Dôme*.

Pascin was suffering from depression and alcoholism and he took his own life when he was only forty-five years old. It was the night before the opening of an important solo exhibition of his. He slit his own wrists, then used his blood to write the words *"Adieu Lucy"* on the wall before hanging himself. Lucy found him. He left his estate and his works, equally divided, to both Hermine and Lucy. His funeral saw a large crowd of people from the art community, but also many bartenders and waiters from the bars and restaurants that he so often frequented. They were all dressed in black when they walked behind his coffin. His remains now rest at the cimetière du Montparnasse."

What a dramatic yet somehow almost poetic story. What brings it even more to life for me is that we can see their photos, not just of their work, but also of who they were. All this thanks to images of photographers who used to live in Paris at the time. Mario suggests that we go to café Le Dôme now, which also played such an important role in the lives of many of the artists that we are talking about, as well as photographers. We pay for our food and drinks.

It is still lively in the streets of Montparnasse even though it has started to rain.

Photography and film

In the 1920s and 1930s

We arrive at café Le Dôme and are lucky to find a seat on the outdoor terrace, but still sheltered from the rain. With the evening lights and the buzzing atmosphere in the streets it's a perfect moment to watch people passing by.

We order a coffee and Mario shows me an old black-and-white photo of Le Dôme on his mobile phone. The image shows the pavement café area heaving with people, no-doubt many of whom are artists, as this was one of their favourite places to meet. We are fortunate being able to witness those images in this digital age, captured by photographers that used to go to these types of cafés.

"Yes, photography had become a popular means of expression also for artists who gave us a glimpse into their past through, sometimes crude, but also sensitive and storytelling photography. Let me tell you about some of them, who to me were the most interesting. Later, on our way to the hotel, we will pass a plaque dedicated to Gerda Taro, Robert Capa and David Seymour, best known as 'Chim'.

These three then young photographers had their studio in 37 rue Froidevaux from 1937 to 1939, close to where I lived. They certainly were part of the Montparnasse artistic scene and lived the nightlife, quite possibly sharing tables with people like Hemingway, who referred to Gerda Taro as *"Capa girl"*, in bars such as Le Dôme. Hemingway, Gerda, Capa and Chim were all witnesses for the world, to show what was happening in the Spanish Civil War.

These photographers are considered to be the creators of modern photojournalism. To me Gerda is very special, and it even makes me a bit emotional sitting here now, where she may have been sitting, talking to Robert Capa. She was so young and so incredibly brave. She changed her own name as she was born in Stuttgart in Germany as Gerta Pohorylle. Some suggest that she based the name Taro on Japanese artist Tarō Okamoto, which is possible, but I'm not sure about that.

However, she certainly was a feminist activist and had even been in prison when she was younger for demonstrating against the nazi regime. When Gerda was twenty-three years old, she moved to Paris as she and her family were forced to leave Germany. Her parents tried to reach Palestine and her brothers went to England. She would never see her family again.

In 1934 Gerda met Robert Capa, here in Le Dôme, and soon she became his personal assistant. Capa taught her how to develop and perfect her photos but she became so good that Capa signed her photos so they could be published. Capa was already an established photographer and with his signature Gerda could sell her photos too.

They both covered what was happening on the front lines of the civil war in Spain and sometimes you can't see from the photo if it's his or hers. Gerda and Capa were lovers, but she was a free woman and loved several men. She refused Capa's marriage proposal. It is said that Capa was jealous of her escapades, which is perhaps understandable. She liked to take risks, both in her personal life and in her career."

Was Robert Capa an American photographer?

"No, he wasn't. Capa actually was a Hungarian photojournalist called Endre Friedmann, who, till this day is seen as one of the best combat photographers in history. As a teenager he moved to Berlin, but came to live in Paris in 1933 because of the rise of the nazis. In Paris he shared a darkroom with both David Seymour (Chim) and Henri Cartier-Bresson. He then also met Gerda Taro.

At some point Friedmann and Gerda decided to change Friedmann's name to Robert Capa, an invented name. They felt this name would give them better opportunities to sell their photos, also to the American market. Capa kept this name which he is now recognised by as the photojournalist who covered five wars. Including the Landing on D-Day and the liberation of Paris.

In 1935, Gerda found work at Maria Eisner's Alliance Photo and learned more about photography. Capa also did assignments for them. Gerda's work meant they had a steady income. Maria Eisner was in fact the co-founder of the famous Magnum Photos, an international cooperative for photographers, and she played an important role in its success. At that time the French authorities granted residency to photojournalists which was important for Gerda to being able to stay. In 1936 she was accredited for her work by an ABC Press-Service agency in Amsterdam which gave her official residency in France and allowed her to work as a photojournalist under her own name."

And what about David Seymore, why did they call him Chim?

"His real name was Dawid Szymin, he was of Polish-Jewish descent, however he adopted the name David Robert Seymour out of fear for retaliation by the nazis against his family who were still living in occupied Poland. But his friends called him Chim, an abbreviation of Szymin. He is best known for his coverage of the Spanish Civil War, but also for co-founding Magnum Photos, together with photographers like Robert Capa and Henri Cartier Bresson. After Capa's death, in 1954, Chim became the director of Magnum, the world's most prestigious photographic agency, until his death in 1956.

In 1936, Capa, Gerda and Chim went to Spain to cover the Civil War. Their photographs were used by the international press. They apparently were among the first photographers to use modern, small hand-held, light-weight camera's such as Leica's, which made it easier for them to travel to war-torn regions. Before that cameras were large and heavy and made it almost impossible for photographers to capture the real action on front lines.

In 2008 a box called 'The Mexican suitcase', containing over four thousand five hundred negatives of the Spanish Civil War, was discovered. This was in Mexico City as the Mexican ambassador of Vichy in France had taken the suitcase with him. It was finally returned to the younger brother of Robert Capa, Cornell Capa, who also was a photographer and the founder of the International Center of Photography in New York City.

In the suitcase there were portraits of war scenes, and of ordinary people living in the Spanish towns and countryside. The pictures were created by Gerda, Capa and Chim. They believed that capturing what was happening in photos could change the world and sometimes it did. Every frame was important to them and of course every picture tells a story. It must be said though that they were not necessarily objective journalists as they were supporting the Republicans in their attempt to defeat fascism. Also interesting to know is that Chim focused more on the social and cultural aspects of the war, whilst Gerda's and Capa's work is mostly reflecting the fighting.

Nevertheless, we can safely say that not just these images but all images taken by these brave young photographers are a testimony of the actual situation of war-time events during their life-time. A bravery which all three of them paid for with their lives!

Gerda Taro was always the closest in combat without fearing death. It's as if she had known she was going to live a short life and that's why she lived it fast and intensely. She knew that the Spanish civil war was the laboratory of the World War that was going to break out in 1939. She wanted to photograph the victory of the republic against fascism. Sadly, when she was only twenty-six years old, she was crushed by a reversing tank whilst covering the *Battle of Brunete*, fought twenty-four kilometres west of Madrid. She was the first female photographer who died covering a front-line war.

Robert Capa stepped on a landmine during the war in Vietnam in 1954 and David Seymour who was credited as a great humanist photographer and who had become a US citizen, was killed by a sniper in 1956 in Suez.

I'd like to show you a picture of Gerda Taro's grave, because it was designed by Alberto Giacometti. It says "*So nobody will forget your unconditional struggle for a better world*". It's beautiful don't you think?"

Oh, I really like that Mario. By the way, did Giacometti not live close to where you lived?

"Yes, he did, and I will tell you more about him later, as he lived so close to me that I must have met him several times. Without knowing who he was of course!

Look, this is a photo of Giacometti in his studio, taken by Robert Doisneau, a French photographer who became well-known for his humanist photography, specialising in photographing the streets of Paris."

What an intriguing picture. I especially like the unusual angle.

"Yes, I feel he is a very interesting photographer who has left us an important heritage of what Paris was like in the 1930s. Together with Henri Cartier-Bresson, he was considered one of the pioneers of photojournalism. He was a master in portraying people's lives.

Doisneau said that you have to look for the wonderful and the magical, even if reality is not that good at all. He also said that to be good at something in life, you have to be disobedient and curious. His photos were mostly black and white because colour film was expensive, but I rather like that. It somehow feels more artistic.

Apparently, he was a very shy man. His parents died when he was still a small child and he grew up with an aunt. He later went to a craft school where he was first introduced into the world of the arts, learning engraving and lithography, but also figure drawing and still life. When he was sixteen, he discovered photography, first as an amateur. He was so shy that he started taking pictures of the cobble-stones in the streets to later also taking pictures of children and adults.

At some point, he had the opportunity to work as a camera assistant for André Vigneau, an advertising photographer and I believe he then became one of the photographers. Doisneau was married to Pierrette Chaumaison, they had two daughters, one of whom became his assistant. His wife died in 1993 and he, only six months later in 1994.

But let's talk about his work. He liked taking pictures of working-class people, like people in a factory where he had worked for some time. People smiled at him because they knew him. He felt as if he was one of them. He used to walk across Paris to go to the humble neighbourhoods and spend hours in bistros. He became friends with many of these people. He often prepared for taking a specific image, staging it, as finding the right angle costs time. And it helped to be friends with those people. He also took pictures in the central market halls and even in brothels. However, he was very serious and a protestant, so he didn't go there to 'have fun'. He used to say "*I can't rest, I always have to do something*".

Doisneau was a photographer of his time. He was also known to be generous, lending out money and it didn't matter if they returned it or not. Since he was twenty-five years old, he had been archiving his photos, which is fantastic as we can now still admire many of his images.

After the war he showed the joys of the liberation of Paris. He could wait up to two hours to see if something would happen and be there just to take those magical shots. He would also stay for days in a gypsy community on the outskirts of Paris, portraying them when they travelled around Paris. He liked photographing the marginal world.

His work is a testimony of life in those days, showing humour, nostalgia and tenderness. He was a humble man though and said that out of four hundred thousand negatives there were only three hundred good ones.

He also loved photographing Picasso, taking him from interesting angles. He absolutely was a craftsman. Many know Doisneau for his photos of people who kiss or hug each other. His best-known photo, world-famous in fact, was a picture taken in 1950. It's called *Le baiser de l'hôtel de ville* depicting a man and a woman kissing on a busy Parisian street.

The photo was commissioned by the American magazine *Life*. They wanted to publish photos of love in Paris. Doisneau asked a couple of lovers on a terrace to pose for him in exchange for about five hundred francs, which would now be about fifteen hundred euros. This kiss is one of the most famous in the history of photography. In 1986, about four hundred thousand posters had been sold. The couple in the picture sued the magazine because they had made so much money out of it, but they couldn't prove that it was actually them.

It's interesting to see the world through the eyes of Doisneau."

I agree, but how about other women photographers Mario? Were there any?

"Yes, there were of course and we have already spoken about Dora Maar, Picasso's lover who photographed him working on his painting *Guernica* but there are other interesting female photographers. For example, Berenice Alice Abbott. She was an American photographer who is best known for her images of cultural figures during the interwar period. She was born in the United States, but in 1921 she came to Paris to study sculpture. She then became Man Ray's assistant in his portrait studio in Montparnasse. She later wrote *"I took to photography like a duck to water. I never wanted to do anything else"*.

She held her first exhibition in Paris, in gallery Au Sacre du Printemps in 1921. Four years later Man Ray introduced her to Eugène Atget's photographs, and she was very interested in his work. She shot a beautiful portrait of him, this was in 1927, shortly before he died. After his death, having purchased a considerable amount of his work, she was the photo editor of a book called *Atget Photographe de Paris*. She also wrote a book called *The World of Atget*, published in 1964. Partially thanks to her work, Atget gained international recognition.

Yet another interesting female photographer was Nora Dumas. She was a humanist photographer from Hungary, but she mainly worked in Paris. She had arrived in the city in 1913 where she first had to spend about three years in an internment camp. After that she went to the United States where she married Adrien-Émile Dumas, a Swiss architect and they moved back to France. Her photos depict mostly rural life in villages along the Seine, which show the decimation of the male population because of wartime and poverty.

In 1929 she was able to work as an assistant to Ergy Landau, also a Hungarian photographer, in her studio in Paris, where they worked together for nearly ten years. Well-known images of this period were of a famous Ukrainian model, Assia Granatouroff, who posed for many artists in Paris, but Nora and Ergy also took fashion photos and portraits of children and adults.

Ergy arrived in Paris in 1923 and soon was able to gain recognition, both by fellow photographers and the public. She was trained as a photographer in Vienna and Berlin, but opened a studio in Paris one year after her arrival. She made a name taking portrait pictures of well-known people which were published in the press.

To me it's a bit sad that there is much more information to be found on male than female photographers, but it is what it is. I still feel it's important to name some of these male artists as their stories are certainly worth mentioning.

We've briefly mentioned Henri Cartier-Bresson, who had a forty-year career as a photographer. He was very much inspired by the work of Eugène Atget and Man Ray. Born in France in 1908 he helped establish photojournalism as an art form with his spontaneous and humane approach. There is an interesting book with his work called *Images à la Sauvette*. I think the fact that he studied literature and painting, and later his travels around the world, influenced his way of taking pictures. But he was known as wanting to remain anonymous when capturing his images, and for covering the shiny metal-coloured parts of his camera with black tape and sometimes a handkerchief, to make it less visible. He liked to be an unseen witness.

Bresson also produced a documentary film which was about medical aid during the Spanish Civil War. It sparked an interest in him for this medium. He was the assistant of Jean Renoir, a film director, for three years. He lived a long, well-travelled life and died in 2004.

One of my personal favourites is Brassaï (Gyula Halász), a French Bulgarian photographer who made his name internationally. He also was a sculptor, writer and filmmaker who claimed he was artistically inspired by Toulouse Lautrec. He studied drawing in Hungary and later goes to Berlin where he meets Kandinsky and many other artists. He is young and dreams of Paris.

He arrives in Paris in 1924. I feel it's important to know that in the 1930s there was a social revolution that led to the Second World War and it was bringing these creatives together to tell us what was happening in the world. Brassaï mostly depicts the nocturnal and popular Paris."

Mario shows me some photos of Brassaï and I must say they are fascinating. Storytelling and mysterious, a story that we can make up ourselves. Mario is telling me what he feels when he looks at these images and I can see that it evokes emotions in him.

"To me art is about observing and feeling with the help of our personal knowledge and the culture we live in. The narrative is born from observing a photo and the story simply becomes real. These images remind me of the songs of Edith Piaf, the world of the 'maisons closes', the women who sell themselves in the streets, the street lights.

Brassaï photographed details, for example, a defect in a wall. He was able to capture such details and express his emotions with that, almost like modern-day graffiti. He was fascinated by the world around him. When he arrived in Paris he felt welcomed by its nightlife and popular atmospheres. He loved the everyday life, and it was during a walk through the night of Paris, that he decided to be a photographer. He loved the night and frequented the neighbourhood cafés. In his photos you see shadows, the light of the streetlights, the love that is sold on the corners.

He creates his images with devotion, highlighting every detail, whilst giving life to the anonymous. He finds the unexpected. In Montparnasse he also becomes friends with Henri Miller, who was a perfect guide for his nights out, no doubt accompanied by lots of alcohol.

Brassaï liked the rain and fog, and his black and white images take us to the unreal, observing the silence in the semi-dark streets of Paris, people seeking refuge in the cafés, served by the coffee garçons, prostitutes waiting for their next client, a heartbreak solved with alcohol, workers finding some solace after a hard-days' work.

We can actually see these nightlife images in his book *Paris la nuit* from 1932. He was the only witness of that life in Paris in the 1930s.

Making the simplest moments unique. Realism that can become a dream which you don't want to wake up from.

He captured the streets of Pigalle, the Mercado Marché Central des Halles, and the lonely streets, but he also shows a glimpse of looking into the windows where the light tells us that love is around. Brassaï has done portraits of other artists and also took images of the lives of prostitutes, always with affection and respect. For example, a photo of a woman undressing, reflected in a mirror. But also, the ones in the streets, as Edith Piaf sang "*Une ombre de la rue*".

Brassaï married Gilberte Boyer in 1948. She was French, and she worked with him, supporting his photography. A year later he was given the French nationality. He was eighty-four when he died and buried at the Montparnasse Cemetery."

Rather special all this. You say he was also a filmmaker? I know you already told me about cinema earlier, but I presume that in the 1930s cinema changed from silent to spoken film. Am I correct to think that?

"Yes, you are right and yes, Brassaï was also a filmmaker and has several films to his name. He even won Most Original Film in 1956 at the Cannes Film Festival with his film *Tant qu'il y aura des bêtes*. And I think we should talk a little about the film industry now.

We previously talked about the birth of cinema and the first screening of the brothers Lumière. Talking cinema would appear at the end of the 1920s, beginning of the 1930s coinciding with the economic crisis of 1929. French cinema had to transform their studios and projection rooms introducing sounds. This sound that was going to change the film industry.

There were some very interesting directors, who were making social cinema. Referred to as Poetic Realism, such as Jean Renoir. He was the second son of impressionist painter Pierre-Auguste Renoir. Jean had two brothers, Pierre, a stage and film actor, and Claude, who also briefly acted in films, mainly in Jean's films.

Jean, who was also an actor and an author, created more than forty films, both silent and with sound. Two of his films, *La Règle du Jeu*, already warning of the threat of war that is going to come, and *La Grande Illusion*, are considered to be among the best films ever made.

Two other interesting directors were René Clair and Marcel Carné. Clair was known for his silent comedy films which were mixed with fantasy. For example, *Paris Qui Dort*, a silent science fiction comedy. He did create some very innovative, early sound films and subsequently worked both in the United Kingdom and the United States. But after a decade he returned to Paris and continued working in the film industry. And Carné was an important figure in the Poetic Realism movement, for example, *Les Enfants du Paradis*, which was seen as one of the greatest films ever made.

The thirties were a decade of development of avant-garde cinema, among which surrealist films such as *Le Ballet Mécanique* by Fernand Léger. I have already mentioned this when we spoke about Kiki de Montparnasse who has a role in this film.

But I'd like to focus on some actresses, in particular Arletty, Michelle Morgan and Danielle Darrieux. Again, there are so many great films, directors, actors and actresses, too many to mention as the film industry was thriving, but I'd like to at least mention a few of them.

Michelle Morgan was actually called Simone Roussel, but she changed her name to Michelle Morgan early on in her career as she thought it sounded more Hollywood friendly. Michelle was a leading figure in both the French and Hollywood film industry for three decades and considered to be one of the greatest French actresses of the 20th century.

Danielle Darrieux was a French stage, television and film actress, as well as a dancer and a singer. At the age of fourteen she got a part in the Musical film *Le Bal*. This was in 1931 and from then on, she was in more than one hundred and ten films. She worked for eight decades, amazing, isn't it? She had the longest film career in history and was one of the greatest French movie stars. She died in 2017 when she was a hundred years old after she had some complications due to a fall."

Gosh , that's impressive. I'm just looking at her long list of film appearances and she was very beautiful. You mentioned Arletty, who was she?

"Yes, hers is also an interesting story. Her name was Léonie Marie Julie Bathiat and she was born in 1898. Her professional name was Arletty. She took on that name because it was one of the heroines in a story by Guy de Maupassant.

When she was young, she had a lot of jobs during the First World War, among others working in an arms factory. At first, she wasn't all that interested in becoming an actress, but one day she meets the art collector Paul Guillaume who encourages her to do theatre and magazine work and to perform as a singer. She had some successful performances in theatre.

Arletty was then chosen for the role of Raymonde in Marcel Carné's drama film *Hôtel du Nord*. It is about two couples in Paris. A prostitute Raymonde and her pimp, and two lovers who don't have regular jobs and are contemplating committing suicide because they can't afford to get married and start a family. The film is considered a work of Poetic Realism. The music, cinematography and dialogue give an almost poetic dimension to the lives of people from a working-class background. The film was partially shot in and around Hôtel du Nord.

It is based on a book with the same title, written by Eugène Dabit, who was the son of the owners of the real Hôtel du Nord. He also lived in the area and is believed to have been inspired by, and even written the novel, when he was in Hôtel du Nord. The hotel is located at the Canal San Martin. Tourists don't normally go there, only people who know about the film and want to see the setting and the atmosphere of the film, a classic French cinema.

Paris is also well-known for its river Seine and its canals. The façade of Hôtel du Nord is one of the most famous facades in the history of French cinema. You could say that the hotel is the main character of the film. Close to the hotel there is a bridge that bears the name of Arletty in honour of one of the most famous scenes of French cinema filmed there.

In 1945 Arletty played a role which was probably her most famous in the film *Les Enfants du Paradis*. This role made her the highest paid actress of her time. But when the war had come to an end, she began to receive insults and even death threats. The reason was her romantic relationship with a German officer during the war.

His name was Hans Jürgen Sohring, he was very cultured and did not sympathize with nazism, but he was a German officer. He and Arletty made plans to be together after the war, but it wasn't meant to be as he died during the war.

She was arrested and was brought before a court and said "*my heart is French but my body is international*". At the time women who had had relationships with Germans during the war had their hair shaved off, but Arletty said "*I'd rather shave my own hair than give someone else the pleasure of doing it*". In the end she was not sentenced because she never collaborated with the nazis, didn't work in German cinema and had even helped friends to get out of German prisons.

Arletty continued working after the war, but she suffered from professional isolation. Something she considered unfair. In 1954 her friend, philosopher Jean Paul Sartre, commissioned her to play in the film version of *Huis clos* (known in English as 'No Exit'), which is a one-act philosophical drama, suggesting that "*hell is other people*" not a place created by God.

After this she was in four more movies, but they weren't well received. She knew it was because of her relationship with Hans and also because of her age. Arletty then began to lose her eyesight and rejected roles in the theatre. She was a woman of character and independence. She died when she was ninety-four, in 1992."

I'm delighted when Mario tells me that we will go and visit Hôtel du Nord tomorrow, and he also has a surprise for me. It's been a long day and I've learned a lot. We are both tired and decide to go back to our hotel.

We walk in the direction of the Montparnasse cemetery towards rue Froidevaux. We stop for a moment in front of the building at number thirty-seven. Mario points out the plaque in honour of Gerda Taro,

Robert Capa and David Seymour who we mentioned before and where they had their studio. Standing here, in front of the plaque, my mind goes out to the brave photographers who had given their lives trying to inform the public of the atrocities of war.

Sculptors of a new era

After our breakfast we go to the Passerelle Arletty. The bridge is named after Arletty, who we talked about yesterday. I like the area and the bridge, it just feels special, moreover because it looks like one of the Amsterdam canals. It has to be said that the film was such an important production that they replicated the area around Hôtel du Nord in the Billancourt film studios, the hotel, the street, the canal and the bridge. To create the canal, they dug ditches on land owned by a cemetery outside the studio and filled them with water. But some scenes in the film were actually taken in the Hotel itself.

We walk in the direction of Brasserie Hôtel du Nord, since it is no longer a hotel, where we will have a coffee.

I cannot believe my eyes, there in front of the brasserie I see my friend Jeanette, who actually lives close-by. She is Dutch but has been living in Paris for over thirty years. Mario has asked her to join us for the day without me knowing this. What a lovely surprise. Jeanette and I have been friends for a very long time. We met in the Netherlands but I have since moved to Spain and she to Paris, but we talk almost weekly on the phone.

Jeanette works as a sworn translator in Paris and she loves art and is an avid reader. She regularly visits the grand museums in the city. After a hug we decide to go inside the brasserie.

The welcoming, cosy atmosphere makes me feel thrown back in time. I love the floor with two types of black-and-white tiles and the wooden bar. I can totally imagine how Eugène Dabit sat here with a coffee or a drink and got inspired by passersby and people working in the hotel. His book became a big success in France and even won the 1929

Populist Prize. And how special that some of the scenes of the film were shot here. We order a coffee and discuss our plan for today.

First Mario will talk to us about Giacometti and some other sculptors that were working in Paris during the Roaring Twenties. Then we will visit Atelier Brâncuși, which is the studio of Constantin Brâncuși, composed of several spaces and located in front of the Centre Pompidou. This famous artist left a large part of his collection to the French state in his will, and it is a great testimony of his work. It's also free to visit. After this we will go to the museum. Mario starts talking and Jeanette and I are all ears.

"Alberto Giacometti was an Italian speaking, Swiss sculptor and painter, but mostly famous for his sculptures. Talking about him is rather personal to me as I'm sure I will have crossed paths with him on rue Alésia, close to the house where I grew up. In my opinion, you can't really put Giacometti in one of the art movements that we've discussed as he had his own style, however, he was part of the Surrealism movement for a while and acknowledged for his surrealist works. In fact, he was considered to be one of the leading surrealist sculptors and it is certainly true that he was inspired by Cubism and Surrealism.

His father, called Giovanni, was a post-impressionist painter which must have influenced Giacometti's choice to become an artist. He was born in 1901 in Borgonovo, close to the Italian border, and grew up with two younger brothers and a sister in Stampa, a nearby town. He studied art at the École des Beaux-Arts in Geneva and then at the École des Arts et Métiers. In 1920 Giacometti accompanied his father on a trip to Venice. His father was a guest of the Biennale. He subsequently visited Rome and stayed there for almost a year, visiting towns such as Naples, Florence and Assisi."

Oh wow, I have to interrupt you for a moment Mario as this brings back memories. I lived in Rome for three months and then moved to Perugia, a town in Umbria and then I was invited for a solo exhibition in Gualdo Cattaneo, a small village close to Assisi. I ended up living there for almost four years. I certainly also visited the inspiring and beautiful towns of Venice, Naples, Florence and Assisi multiple times. I can totally imagine how his stay in Italy could have influenced Giacometti's work, but when did he arrive in Paris?

"He arrived in Paris in 1922 and studied sculpture at the Académie de la Grande Chaumière. He lived and worked mainly in Paris, but also regularly went back to his hometown of Borgonovo to visit family.

He then met Jeanne Bucher. Now she was an interesting lady as well. She was from Alsace, a French region. She had worked in libraries in Switzerland and later as a nurse during World War I, but moved to Paris in 1920 where she was introduced into artistic and literacy circles. In her forties she decided to become an art collector and dealer. When she was fifty-one, she opened a library gallery in the interior design store of Pierre Chareau at 3 rue du Cherche-Midi.

At first, she represented cubist artists, including Jules Pascin, Picasso and Piet Mondrian, although the latter is not really considered a cubist. There were many more artists of course, too many to mention them all. She also became a publisher of artists' books. In 1929 Jeanne opened her own, independent gallery in 5 rue du Cherche-Midi, so next door to the library gallery. During the inauguration she showed work of, among others, Braque and Picasso.

Sadly, in the summer of 1932, she had to sell the gallery due to the global economic crisis, but she continued working in the art scene. Three years later she opened yet another gallery at 9 boulevard du Montparnasse. The gallery still exists today but is now located in 5 rue de Saintonge.

She also supported young upcoming artists like Giacometti and in her gallery, she exhibited his *Tête qui regarde* sculpture, which attracted the attention of important surrealist artists and writers. This resulted in Giacometti being part of the Parisian avant-garde and introduced to the surrealist circles.

I believe Giacometti was close to his family and in 1930 Giacometti's brother Diego came to live in Paris and became one of his favourite models. He also shared his studio with his brother. His artistic career took off, and he took part in many group exhibitions, both in France and abroad. To me it is interesting that such a brilliant artist had self-doubt about his work and felt that he wasn't able to do justice to his own artistic vision, but this at the same time hugely motivated him to continue and create a large body of work.

From 1938 to 1944 his sculptures were extremely small, only seven centimetres high, and he said it reflected the distance between him and his models. In that same period Giacometti also created his view of the human head in his unique way of viewing reality. He preferred models he was close to, like his sister, and artist and model Isabel Rawsthorne, better known as Isabel Delmer. She was a British painter who came to live in Paris in 1934. She also posed for artists like Derain and Picasso.

It was a sad moment for Giacometti when his only sister, Ottilia, died in 1937 while giving birth to Silvio, Giacometti's only nephew. Silvio later posed for him and is represented in his sculptures during the war when Giacometti and his brother had returned to Switzerland.

In this period, he met Annette Arm, a secretary who worked at the Red Cross. They got married in 1949. A new phase in his work emerged as he started to create taller, very thin statues with elongated limbs. Annette became one of his favourite models and they lived together in Paris till the end of the artist's life.

Giacometti who is known for his numerous exhibitions internationally, died when he was only sixty-four years old in Switzerland of cardiac exhaustion. He is buried in the cemetery of Borgonovo. As one of the most important sculptors of the 20th century he has left us an amazing legacy. Since he had no children, Annette inherited the property rights for his work and when she died the French state set up the *Fondation Giacometti*."

Jeanette asks Mario whether there were many female sculptors during the thirties in Paris. He replies.

"To my knowledge, there isn't a lot of information available about female sculptors in Paris apart from perhaps Chana Orloff. I will tell you more about her later. We mustn't forget these were still male dominated times. As I've already explained to Renate, Paris attracted artists from all over the world and became the capital of the art world. But there was also a very specific group of artists of Jewish descent who had fled from Poland, Russia and Central Europe. Think about artists like Soutine and Chagall. Among them were also women artists including Chana Orloff.

But I know of some female sculptors that are worth mentioning too, even if only briefly. One was Irina Codreanu, a Romanian artist who came to Paris with her sister, a dancer, in 1918. She studied at the Académie de la Grande Chaumière and was able to exhibit her work at the Salon d'Automne in 1921. She also worked in Brâncuși's studio for four years and created portrait sculptures, for example, of Man Ray. She became close to Marguerite Bayser-Gratry, a sculptor who won the Decorative Arts Grand Prize in 1925. But there is not much information to be found about her personal life.

Irina was inspired by Rodin and known for her sensitivity in portraying portraits of people. We can see that she was influenced by Egyptian art. Over the years Irina had exhibitions internationally and many of her artworks can be seen in museums in different countries, including at the Musée d'Orsay in Paris.

Another female sculptor who is interesting to mention was Augusta Savage, an American sculptor. She started working with clay when she was still a young teenager. Her father, a Methodist minister, didn't approve of this as he saw it as a sin. So, she must have been a very strong-willed character to pursue her career as an artist. It can't have been easy for her, the more so, because she was a black artist.

An amazing woman I feel, as she became a teacher as well and influenced the careers of a generation of artists. She was also an important advocate for equal rights for African Americans in the art world.

She won numerous prizes and received many commissions but also had several setbacks. One was when her acceptance for a summer art program in France was cancelled after the committee found out that she was black. She fought the decision and did get a lot of press coverage both in the US and Europe, but it was to no avail.

In 1929, at the age of thirty-seven and with the help of some grants and donations from former teachers and friends, Augusta was able to travel to France and enrolled at the Académie de la Grande Chaumière. She lived in an apartment in Montparnasse.

At first her teachers were encouraging her work but later in life she wrote: *"the masters are not in sympathy as they all have their own definite ideas and usually wish their pupils to follow their particular method"*. She won two awards in Paris during her exhibitions. She also visited other parts of France and Germany and Belgium especially to study sculpture in museums and cathedrals.

Augusta returned to the United States in 1931 and despite the Great Depression she continued working as an artist. She was the first African-American artist elected to be included in the National Association of Women Painters and Sculptors. She received a grant from the Carnegie Foundation and opened the Savage Studio of Arts and Crafts, open to anyone who wanted to sculpt, draw or paint.

Despite many setbacks and clear discrimination, she continued to create prolific artworks. However, even though she had been acknowledged and won prizes, it was still a financial struggle for her. The last large exhibition of her work was in 1939. In 1945 she decided to move to a farm house in Saugerties in the state of New York. She also found a job as a laboratory assistant in a cancer research facility. Although she continued sculpting, it was no longer her major occupation. Despite the fact that there is quite a bit of documentation about this interesting artist, the whereabouts of many of her artworks are unknown.

Augusta Savage died of cancer in 1962, but she is remembered as the great artist, teacher and activist that she was."

Oh wow Mario, what a woman, I would have loved to have met her. I'm glad you have told us about her. Jeanette agrees with me.

"Yes, she certainly was special. There is another rather amazing sculptor which I would like to talk about now. Her name was Chana Orloff. She was one of nine children born in Ukraine. As a teenager she already learned sewing and dressmaking. In 1905 she and her family moved to the Ottoman Empire, Palestine.

She started working as a seamstress and clothing designer. She was then offered a job in Jaffa as a teacher. It was 1910, and she decided to go to Paris to study fashion at the L'École nationale supérieure des arts décoratifs. During her study she worked at Maison de Couture owned by Jeanne Paquin.

She also enrolled for classes at the Vassiliev Academy in Montparnasse where she discovered her love for sculpture. She became well-integrated in the Paris artist's scene and met artists like Modigliani, Foujita, Picasso, Chagall and sculptor Ossip Zadkine to name but a few. She was able to exhibit her work in Salon d'Automne in 1913. Her sculptures are best described as fresh, with a simple and geometric appearance, almost cubist.

In 1916 she married Ary Justman, a writer and poet. They had a son together called Elie, also called 'Didi'. Ary died of the Spanish flu in 1919. It can't have been easy for Chana to be left with a small child. Nevertheless, her art career started to flourish. She was extremely productive during the interwar period, created more than five hundred sculptures and was very successful. She had a very innovative style, sometimes ironically grotesque, sensual forms and with an influence of African art. She experimented with different types of materials, including concrete, terracotta, bronze, and she knew how to work wood as it was done in her native Ukraine.

In 1925 she was already appreciated by the public and critics and had a house built in rue Villa Seurat, a street where many artists lived, near Montparnasse.

During the war, in 1942 she managed to flee to Switzerland with Didi and Jewish painter George Kars. They were given refugee status. Sadly, Kars committed suicide in 1945. After the war Chana returned to Paris, but her house had been completely ransacked and hundred and forty-five sculptures were stolen."

Mario shows us some photos of her mother and child statues, the sensitive statue *my son* and some stylishly shaped figures. We are both impressed. Jeanette asks *"Did she only do these types of sculptures or also portraits?"*

"Not just these, she was actually really in demand as a portrait sculptor and throughout her long career she made busts of quite a few famous artists, including Matisse, Picasso, Per Krohg and many well-known people.

In 1968 Chana Orloff flew to Israel for a retrospective exhibition of her work at the Tel Aviv Museum. It was also to honour her on the occasion of her 80th birthday. Sadly she became sick and died. She was then buried in Tel Aviv."

I think it's beautiful that we get to know a person thanks to what Mario tells us and the images we see on our telephones. It's time to move on though, so we decide to pay for our coffee and take a metro to the Centre Pompidou.

One of the main reasons why we are going there is to view the studio of Constantin Brâncuși, but we have planned to spend the rest of the day in the Centre Pompidou. When we arrive, I can't believe what I see. I really love old architecture, but the centre has a unique design showing its structure on the outside and covered in bright colours. It's not just a museum, but a cultural centre.

We will also visit the museum known for its large collection of modern art, including work of Picasso, Duchamp, Giacometti, Chagall, Robert Delaunay, Mondrian and also Frida Kahlo, but we decide to go to see Atelier Brâncuși first. On our way there Mario explains...

"Brâncuși is sometimes referred to as the patriarch of modern sculpture. He was a Romanian sculptor, photographer and painter but best known for his sculpture. He was born in a small village in a region known for its woodcarving tradition, which possibly is the reason why he already did woodcarving when he was still young. His family was very poor and as a child he had to herd sheep. He left the village to work somewhere else when he was nine years old.

When he was eleven, and during his teenage years, he worked as a domestic servant. Then, encouraged by someone who saw a violin that Brâncuși had made from scrap wood, spotting his talent, he enrolled in the Craiova School of Arts and Crafts when he was eighteen. He went on to get an academic training in sculpture at the Bucharest School of Fine Arts. He was very talented.

He continued his study first in Munich in Germany and then went to the École des Beaux-Arts in Paris. This was from 1905 to 1907. His work was inspired by non-European cultures, but in some of his art we can see the influence of Romanian folk art.

In Paris he was invited to work in the studio of Rodin, but he stayed only for two months, apparently saying "*Nothing can grow under big trees*". He started to step into his own style of sculpting. Some very famous works of his are *La muse endormie*, a simply but beautifully carved laid down head, *Le Baiser*, one of his earlier non-literal representation works in a cubist style and *La Prière* which was his first commission and part of a gravestone memorial, depicting a young woman or girl kneeling down, slightly bent forward, with crossed arms.

What I find interesting is that he was familiar with modelling in clay or plaster, then to be cast in metal, which was what many sculptors did, but as of 1908 Brâncuşi's favourite way of creating his sculpture was through carving. Although he was an idealist offering visitors to his workshop an almost spiritual experience, he was also a womaniser and loved to go out, enjoying good wine and cigarettes. He did have a child, John Moore, with Vera Moore, a New Zealand pianist who had gained international recognition, but he never acknowledged him.

His art soon became popular in France, the United States, but also in Romania. But some of his works caused quite some controversy and gave him a bit of a bad reputation. I'm referring to his entry of a sculpture called *Princess X* into the Salon. It's a large shiny bronze phallic looking sculpture. Although Brâncuşi claimed it just represented the essence of womanhood, they removed it from the exhibition. Apparently, it was inspired by his relationship with Princess Marie Bonaparte who was a great-grandniece of Emperor Napoleon I.

Princess Marie was a psychoanalyst and a devotee of Sigmund Freud. She was able to use her influence to help Freud escape Austria in 1938, to avoid him being caught by the nazis. She also was interested in issues of sexuality and is said to have been on a lifelong quest to achieve vaginal orgasm. Some say that Brâncuşi's sculpture *Princess X* symbolised her obsession with the penis.

Although his fame had grown, Brâncuşi became a bit of a reclusive. He was given French citizenship in 1952 and had his first retrospective exhibition in 1955 at the Guggenheim Museum in New York. In his later years he was looked after by a refugee couple from Romania. His French citizenship made it possible for him to make the caregivers his heirs and as we already said, he left his studio and contents to the Musée National d'Art Moderne in Paris, where we are now. He was eighty-one when he died and was buried in the cimetière du Montparnasse."

I decide that I must visit the Montparnasse cemetery before I leave Paris as there are so many interesting artists laid to rest there. Moreover, there are several statues of deceased artists created by Brâncuşi. I also want to see the house where Giacometti lived and the studio of Chana Orloff. But right now, we enter Atelier Brâncuşi.

All three of us stand there quietly for a moment. It feels unreal, as if this great artist could walk in any minute now and continue to work on one of his artworks. I understand why they say that it's an almost spiritual experience. It certainly is for me.

Art Deco

And American women who put their mark on Paris

When we leave Atelier Brâncuși, we walk to the Centre Pompidou just opposite the Atelier, to visit Musée national d'Art moderne whilst Mario tells us about Art Deco. We plan to see artwork by Tamara de Lempicka, and other artists. Mario will explain about the connection between France and America and, more specifically, female American artists, like Josephine Baker. Art Deco even influenced the fashion industry during the 1920s and 30s, something Jeanette and I are eager to find out about.

It has started to drizzle, but inside the Centre Pompidou we are sheltered from the rain. We take the glass lift that goes up the façade. It looks like a giant caterpillar (chenille) climbing like a plant from the floor to the terrace. From here we can clearly see the Stravinsky fountain just below with its moving mechanical figures created by artists Jean Tinguely and Niki de Saint Phalle, like a ballet on water full of colour.

"Art Deco is a design style that emerged in the early 20th century. I think most people have an idea of what it is although it is sometimes confused with Art Nouveau. Art Deco is characterised by its bold geometric shapes but also by the use of luxurious materials and rich colours. Art Deco originated during the 1925 Exposition Internationale des Arts Décoratifs et Industriels Modernes in Paris, showcasing the latest innovations in decorative arts and consequently giving this new style its name.

You could say it's a mixture of modernism, opulence and luxury. It took inspiration from different cultures, including African and ancient art but also from Oriental design. Not only that, the discovery of

Tutankhamun's tomb in 1922, created an interest in Egyptian motifs which quite possibly contributed to the Art Deco style, as well as new materials such as chrome, stainless steel and glass, which helped to streamline the aesthetics of Art Deco.

Paris was a central hub for the development and popularisation of Art Deco during the 1920s and 1930s. You can still see great examples of Art Deco architecture throughout the city. For example, the Théâtre des Champs-Élysées and Palais de Chaillot. Moreover, we can see it in furniture, jewellery and fashion. Think about the iconic French designers René Lalique and Jeanne Lanvin, to name but a few. They embraced Art Deco in their creations, emphasising geometric patterns.

However, if you like we can first go and see the Art Deco style art of Tamara de Lempicka here in the museum."

I'm already familiar with her work and I love her strong colours and very recognisable Art Deco style. Great that we can see her work today in real life!

"Tamara originally was from Poland but she spent most of her adult life between France and the United States. She is best known for her Art Deco portraits of mostly aristocrat and wealthy people.

She came to Paris with her first husband, a Polish lawyer, and studied painting. Her art soon became a mixture of Cubism and Neoclassical art. It didn't take her long to become active in the Paris art scene. She also met and became the mistress of Baron Raoul Kuffner, a wealthy art collector. After the death of his wife and Tamara's divorce from her first husband they were married. This was in 1934 and she was soon given the nickname 'The Baroness with a brush'.

Her breakthrough in the art world came in 1925 which, you could argue, was the year that Art Deco was born. Tamara held exhibitions of her work in two major salons, namely the Salon des Tuileries and the Salon des femmes peintres. At the start of World War II in 1939, Tamara and Kuffner moved to the United States where Tamara worked as a celebrity portrait and landscape artist. Her art was subsequently discovered by various fashion magazines and she made herself a name in the States.

In 1974 they moved to Mexico where Tamara died in 1980. On her request her ashes were scattered over the Popocatépetl volcano.

How best to describe Tamara de Lempicka's style? Her art blends neoclassical elements with a modern sensibility, using geometric shapes in a luxurious setting. Tamara's distinctive style, can be recognised by strong lines and vibrant colours. Two of her iconic works, *La Belle Rafaela* and *Autoportrait* (Tamara in the Green Bugatti), reflect both the opulence of the era and the artist's unique vision that continues to resonate in the world of modern art."

Jeanette says that it's fascinating that so many female artists found their way to Paris, considering the male dominated society they lived in. And we also wonder how these women, and of course also men, heard about Paris. In our times it's easy, if we want information, we can simply search online, but how did they get their information back then?

"That's an interesting point. I presume from hearing about it by fellow artists, travellers, writers and journalists who had been to Paris. But they must have had courage to just give up the life they knew to replace it for an exciting and no-doubt challenging adventure.

During the 1920s and 1930s there was an influx of Americans who came to Paris as well, including women. Americans dreamed of Paris because they knew it was a hotspot for artists and they liked European art. In a sense they brought liberation to Paris in two ways, American women went out without a hat and also visited bars on their own, setting an example to other women in Paris. Ironically, they came to Europe to look for a sense of freedom that they didn't have in the United States. This was true especially for African American artists as in France, and particularly in Paris, they were free to go where they wanted.

Perhaps some of them had heard of Paris thanks to Meta Vaux Warrick Fuller, an African American sculptor who moved to Paris in 1899 to study sculpture. Her art celebrates her African American identity and cultural heritage. She was the first African American to receive a federal art commission and was part of the Harlem Renaissance. Not only was she a sculptor, but she also wrote poetry, painted, and designed for the theatre, though she is especially known for her style rooted in themes of horror.

She was the first African American sculptor in Paris, and as you might expect, Meta became a protégé of Auguste Rodin in 1902. She used her art to depict the racial injustices and social traumas faced by African Americans, such as the lynching of Mary Turner, a young pregnant black woman. The statue represents a protest against violent racist groups.

Meta's work flourished in Paris, with the French press dubbing her *"the delicate sculptor of horror."* While in Paris, she met W.E.B. Du Bois, an American sociologist who became a close friend and confidant. He undoubtedly encouraged her in her work. And for Meta, as a black artist, it must have been a true relief that her race and gender did not inhibit the French public's response to her racially themed artworks. This would have been very different in the United States.

Other artists, including Mary Cassatt and Toulouse-Lautrec, recognised her talent and supported her solo exhibition at the Salon de L'Art Nouveau. In 1903, some of her works were exhibited at the Paris Salon. She became quite well known on the Parisian art scene, and her works were displayed in many galleries.

She was born in Philadelphia into a well-to-do family. Her mother owned her own beauty salon, where her clients included upper-class white women; she was also a wigmaker. Her father owned several barbershops. Due to her parents' prominent position in society, she was able to study art, dance, and music, and even learned to ride horses. Her older sister also studied art, and her father encouraged his daughters, as he had a keen interest in the arts. It is said that her grandfather and brother loved sharing horror stories, which may have partially influenced her choice of themes in her art.

Meta married a prominent doctor and psychiatrist who was one of the first black psychiatrists in the United States. Despite becoming a housewife and mother of three, she continued to create art. She was involved with her church, where she also helped organise plays, directing and designing the costumes. Inspired by her faith, she began sculpting traditional biblical scenes.

She is described as a literary sculptor and portraitist, and her work expresses the complexities of life, such as religion, nature, and identity. Here, let me show you some photos of her sculptures—they're impressive, aren't they?

Her work was, and remains, powerful and important. But what is truly a shame is that in 1910 she lost sixteen years of her work in a fire at a warehouse where she stored many of her sculptures and paintings. This was, of course, devastating for her.

She was indeed a special woman who used her art as activism. Although she is now receiving recognition, in her time she was much more encouraged in Paris than in her own country. But I feel that now she is finally being given the justice she deserves for the incredible work she accomplished in the field of art.

But let's get back to Americans in general, they played an important role in Europe. They also brought jazz music to Europe and, let's not forget, they freed Paris from the Germans, both in the First and Second World War. I think it's fair to say that Americans loved Europe and especially Paris. They felt inspired by French art, such as the impressionists and Art Deco.

Let me tell you about several female American artists who came to Paris. Some are more known than others, for example Isadora Duncan and Josephine Baker. Isadora Duncan was a revolutionary figure in the world of dance, at a time of artistic freedom and the cultural revolution. She was born in America and was both a dancer and choreographer, and one of the pioneers of modern dance. Isadora was born in San Francisco in 1877 and loved dancing already when she was a very young child. But she didn't like the constraints of classical ballet and felt attracted to a more expressive and natural form of dance.

She was adventurous and came to Paris in the early 1900s. It was easy for her to be welcomed into the like-minded, avant-garde scene of writers and artists.

In 1902, Loïe Fuller invited Isadora to tour with her. Loïe Fuller was an American dancer specialised in modern dance and theatrical lighting.

She was born in 1862 and had already started performing as a toddler in dance acts. She even toured with Buffalo Bill's touring act when she was nineteen. Looking for serious artistic recognition that she felt she didn't get in America, she came to Europe in 1892. She was one of the first of many American modern dancers to come to Paris, where she received a warm reception.

Loïe was well-loved for her shows where her costume and lighting were the principal elements in her performance, using a lot of fabric in her dresses and different lighting to enhance the effects of her costumes in movement. She designed it all herself.

For thirty years Loïe was in a romantic relationship with Gabrielle Bloch, known professionally as Gab Sorère, who was a French choreographer, visual effects artist, art promoter and filmmaker. Despite initially creating some controversy for openly having a lesbian relationship, they soon were accepted and were able to live a normal life as a couple. Loïe Fuller and Isadora Duncan toured all over Europe where they showed new dance performances using innovative techniques and emphasising natural movement.

Isadora certainly had a turbulent life and had to overcome some terrible losses. She had three children, all born out of wedlock. Sadly, her daughter and son, still young children, drowned when they were in the care of their nanny in 1913, when their car went into the river Seine.

Isadora, naturally, was devastated and after the tragedy she spent a few months in Corfu with her brother and sister. She was close to her family. After this she went for a few weeks to a resort in Italy where she slept with a young Italian sculptor and fell pregnant again.

She gave birth to a son in 1914, but he died shortly after his birth. She was left heartbroken by the loss of three children, but continued to dance, which gave her some solace. However, she was depressed by the deaths of her children which meant that her performing career wasn't as strong as it used to be. The last years of her life she lived a rather scandalous love life and had episodes of public drunkenness, spending her time between Paris and the Mediterranean, apparently leaving debts in several hotels.

Then, in 1927 Isadora herself was involved in a freak car accident in Nice. She was a passenger in a cabriolet type car and her long scarf became entangled in the wheels, which led to her death through strangulation.

Her legacy remains and to this day she inspires dancers and artists with her courage to break free from tradition and taking the path of individual expression. She was, so to speak, reunited with her children at the Père Lachaise Cemetery in Paris."

Jeanette asks rhetorically, *"wouldn't it be fascinating to visit the various cemeteries in Paris, where so many great artists are laid to rest?"*

"Yes, that certainly would be interesting, also because many of the tombstones are amazing works of art, some of them made by artists that Renate and I have already talked about! And what is truly special is that Josephine Baker was one of the very few people to be honoured and included symbolically in the Panthéon in Paris.

Josephine Baker, who many people will have heard about, was mostly known for her dance performances and her singing and acting, but she was so much more than that. There are plenty of images of hers to be found with short hair, sometimes topless and wearing a skirt made of bananas, whilst dancing the Charleston.

Her show was an instant success in Paris and she became the most successful American entertainer in France. She also mingled with quite a few of the great artists that we are discussing during our trip to Paris, for example Hemingway referred to her as *"the most sensational woman anyone ever saw."* He used to spend time with her in the bars, no doubt having deep conversations.

Other artists were inspired by her as well, for example Picasso. And she was the first black woman to star in an important silent movie called *La Sirène des tropiques* in 1927.

Many don't realise that she was part of the French Resistance, gathering information during meetings and parties at embassies and ministries. Charming the socks off those attending and trying to get as much information as she could, in order to pass it onto anti-nazi forces, which were led from London by General Charles de Gaulle.

As a successful entertainer she had the privilege to travel throughout Europe and to visit neutral countries like Portugal. Whilst travelling she carried information about airfields, German troop locations in France, etc., written in invisible ink on her music sheets.

Also, when France was invaded by the Germans, Josephine went to stay in her Château des Milandes in southern France and she allowed people who were working to free France to stay with her and helped them obtain visas. By then she already lived permanently in France.

Later, during the 1950s she became involved in the Civil Rights movement in the United States. One story tells that at some point she went to New York with her husband Jo, but they were refused to reserve a room in no less than thirty-six hotels, clear racial discrimination. But being the strong woman that she was she started writing several articles about the segregation in the United States.

In 1963, she was invited as a speaker during the march on Washington, and gave her speech just before Rev. Martin Luther King gave his famous 'I Have a Dream' speech. She was the only official female speaker and wore her 'Free France' uniform with her medal of the Légion d'honneur.

She spoke about the 'Negro Women for Civil Rights' also mentioning Rosa Parks. Some criticised her saying she was now a French woman and not really connected to Civil Rights issues happening in the United States. Her reaction was *"I have walked into the palaces of kings and queens, and into the houses of presidents and much more. But I could not walk into a hotel in America and get a cup of coffee, and that made me mad. And when I get mad, you know that I open my big mouth. And then look out, 'cause when Josephine opens her mouth, they hear it all over the world"*.

After King's assassination, his widow asked Josephine Baker to replace him as a leader of the Civil Rights Movement, but she declined as she felt her children were too young to lose their mother!"

I didn't know about this to be honest and I also didn't know that she had children. Do you know about that as well, Mario? And you also said she was married?

"Yes, for sure. Josephine Baker had quite a remarkable life. She was actually born as Freda Josephine McDonald Missouri in the United States. Her mother, Carrie was adopted, so little is known about her ancestry. It isn't sure who her father was, but it was fairly sure that he was a white man.

This is also based on the fact that her mother gave birth to her in an exclusively white, female hospital in 1906. It was totally unusual at the time, as black women had their babies at home. Some suggest that her mother had worked for a German family around the time she became pregnant. We can only guess, but apparently Josephine herself believed that her father must have been a white man.

Josephine was first married when she was only thirteen years old, but it was a very unhappy marriage and they divorced soon after. Then, when she was fifteen, she married William Howard Baker. This marriage didn't last either, but at the time she had already started a career as a dancer and she decided to keep his surname. She was married four times in total.

In 1937 she married Jean Lion, a French industrialist and this is when she became a French national. She also started to adopt children. Apparently, she couldn't have children herself and had lost several due to miscarriages.

Josephine ended up adopting eleven children in total. She referred to them as "*The Rainbow Tribe*" as it was important to her to adopt children of different religions and ethnicities. She wanted to show that they could still be brothers and live in peace together.

Towards the end of her life, she performed in a retrospective revue in Paris, called *Josephine à Bobino 1975* to celebrate her fifty-year long career in show business. The show was financed by Prince Rainier of Monaco. He and his wife Princess Grace were friends of Josephine and had helped her when she was in a financially unstable time in her life. The audience at the opening night included Princess Grace, Jacqueline Kennedy Onassis and also stars like Mick Jagger, Liza Minnelli, Shirley Bassey, Diana Ross and Sophia Loren.

Only four days later, Josephine was found in a coma after having suffered a cerebral haemorrhage. She apparently was lying on her bed peacefully, surrounded by newspapers with glowing reviews about her last show. She was taken to hospital, but died at the age of sixty-eight. She will always be remembered and Paris certainly will remember her as well.

There is a Square named after her in Montparnasse, place Joséphine Baker, and although her body remained in Monaco, a symbolic casket with soil from different locations where she had lived was interred with a special ceremony at the Panthéon in Paris. This was in 2021. This means that she was the first black woman honoured to be part of this place of 'great men' of the French Republic. Joséphine Baker always sang... "*J'ai deux amours, mon pays et Paris*" (I have two loves, my country and Paris")."

Jeanette and I both agree that it's very special to hear her story. This important woman, coming from such a humble background, gracing the world with her talent and charm. She probably is the most famous of black woman who came to Paris.

"Yes, I certainly think she was, but there was yet another African American woman that I would like to tell you about. Her name was Loïs Mailou Jones, and she is thought to be the only female African American painter who achieved fame abroad in the 1930s and 40s, and till today, her work is valued by art collectors and can be found in the permanent collections of many important museums all over the world.

She also was a friend of Josephine Baker and is considered to be part of the Harlem Renaissance, a culturally and intellectually flourishing period of African American art, music, but also dance, fashion, literature and even politics, in Manhattan's Harlem. This was during the 1920s and 1930s. She left a large body of work as she produced art till she died at the age of

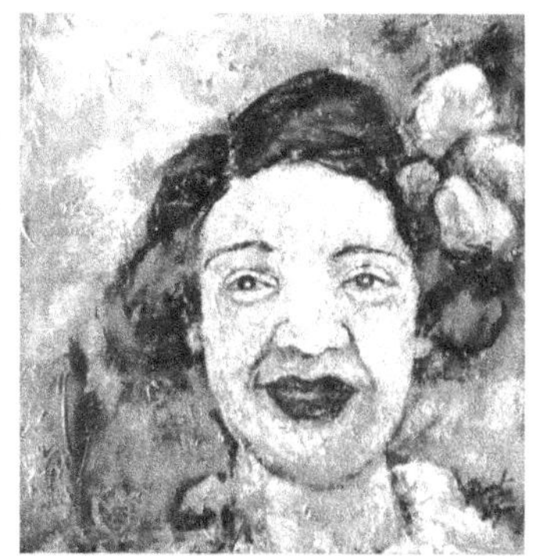

Loïs Mailou Jones

ninety-two. Throughout her career her style did evolve and changed many times and you can see the influence of her extensive travels in her work.

Loïs Mailou was an art teacher at the Howard University in Washington, D.C. She was then offered a fellowship to go and study at the Académie Julian in Paris and during the year she was in Paris, she produced around forty paintings, many of which were created working outside. Some of her paintings were included in the annual Salon de Printemps and at the Société des Artists Français.

Loïs Mailou was really enjoying her time in Paris, moreover as she felt fully accepted, and she could walk, eat and paint wherever she wanted. Something that wasn't the case in the United States with so much racial prejudice at the time. She said "*The people would stand and watch me and say 'mademoiselle, you are so very talented. You are so wonderful.' In other words, the colour of my skin didn't matter in Paris and that was one of the main reasons why I think I was encouraged and began to really think I was talented.*" There is a beautiful book, published in 1952 also containing images of her paintings that she made whilst in France. It's called *Loïs Mailou Jones: Peintures 1937–1951*.

When the Second World War started, Loïs Mailou had to leave Paris and return to Washington D.C. While she was in Paris, she studied with Céline Tabary, a French artist. They became very close friends and Céline came to Washington D.C. with Loïs Mailou. Thanks to Loïs Mailou, Céline was able to get a teaching job at the Howard University.

We know Paris was important to Loïs Mailou because when she was back in the United States, she and Céline Tabary, founded the *Little Paris Group* which they hosted in the studio in the attic of Loïs Mailou's home, in the style of a Parisian salon. Black artists were able to use it to create and exhibit their work.

Céline Tabary, who was a white émigré, submitted the work of Loïs Mailou into various prestigious art competitions where African American artists were not allowed to take part, as Loïs Mailou really wanted to exhibit her art in the States and receive the same recognition she had received in France. When she won a prize, Céline had to secretly mail it to Loïs. Fifty years later the Corcoran Gallery of Art made a public apology to Loïs Mailou during the opening of an exhibition *The World of Loïs Mailou Jones*.

She died when she was ninety-two years old and wanted to be remembered as an American painter with no labels.

Loïs Mailou certainly wasn't the only female African American to come to Paris. I've already mentioned Augusta Savage, but Elizabeth Prophet, who came to Paris in 1922, also was a female black artist, a sculptor. She first settled in Montparnasse, but she had very little money and her time in France apparently was a struggle, moreover because she suffered from anxiety and depression."

We check out some of Elizabeth's statues on our phones and I personally like her style very much. It surprises me that she had a hard time receiving recognition. Perhaps it was because she wasn't extreme or inventive enough? I'm not sure. I also wonder whether there were American female writers in Paris.

"Yes, there were, and I think it is important to mention Natalie Clifford Barney. She was an American writer, but she is known for hosting a literary salon at her home in 20 rue Jacob in Paris for over sixty years. She has been called one of the most intriguing literary hostesses of the previous century. Her salon became a favourite place for many international and French writers. Although many famous writers came to her salon, she worked hard to promote the work of female writers and decided to host L'Académie des Femmes in her salon as well.

Natalie was born into a wealthy family and her mother was an American painter, who helped turn Washington D.C. into a centre of the arts. Her father, who owned Pike's Opera House in Cincinnati in the United States, was an art lover, something he installed in his daughters, Laura and Natalie who both became writers. The girls were educated in the English and French language. Natalie discovered she was a lesbian at a young age and made the choice to openly live her life in that way. She in fact came to Paris with Eva Palmer, her first love relationship.

Already in 1900 Natalie published some love poems, writing in both the English and the French language. She also was a great supporter of feminism and pacifism and was against monogamy which was not always appreciated by her long-term partners. Natalie had many long and short-term relationships, among which was Colette, whom we've already spoken about, and with poet Olive Custance, poet Renée Vivien, writer Duchess Élisabeth de Gramont, Dolly Wilde who was the niece of Oscar Wilde, and painter Romaine Brooks.

During the occupation of the Germans during the Second World War the salon was closed and Natalie lived in Italy with her then partner Romaine Brooks. After the war, she returned to Paris and reopened the salon continuing to inspire young writers. She literally was the inspiration for many novels written by others, for example, *The Well of Loneliness*, considered to be the most famous lesbian novel of the twentieth century, written by English author and poet Radclyffe Hall. She lived a long life as well and died at the age of ninety-two.

I really love bookshops, especially the old ones. So there is one more American lady I would like to point out. Silvia Beach opened a bookshop in Paris in 1919, called Shakespeare & Company. Today we can still find a bookshop bearing that name. It was opened by George Whitman, who gave the bookstore its name in honour of Silvia Beach. It's on 37 rue de la Bûcherie very close to the Seine and right opposite the Notre-Dame Cathedral. And arguably the most famous bookshop in Paris with a very authentic and specific atmosphere that is nowhere else to be found.

Whitman's daughter, who was named after Silvia Beach, now owns the bookshop, which some say is the most famous and certainly worth a visit in Paris.

Silvia Beach, who was born in Baltimore, moved to France with her family when she was still a teenager, as her father became a minister of the American Church of Paris. They lived here for three years and then returned to the United States. Silvia returned to Europe several times, and finally came back to Paris to study French literature.

She then met Adrienne Monnier, the owner of a lending library and bookshop called La Maison des Amis des Livres, in fact I think she was one of the first females to own a bookshop in Paris. Silvia and Adrienne became a couple and stayed together for over thirty-five years.

Silvia dreamed of opening a bookshop similar to La Maison des Amis del Livres in the United States, but it was cheaper to rent a space in Paris. So she opened her own place which soon became one of the best loved places for English literature. At some point she met James Joyce, the Irish novelist and she ended up publishing his novel *Ulysses*. Although he later signed a contract with another publisher, after this Silvia's shop became a favourite for writers of The Lost Generation, but also of many French authors.

Near the end of 1941 she was forced to close the shop and spent six months in a camp for American and British prisoners, but was released again in 1942. Sadly, her shop did not reopen after the war. In 1956 Silvia Beach published a biography about her life as the owner of Shakespeare & Company. She died in Paris in 1962."

I loved listening to the stories of all these women, whilst walking to the space where the work of Tamara de Lempicka is displayed. When we are there, I have to say that it makes my heart sing. I don't really know why I feel so attracted by both Art Nouveau and Art Deco, I always have been, but it's nice to see such an obvious reference to this artistic style in a painting.

We admire her work for a while, and decide to have a drink in a café outside Centre Pompidou. The rain has stopped and we are watching people, a colourful mix of fashionable Parisian men and women and tourists, dressed in comfortable clothes, keen to soak up the atmosphere of Paris. It's a colourful mixture of fashion statements.

I wonder whether fashion is art or, in other words, are fashion designers' artists. I've read somewhere that some museums are recognising that fashion is not only applied art, it also is an artistic gesture. The three of us decide, that for us, fashion designers are artists. The Musée de la Mode de la Ville de Paris in the Palais Galliera is a testimony to this.

Fashion

An art form on its own

On our way out of Centre Pompidou we look for a place to enjoy a drink and perhaps something to eat. We pass the Stravinsky Fountain just outside of the Centre Pompidou. Mario says that there is an interesting link with fashion. I wasn't even aware that Igor Stravinsky lived in France and that he obtained French citizenship as well as United States citizenship.

"Yes, indeed he did. Stravinsky was a key figure in modernist music. His family had an upper-class Polish and Russian background. His father was actually an established bass opera singer, and Stravinsky started taking piano and music lessons from a very young age. Despite disapproval of his family, he married his first cousin, and they had two children. They lived in France from 1920 until 1939 and spent a lot of time in Paris.

At first academics and other composers criticised Stravinsky's avant-garde music, but later his importance was undeniable and he has influenced many composers. He created quite a few compositions in commission of Sergei Diaghilev, the owner of the Ballets Russes.

It was his third ballet for Diaghilev, *Le Sacre du Printemps*, based on Pagan myths that almost caused a riot, because of the music, the costumes and the choreography. Its premiere was in the Théâtre des Champs-Élysées. Many people were booing when they watched the unusual spectacle with colourful, folklore type costumes, modern dance moves and the strange rhythms and dissonance of Stravinsky's music. People were getting up, and many walked out.

Coco Chanel was in the audience. There actually is a movie called Coco Chanel & Igor Stravinsky from 2010 showing this moment, but also explaining about their passionate affair. By the time Coco Chanel met Stravinsky she had already made her fortune and a name for herself in the fashion world. I don't think there are many people who have never heard of Coco Chanel."

I certainly had already as a young child, as my mother's favourite perfume was Chanel 5. And recently I saw a documentary about her called *Coco Chanel Unbuttoned*. They are referring to her as the original influencer whose designs still stand strong today, representing female sensuality, style and power. One interviewee said *"she turns her trade into an art and she turns the art into a multi-million fortune"*.

What a life this woman has led. And yes, her affair with Stravinsky was also mentioned. He came to France with his family, fleeing Russia's revolution. They arrived with nothing and were homeless, but Coco Chanel took the entire family in. So Stravinsky and his wife, who was ill with tuberculosis, and their four children were living in her country house in Garches, just outside of Paris. She even bought him a piano.

I presume you could say that she was a generous woman, and she did support various artists, including Diaghilev, of the ballets Russes and Picasso. I didn't know anything about her past and was fascinated to learn about it. How she came from a very poor family and that her mother died when she was very young, possibly in the presence of her five children. Her father was an alcoholic and a travelling merchant.

Coco Chanel never revealed much about her past. She was good at keeping her life secret, mysterious. And she told people she was raised by an aunt, that her father had dropped her off to seek his fortune in America but that he never came back. In reality, she was taken to an orphanage and raised by catholic nuns. You could say she learned her trade there as they taught her how to sew and do embroidery.

In the documentary they show a window in the convent, the former orphanage, which has a pattern that looks very similar to the famous Coco Chanel two C's logo and it's quite possible that this inspired her later in life. Some also speculate that her famous preference for black and white could have come from living with nuns.

We do know for certain, also thanks to photos of her, that she started working in a garrison, a concentration of army troops that was stationed in a specific location, when she was twenty. She was sent there to work as a seamstress, but ended up dancing and singing in a cabaret. This is where she met Étienne Balsan, a rich cavalry officer. She moved in with him in his chateau near Paris, but she was one of several mistresses. The main mistress was a famous 'horizontal' from the Belle Époque, called Émilienne d'Alençon, who apparently taught Coco how to make a living using her charm.

Coco's two sisters had both died, one as a result of alcohol abuse and the other by suicide. One of her sisters had a son, André Pallasse. Chanel raised the boy as her own, and some even suggest that perhaps he was her real son, as she loved him a lot.

Whilst living in the chateau with Balsan she learned horse-back riding as well, and this is how she met the Englishman Arthur Capel, called 'Boy' by many. She fell in love with him and she became his mistress. There exist quite a few pictures of them together.

In this period Coco Chanel already started to distinguish herself in her style of clothing. She didn't want to dress like a courtesan and started to wear more masculine clothes. Capel then lent her the money to start a hat shop. He clearly saw her potential as a business woman and supported her in this. She later said that she owed him a lot.

Soon she didn't just design hats, but also general women's fashion. Coco wanted women to wear more comfortable outfits and introduced jersey. She became her own brand very early on and modelled her own line of clothing. She even cut her hair and wore trousers!

In 1918 she bought her first property in rue Cambon in Paris and ended up owning five properties in that same street. She understood that money was the key to independence and freedom.

Capel did marry a woman from his own social circle, but Coco remained his mistress. He sadly was killed in a car crash. Coco said that he was the only man in her life she had truly loved and this event marked the start of her black period. She painted the shutters of her country house black and only wore black. But the strong woman she was turned her grief into something positive. This is when she created her famous *la petite robe noire* (little black dress).

Apparently, the original or one of the original dresses she made, is now in a museum and is considered an art object.

She was already famous, and she mingled with many artists and clearly was at the heart of modernism. Normally fashion and perfume were not linked together, but Coco Chanel turned her perfume into part of her fashion. Chanel no.5 was launched in 1921. The number five was special to her. Around this time, she also met the Grand Duke Dmitri Pavlovich who was one of the assassins of Rasputin. He later escaped the Russian Revolution and emigrated to Western Europe. When he came to Paris he was also invited to come and live in Coco Chanel's house, with Stravinsky and his family. He and Coco both liked horse-back riding, and she supported him financially as well. You can see the Russian influence in her fashion designs from that time.

In 1923 Coco met the second Duke of Westminster, Hugh Grosvenor, at a dinner in Monte Carlo and became his mistress. They stayed together for a decade. She was forty years old at the time and was even introduced to the Duke's friend Winston Churchill. She was clearly a workaholic and didn't want to stop working, even though the Duke would have preferred her to spend more time with him. She continued to produce two new clothing lines every year. Thanks to her time with the Duke of Westminster she came into contact with tweed and started using it in her fashion.

The Duke ended up marrying a younger woman and Coco Chanel returned to Paris. She went to live in the Ritz, a famous luxurious hotel.

The 1930s marked a social and political division among the Parisians. She met and started a passionate affair with Paul Iribe, who was very right wing. They even planned to get married. One day he came to visit her in her country house. She was waiting for him, but he then unexpectedly died, he just fell to the floor...right in front of her.

When the Germans came to occupy Paris she fled the city, but she came back when the atmosphere had calmed down. She returned to the Ritz and although it was now occupied by high-ranking German officers, she was able to get a space to live there as well. She actually spent thirty-five years of her life living in the Ritz.

This is when she started a relationship with Hans Günther von Dincklage, also called Spatz, a German officer and secret agent. After the war Coco Chanel was arrested, but released shortly after. She then went to Switzerland where she stayed ten years before returning to France.

She absolutely was a survivor, and she was able to make her comeback in 1954, partially thanks to her success in the United States with famous women, such as Jackie Kennedy, buying and wearing her outfits. And it is certainly special that the House of Chanel still is a success today, bigger than ever actually!

She died in 1971 the day after she told one of her workers..."*I am working tomorrow*". I think we can conclude that, although she was conservative, she was also all about freedom of expression for women. Did you know all this Mario?

"I knew quite a bit of this story, but not everything. Many think that she was the first female designer, but this isn't true. There were quite a few women fashion designers at the time. Such as Madeleine Vionnet, who has now more or less been forgotten, Madame Grès, Jeanne Lanvin, and one of Coco Chanel's biggest rivals, Elsa Schiaparelli, who came from an elite Italian family and was working with different surreal artists to create her fashion. But unlike most of the others, Coco Chanel became famous for her personality. Apparently, Karl Lagerfeld once said, "*Jeanne Lanvin was a great dressmaker, but by the 1920s she was a nice old lady*".

I do think though that it's worth mentioning these other designers because Madeleine Vionnet, for example, also put her stamp on fashion and created the so-called 'bias-cut' dress which helped change women's fashion. This also thanks to her use of fabrics such as satin and crêpe de chine, which were unusual in women's fashion of that time.

There was a man who was a very successful designer as well. His name was Paul Poiret. He was the couturier who freed women from the corset and who was inspired by Fauvist and Cubist artists for his creations. He certainly was a rival of Coco Chanel and knew fame and fortune, but unlike Coco he died in poverty and forgotten.

At the height of his career, he was well-known. Something that Coco didn't like is that he was the first to launch his own perfume before she did. He had founded his own brand in 1903 or 1904, helped by his wife Denise who was his muse. He focused on bright colours and extravagant designs. Poiret managed to attract attention thanks to his loose-fitting clothing and his kimono coat.

There is an interesting illustration by Georges Lepape from 1911, showing a Poiret turban, which became highly fashionable at the time. You can also see the decadence of Art Deco in his fashion. In fact, he is sometimes referred to as *"the father of Art Deco"*. He used to surround himself with artists, but also designers and architects. You could say this was a clever way to develop and promote his work. In his autobiography he stated that he was friends with, among others, Van Dongen, Brâncuşi, Delaunay, Derain, Matisse, Modigliani and Picasso.

Poiret turned his haute couture fashion into a lifestyle as he started to create luxurious furniture and accessories as well, even using fabrics in his interior designs. He also did some interior design work for Isadora Duncan.

In 1911, a photographer called Edward Steichen started to promote fashion as a fine art, taking pictures of dresses designed by Poirot. This is still considered to have been the first modern fashion photography.

Early on in World War I Poirot had to serve in the military. When he returned in 1919 his fashion house was nearly bankrupt. Designers like Coco Chanel were producing more simple clothes that became fashionable. He did go to New York in 1922, where he designed some costumes for Broadway stars. However, he didn't feel at home and returned to Paris, but he became very unpopular. He fell into debt and was left with no support. He had to close his fashion empire and even had to do odd jobs, such as selling drawings in Parisian cafés. He died in Paris in 1944 when he was sixty-five years old and some say that his friend Elsa Schiaparelli paid for his funeral."

That's quite a sad story, isn't it? says Jeanette. *So, all those artist's friends, that were still living in Paris, weren't really there for him either, apart from Schiaparelli?*

"That's presumably the case. In 1927 Elsa Schiaparelli created the house of Schiaparelli in Paris. She started with knitwear but was known for her surreal and eccentric fashion items. She would use different themes in her collections including insects and the human body, and she used very bright colours. For her designs she worked together with Salvador Dali and Jean Cocteau and she was one of the most prominent figures in fashion between the two world wars. Among her clients was the famous actress, Mae West.

She was very imaginative, which quite possibly stems from her childhood years. She came from a rather special family. An aristocratic mother, a father who was an authority on Sanskrit and curator of medieval manuscripts, an uncle who was a well-known astronomer and a cousin of her father was an Egyptologist who discovered the tomb of Nefertari.

Her rich cultural background no doubt inspired her, and she loved adventure and exploring. At some point she went to London and attended a lecture by a man who turned out to be a conman. She fell for his charms and one day after they met, they got engaged and then got married not long after that. Her husband worked as a psychic but they mostly lived from the allowance of Elsa Schiaparelli's wealthy family. Because fortune telling was illegal in the United Kingdom, they were forced to leave and lived in various cities such as Paris, Nice and Monte Carlo ending up in America in 1916.

After their daughter, nicknamed Gogo, was born in 1920, her husband left her and she went to live in New York, where she became close friends with Gabrielle Buffet-Picabia, who introduced her to people like Man Ray and Marcel Duchamp. Elsa felt highly attracted to Dada and Surrealism.

In 1922 she and Gogo returned to Paris, just as some of the other artists she had met in New York. Although she could always rely on the financial support of her family, she wanted to be independent. Through

Nicole Groult she was connected to Paul Poiret, who was the brother of Nicole, and Paul mentored Elsa in her fashion design career, but he also became a dear friend.

Without any technical training in creating patterns, she worked purely from her intuition, often draping fabric directly on a body. Elsa began making her own clothes. In 1927 she created a collection of knitwear. Her first designs did appear in *Vogue*, but her business really took off with her *pour le Sport* collection and after that she became increasingly more successful. Elsa certainly was a rival to Coco Chanel and they must have met during lavish parties thrown by artists and rich people.

By 1939 Elsa Schiaparelli was well known in intellectual circles, but in 1940 she moved to New York after the invasion of the Germans. She returned after the war, but fashion in Paris had changed. Christian Dior was rejecting the pre-war fashion putting a stamp on a new era. Elsa struggled with her business and closed her design house in 1954. This was the same year that Coco Chanel had returned to the Parisian fashion scene.

Elsa also published her autobiography called *Shocking Life* in 1954, and she lived a relaxed retirement dividing her time between her apartment in Paris and her house in Tunisia. She died at the age of eighty-three.

Both Coco Chanel and Elsa Schiaparelli were very interesting personalities which surely added to their success, but I would also like to talk about Jeanne Lanvin. She was a haute couture fashion designer and also had a perfume company called Lanvin Parfums.

Jeanne Lanvin was born in Paris in 1867 and when she was a young teenager, she started working as an apprentice hat maker. She quickly worked her way up and opened her own hat shop in 1885 in rue du Faubourg Saint-Honoré. Her hats were in high demand by Parisian women.

In 1895 she married an Italian nobleman, Count Emilio di Pietro and two years later she became a mother. Her daughter Marguerite di Pietro later became an opera singer and also married a Count. When she was a little girl, Marguerite loved nice clothes and her mother created a unique wardrobe for her. Customers to the hat shop noticed this and wanted to buy her children's clothing for their own children. Jeanne didn't take long to design fashion for those mothers as well. In 1909 she was able to join the prestigious *Chambre Syndicale de la Couture*, which made her a formal couturière.

Only eight years into their marriage Jeanne and di Pietro divorced, but four years later she married a journalist, who worked for the *Les Temps* newspaper. He later became the French consul in Manchester in England. In the 1920s Jeanne Lanvin branched out into home décor, lingerie, but also menswear. Till this day there is a Lanvin shop in Paris, still in the same street, which is quite a legacy don't you think? Jeanne Lanvin died in 1946, but her brand is still well-loved by many."

Good for her, although her story doesn't sound as exciting as that from Coco Chanel and Elsa Schiaparelli, the fact that she is still present in Paris, to me, is great. But you also mentioned Madame Grès. Who was she?

"Madame Grès, also known as Alix, was an important French couturier as well. She's referred to as the Sphinx of Fashion. Although not much is known about her personal life, we do know that she was a workaholic and loved attention to detail. She is especially known for her Greek Goddess type dresses, which she kind of draped around the female body. With her technique she is still inspiring modern-day designers.

She was born into a Jewish, middle-class family and raised in Paris. Her actual name was Germaine Émilie Krebs. She studied sculpting and painting and it was her dream to become an artist. Possibly because of her family insisting to take another path, she moved to fashion design. Like many of these women we are talking about, she too started out as a hatmaker, but soon went on to couture dressmaking. She received her training in Maison Premet, a fashion house.

Germaine opened La Maison Alix, her first couture fashion house, in 1932. She became highly sought after and among her clients were Marlene Dietrich, Paloma Picasso, the Duchess of Windsor, but also

Greta Garbo. You can almost imagine these women in those Greek style dresses.

There is a remarkable story about her as well. She married Serge Czerefkov Gres, a Russian painter in 1942 and this is when she started designing under the name 'Madame Grès'. During the Second World War, the Germans demanded that her designs would be bleaker and more practical, which was the opposite of what her collection was at the time. The wives of German officers wanted her to design dresses for them, despite the fact that she was Jewish, but Germaine refused to do so. And, apparently one of her gowns from this period had two small Stars of David sewed on the inside. She continued to create garments which had the colours of the French flag in them. Not surprisingly she was ordered to close her fashion house by the German forces. She then fled Paris and went to the Pyrenees. As soon as the city was liberated, she returned and reopened her fashion house.

She continued her fashion career till she was in her eighties, which again, is rather remarkable. When she retired from actively working in her fashion house it was taken over by Bernard Tapie and later Jacques Esterel, but it was badly managed and it went bankrupt. When the assets of the house were liquidated, they were sold to a Japanese company.

Germaine lived the rest of her life in poverty, but thanks to friends like Hubert Givenchy, a French aristocrat and fashion designer, and also thanks to Yves Saint Laurent and Pierre Cardin she was able to continue to live in Paris, where she still created dresses for friends. Her final dress was designed on commission by Givenchy, I believe this was in 1989.

She died in a retirement home near Toulon in France in 1993, but her daughter Anne kept that secret for a year as she forged her mother's handwriting in documents. It was quite the scandal!"

Gosh, I can believe that. Mario you also mentioned that Poiret had a sister, Nicole Groult? Was she also a fashion designer?

"Yes, but I get the impression that not many people know about her. Yet it is interesting to mention her, as she was the one who was known for promoting *la garçonne*, a youthful, boyish fashion style. She was also the, more or less, secret partner of painter Marie Laurencin for over forty years.

Nicole was born in Paris and the sister of Paul Poiret. It obviously ran in the family as she also became a fashion designer and a theatre costume designer. Some people might recognise the name Groult as she was the mother of two feminist writers, Benoîte Groult and Flora Groult. Nicole married André Groult, a decorator, when she was only twenty years old, and they had the two daughters.

In 1911, she became friends with the painter Marie Laurencin, the lover of Apollinaire, who introduced her to the art scene. Marie Laurencin even became Benoîte's godmother and André Groult produced wallpapers with designs by Marie, so I guess they were all pretty close friends.

Then, during the First World War, André Groult was sent to the front, and Marie, who had by then married German painter Otto von Watjen, had to flee to Spain, where she collaborated with Picabia's dada art and literary magazine *391*.

Nicole Groult started creating dresses for friends, but after the war she opened a couture house in Paris. Being an emancipated woman, but also extravagant and inventive, she soon made a success of her fashion house. We can certainly say that Nicole Groult, fought for women's liberation and contributed to the reason why the 'S' silhouette, created by the corset, fell out of fashion. Nearing the end of her life, Nicole Groult suffered from Alzheimer's disease.

I guess it's interesting to mention Marie Laurencin in this chapter about fashion as she too designed theatre costumes. But she was of course best known as a cubist painter and because of her relationship with Apollinaire. Also interesting, I feel, is that she was commissioned a portrait painting by Coco Chanel. I don't think this painting is in the Centre Pompidou, I believe it's in the Musée de l'Orangerie.

Maybe we should pay and go back to the Centre Pompidou to the Musée national d'Art moderne. We will be able to see some art of Marie Laurencin there as well, and I can tell you something about her on our way there."

Oh, that would be great. I do know her work, it's not so much to my taste, mostly because of her use of very soft and pastel colours, but I would love to see her art in person.

"Yes, to me it's interesting that she studied porcelain painting in Sèvres, but later she returned to Paris, where she was born, and studied art at Académie Humbert. It was here she started to use oils. But porcelain painting must be a quite delicate job, so perhaps that stayed with her in her later painting career and style. As to me it does look somewhat delicate. Her work was considered very naive, childish, full of fairies and flowers. We know that she was fascinated by the dolls in her childhood as well and she painted mostly women and animals. Her paintings always have a dreamlike feel to it, don't you think?

One day Georges Braque found a drawing in a room and went to Moulin de la Galette in Montmartre. He showed it to his friends and Marie was there as well. She told him it was hers, upon which he told her that she was very talented. She and Braque went to see many exhibitions of impressionist painters and she also received advice from Matisse.

She was part of the circle of Picasso and met artists like Picabia and Delaunay. In those times it must have been easy to meet fellow artists because they were so concentrated in certain districts of Paris. She participated in exhibitions in Salon des Indépendants, but also in the Salon d'Automne and the first cubist exhibition in Barcelona, in Galerías Dalmau.

Marie Laurencin was with Apollinaire for six years and even wrote a poem for him to publish. She said "*poets know the whole truth and if they don't, they invent it*". She is known for having had relationships both with men and women, I guess you can see her love for women in her work.

After their exile to Spain and having lived in Germany for a while she was able to return to Paris after her divorce in 1920. She gained financial success with her artwork till the 1930s economic depression started. Something that obviously affected quite a few artists. I guess she was lucky to have found a job as an art instructor at a private school.

She lived in Paris till she died in 1956. Marie's works are in collections of important museums in France, but there is one museum in Nagano,

Japan that exclusively collects her paintings. It's called Musée Marie Laurencin.

She did create an interesting painting called *Apollinaire et ses amis* in 1909. In the painting we can see Gertrude Stein, Fernande Olivier, Apollinaire, Picasso and the poets Marguerite Gillot and Maurice Cremnitz and in the foreground, she painted herself. The painting was bought by Gertrude Stein, but I've read that it's now part of the collection of the Musée national d'Art Moderne in Centre Pompidou. Let's see whether we can find it.

Surrealism and Abstract Art

In turbulent times

With Marie Laurencin we are back to painting and continue our visit to the museum in Centre Pompidou. I feel that both for abstract and surreal art you have to develop a taste. Knowing the story behind the final piece of art can be the intriguing part viewers need, in order to love or perhaps strongly dislike a work of art. However, Mario, Jeanette and I love the work of Marc Chagall. And his story is also quite remarkable, especially how his wife Bella Rosenfeld played such an important part in his art. Is it true Mario that Chagall is considered to be the father of Surrealism?

"Yes, I've heard that as well, but he never referred to himself as belonging to any specific art movement and in a sense, you can see several styles in his work, such as Fauvism, Symbolism, Cubism, but of course also Surrealism. Chagall was born in 1887 in Vitebsk, which today is Belarus.

He created art in many formats, not just painting, but also book illustrations, ceramics, stained glass and tapestries. Early on in his art journey he used a mixture of modern art, inspired by both Jewish and Eastern European folk art. And he became known for his rich use of colours and for the dreamy like scenes in his art.

He was the eldest of nine children, born into a humble family with a hard-working father who did heavy work like carrying barrels at a herring merchant. His mother sold groceries from their home, and he refers to his early home as a place where there was always 'buttered bread'.

At that time Jewish children were not allowed to go to a regular school or university, but his mother paid a headmaster to let him attend anyway. At school he saw another boy making a drawing. He was fascinated as where he grew up there was no art in his home so he had never heard of it. He asked the boy how he learned how to draw and was told "*just go to the library and copy the images*". This is what he did, and he loved it. He then told his mother "*I want to become an artist*".

In 1906 the young Chagall was offered free classes by Yehuda Pen, a realist artist who conducted art classes in Vitebsk and already as a young man, Chagall's art career took off. He had many exhibitions throughout his life, too many to mention here, but his artwork always reflects some of his childhood memories. He later said this himself as he published an open letter when he was fifty-seven years old. He wrote "*To My City Vitebsk.... I did not live with you, but I didn't have one single painting that didn't breathe with your spirit and reflection*". Also good to know is that one of the artists that inspired him early on was Paul Gauguin.

Chagall studied and stayed in Saint Petersburg until 1910, but he often went back to Vitebsk where he met his future wife, Bella Rosenfeld. She wasn't his first love, but when he saw her, it was love at first sight. In his biography *My Life* he described meeting her with the following words... "*Her silence is mine, her eyes mine. It is as if she knows everything about my childhood, my present, my future, as if she can see right through me.*"

Bella was a writer and was also born in Vitebsk. Her family were jewellers, and it took Chagall some convincing that he would be able to look after their daughter. Bella later wrote about their meeting "*When you did catch a glimpse of his eyes, they were as blue as if they'd fallen straight out of the sky. They were strange eyes ... long, almond-shaped ... and each seemed to sail along by itself, like a little boat.*" Bella and Chagall certainly were on the same wave-length.

Chagall came to Paris in 1910 as he wanted to further develop his art style. He moved into artist's residence La Ruche in Montparnasse where he met a lot of other artists, including Modigliani and Chaïm Soutine.

He also became friends with Robert Delaunay and Apollinaire. Chagall was only twenty-three years old at the time, but it was an important time for him to experience freedom in this city of art and light.

Cubism was becoming increasingly popular by painters and you can see in his work that he was inspired by it as well. However, he always added his exceptional use of colours, his poetic images and even the use of humour in his work, which kind of explains why he was at first mostly appreciated by poets such as Apollinaire and Cendrars.

There were many foreign artists during his first period in Paris. Many enjoyed going out, living a life of partying, but Chagall worked day and night, sleeping only a few hours. He once said "*My homeland exists only in my soul*". He painted Jewish motifs and scenes from his memories of his home town, Russian landscapes with characters from his childhood, but then he mixed them with Parisian scenes, for example, the Eiffel Tower. He missed his family, the riches of Slavic folklore and Bella. Apparently thinking about her all the time.

In 1914 he went to Berlin on invitation from an art dealer, with the intention to travel to Belarus afterwards, marry Bella and return to Paris with her. His exhibition in Berlin was a big success and the German critics loved his work.

When he had returned to Vitebsk, the First World War had broken out and the Russian border was closed. One year later Bella and Chagall married and in 1916 their only child, Ida, was born.

Bella was hugely important in Chagall's work, as he once said *"in painting there is only one colour that gives meaning, and that is love"*. He was a passionate man, faithful. She was always present in his work; he painted hardly anything else. She was his muse, his accomplice, and his wife, let's say it was pure love. It is very difficult to find an artist who has dedicated so much talent in his work to a woman.

In 1923 they moved back to Paris to develop his art further. Whilst waiting for their visas, Chagall wrote his autobiography *My Life*. On their way back to Paris, he stopped in Berlin to pick up his paintings from the exhibition ten years earlier, but they were all gone. With all his early artworks lost, he started painting from his memories in Vitebsk again. He also started creating illustrations for books.

Already an achieved artist, his first exhibition took place in New York with hundreds of his artworks. He didn't attend the opening though, he stayed in France, continuing painting. They also travelled to nearby countries and to regions like the Côte d'Azur. He later wrote that there, in the south of France, he saw the lush nature, with all the greenness, that he had never seen in his life. He loved going there taking his sketchbook to create memories. But he went to Holland, Italy, Spain and the Middle East as well.

When Hitler had gained power in Germany modernist art was immediately abolished and many thousands of artworks from museums in Germany were confiscated. Chagall's art, after having been praised many years before, was now mocked.

After Germany had occupied France, at first the Chagalls, who were living in Vichy, weren't really aware of the seriousness of the situation. And it wasn't until their daughter Ida urged them to act fast that they tried to leave France. They were saved by having Chagall's name added to the list of prominent artists whose lives were in danger and who would get a forged visa for the United States. Chagall, Bella, and Ida and her husband managed to flee France in 1941. They were also able to take quite a few paintings with them.

In the United States he found out that he already was known internationally, he had become a celebrity almost without wanting to. They settled in New York which was of course a hotspot for many artists who had fled Europe during the war, and he loved spending time in museums. During this time, he also met André Breton and Piet Mondrian.

Pierre Matisse, the son of Henri Matisse became his agent and organised exhibitions for Chagall both in New York and Chicago in 1941.

He even worked on the décor for Aleko, a ballet commissioned by choreographer Léonide Massine. To save costs they worked in Mexico which hugely inspired Chagall as he could relate to the colourful art of the Mexican people.

Sadly, in 1944, Bella was infected by streptococcus and as there were restrictions on penicillin due to the war, the Mercy General Hospital didn't have any. She died when she was only fifty-five years old. Following this we can only imagine his grief. He did stop painting for many months but later he created artworks to preserve Bella's memory. After her death, her influence on him would continue; it was like love, influence and inspiration beyond her death.

There is a really interesting painting that he painted, some years after her death called *Les Amoureux de Vence* from 1957. In the painting you can almost see that she is no longer there, but she is in his work, and in her face, which is very close to him, to me it seems that she is probably not alive, it seems as if only her soul is there.

Bella has appeared in many of his paintings where you always see lovers escaping through a window, floating. Bella is the eternal woman dressed as a bride with her lover, and in a way, which is quite spiritual, as if he wanted to give Bella a sacred dimension.

Despite two other women being in his life after her, Bella will always be present. Let's say that she lives beyond her death.

It's in a sense very appropriate for Chagall's work in general, as he always liked to include religious symbolism. He did try to create an almost universal message, using both Jewish (although he wasn't a practising Jew) and Christian themes. We also mustn't forget that some major contributions in art are his stained glass works in cathedrals in France, the United States, Israel and Germany.

After Bella's death he moved in with his daughter and her husband but soon he started a relationship with Virginia Haggard, who was a great-niece of the famous writer Henry Rider Haggard. They stayed together for seven years.

By 1946, Chagall's work was celebrated by many and a large exhibition of forty years of his work was shown in the Museum of Modern Art in New York. After the war, he went back to France and in 1947 he was present at the exhibition of his art at the Musée National d'Art Moderne, where we now are. Although at the time it was housed in Palais de Tokyo. Back in France he went to live on the Côte d'Azur which had become a favourite spot for many artists, like Matisse and Picasso.

Virginia Haggard and Chagall broke up in 1952 and his daughter Ida felt her father might be a bit lonely and introduced him to Vava

Brodsky, who came from a similar background. First, she became his secretary, but they soon became a couple and got married. They stayed together till the end of Chagall's life in 1985.

Now I do think it is important to mention that Chagall painted the ceiling of Opera Garnier in 1963. Initially it created controversy as some didn't feel it was correct that a Russian man decorated a French national monument. It took him a year to complete the work. He was already seventy-seven years old by then.

When revealing the ceiling to the public, the press unanimously agreed that the work was a great contribution to French culture. Chagall gave a speech, explaining what he had painted and why. "*Up there in my painting I wanted to reflect, like a mirror in a bouquet, the dreams and creations of the singers and musicians, to recall the movement of the colourfully attired audience below, and to honour the great opera and ballet composers... Now I offer this work as a gift of gratitude to France and her École de Paris, without which there would be no colour and no freedom*"."

What a great artist and I think also a nice man. I like his story, but I'm intrigued about Surrealism. I'm personally more a fan of surreal art than abstract art, but I realise that's a personal thing. So, can you tell us a bit more about the surrealist movement?

"When we talk about Surrealism, we have to talk about André Breton as he co-founded the surrealist movement, and published the *Manifeste du surréalisme* in 1924. His description of Surrealism was something in the lines of "*Psychic automatism in its pure state, by which one proposes to express the actual functioning of thought in the absence of any control exercised by reason, exempt from any aesthetic or moral concern*". In other words, breaking the bounds of reality, uncovering the philosophy behind the surrealist movement, advocating for an art form that breaks from the constraints of the rational mind.

Well, we can ponder that for a moment whilst we look for the re-creation of part of his apartment, a 'wall', in the museum. It is a collection of two hundred and fifty-five artworks and other objects from

Breton's apartment on rue Fontaine, that were placed on the wall behind his desk and is conserved as an artwork in the Centre Pompidou."

Mario, I came across the work of Dutch artist Hieronymus Bosch, who lived from 1450 to 1516.To me it looks very surreal. Would it be correct to suggest that he inspired later surrealist artists?

"Personally, I believe this is the case and I recall Breton mentioning Bosch as well. Breton was a French writer and poet who also became the leader of the surrealist movement. He was born in Normandy in France. His father was a policeman and his mother a seamstress, so he came from a humble background. He was a well-known author, but he also became an art collector and ended up owning over five thousand objects, like modern art, photographs, books and much more, including popular and oceanic art. He was considered an important figure in French literature and art in the twentieth-century.

Rather curious to me is that as a young man he went to medical school, but he didn't finish because he was enlisted compulsorily for the First World War and worked in a neurological unit in Nantes.

Breton married Simone Kahn in 1921 and they lived in 42 rue Fontaine in Paris till their divorce in 1931. Simone was also seriously interested in collecting art objects and after divorcing Breton she continued collecting and supporting artists. She had formed close friendships with people like Picabia and Man Ray. Later on, she became a gallerist and opened two galleries in Paris, showcasing the work of many famous and upcoming artists.

Breton was first associated with the Dada movement and worked together with Tristan Tzara. Then, in 1929 he published the *Second manifeste du surréalisme*. He wasn't loved by everybody, as in this manifesto he wrote "*The simplest surrealist act consists, with revolvers in hand, of descending into the street and shooting at random, as much as possible, into the crowd*", which many surrealist artists were not happy about. Some of them published a number of pamphlets against Breton. Some felt insulted by him or didn't agree with his leadership. But he continued to be revered and played a major role in the international art world.

Breton travelled to Mexico on a cultural commission from the French government in 1938 to attend a conference about Surrealism. An interesting fact is that he stated that he got lost in Mexico City as there was no one to pick him up from the airport and apparently, he said *"I don't know why I came here... Mexico is the most surrealist country in the world."*

Nonetheless, this visit allowed him to meet Frida Kahlo and her husband Diego Rivera, a prominent Mexican painter who, through his work, inspired the mural movement in Mexico, but also internationally. Breton also met Leon Trotsky, a Marxist and Leninist prominent Russian politic figure. Together they wrote *Manifesto for an Independent Revolutionary Art*, which was published under the name of Rivera and Breton. With this manifesto they were calling for complete freedom of art, which was necessary as at the time, with the upcoming restrictions of the German invasion, art became increasingly restricted. Breton was certainly politically involved and apparently quite a few surrealist artists were considered communists.

In 1934 he met Jacqueline Lamba, a surrealist painter, in Café de la Place Blanche. Jacqueline was born in Paris and already as a little girl she, her mother and her sister visited the Louvre. She was well-read and opiniated. Before meeting Breton, she had already read some of his books and had become fascinated by his words, rather than by him as a person. She felt he was saying things that she was thinking.

The second time they met was at the Coliseum at *Duque's Dancing* event, in rue Rochechouart, where she performed as a nude underwater dancer. Breton referred to this first meeting in his book *L'Amour Fou*. He described Jacqueline as a *"scandalously beautiful"* woman. Three months after their meeting they got married, and Giacometti was their best man.

Jacqueline Lamba had studied at the École de L'Union Central des Arts Decoratifs and at first, she worked as a textile and paper designer. Later she became a painter. She also was politically active and joined the French communist party, so it is no surprise to me that she and Breton got on. He wrote about her quite regularly in his poetry. In 1935 their daughter Aube was born. She later became an artist herself.

At the start of the Second World War Breton was part of the medical unit of the French Army again, but at some point, his writings were banned and he and Jacqueline were wanted by the nazis. Luckily, they were able to escape with Aube. They lived in New York City for a few years and Breton organised an important surrealist exhibition at Yale University. Jacqueline was close friends with Dora Maar and a letter from her to Dora explains a lot about her situation in exile.

Breton and Jacqueline did create some works together, for example *Le petit mimétique*, a collage of an insect, dry leaves, paper and cellophane. I believe this is part of the Breton collection in the museum, so we can check that out.

He was pretty much obsessed with Jacqueline, but I guess she found him hard to handle as she left him several times, even leaving their daughter with him, each time to return to try to recover the relationship. An example is when she left him in 1939 and went to stay with Picasso and Dora Maar. Some suggest that a work by Picasso where he painted two women watching some fishermen is based on this stay. It's called *Pêche de nuit à Antibes.* I believe that it's in a museum in New York. It's quite a large painting.

Jacqueline Lamba and Breton separated in 1943 as she felt overshadowed by her husband, it was as if she didn't exist and was either referred to as 'the woman who inspired Breton', or as 'Breton's wife'. I've read somewhere that after her divorce, Jacqueline and Aube stayed for around seven months in Mexico, invited by Frida Kahlo and Diego. She had become friends with Frida as they both understood their struggle to be acknowledged for their own artistic identity whilst living with famous men who, I imagine, weren't easy to live with.

Some suggest that Jacqueline and Frida even had an affair, but I'm not too sure whether this is correct. Frida Kahlo did create a painting about Jacqueline in 1943. The painting is called *La novia que se espanta de ver la vida abierta* with Jacqueline shown as a small figure behind large fruits that apparently suggest the shapes of both the female and male intimate parts.

Jacqueline Lamba was part of the surrealist movement till 1947 and also exhibited at the Art of This Century gallery in New York. After breaking up with Breton, she met and later married the American sculptor, David Hare with whom she had a son, called Merlin. They were living in Connecticut and even exhibited together. Hare was known to have many affairs and also used drugs. Eventually, they divorced in 1954 and Jacqueline returned to Paris. Hare was financially supporting her for the next forty-two years.

Her painting style over the years had evolved from Surrealism to expressionist landscapes to cityscapes that were very detailed, but at the same time softer, with gentle strokes. She painted till the end of her life despite suffering from Alzheimer's disease and a stroke. She died in 1993. In a sense I feel it is important to talk about her, and give her some justice, as despite her efforts and a great body of work, she is not acknowledged like her female contemporaries Frida Kahlo, Dora Maar and Claude Cahun and is usually only referred to as the muse and second wife of Breton.

And there is another very influential surrealist writer, a woman, who has more or less been forgotten and, so to speak, 'lives in the shadow of Breton's fame', much like Jacqueline Lamba. Her name is Lise Deharme. She was born in Paris as Anne-Marie Hirtz into a well-off family. Her father was a quite famous doctor.

In 1927 she married Paul Deharme, who was a radio pioneer. He was working with a French surrealist poet, called Robert Desnos. Lise was fascinated with Surrealism and published her first book under the name Lisa Hirtz in 1928. It is called *Il était une petite pie* (There was a little magpie) and it includes eight illustrations by Joan Miró, a Catalan abstract and surrealist painter.

Miró who is of course world famous, joined the Surrealist group in 1924. His work fitted in very well, with his symbolism and poetic style of depicting things. It was in line with the sort of dreamlike automatism that was something the surrealist group was supporting, in other words creating art without a conscious intention.

Whilst he lived in Paris, Miró was influenced by the surrealist artists he met, which you can clearly see in his work. Although Miró himself didn't want to be seen as part of a specific movement, André Breton once described him as *"the most surrealist of us all."*

But we were talking about Lise Deharme. Sorry to get side tracked, but there are so many interesting figures during this time, that I keep being reminded of people I should perhaps tell you about. But again. I cannot name them all. Nevertheless, Lise Deharme deserves a mention as she was only known as the muse and the impossible love of André Breton. But she was much more than just part of a failed love story. At the time in Paris, she was well-known as the organiser of surrealist salons.

In 1933 she published and edited *Le Phare de Neuilly*, a surrealist magazine with political and subversive articles, among which were writings about the socio-political situation in the early 1930s.

Later Lise created a book in collaboration with Claude Cahun, called *Le Cœur de Pic*. She subsequently became known as 'La Dame de Pique' (The Queen of Spades). She met many surrealist artists, including Man Ray, who took a photo of her in which she is shown as the Queen of Spades."

I'm glad to get to know these, in my opinion, intriguing women Mario. So did Breton marry again as well? And also, who is Claude Cahun?

"I will tell you later about Claude Cahun, but yes, he did. Whilst in New York Breton met Elisa Bindhoff, she was from Chile. She also was an artist and a writer, but a very good pianist as well. She was married to a Chilean politician and had a daughter who sadly drowned in 1943 during a boat trip. Elisa tried to take her own life, but a friend came to New York to support her. That same year she met Breton in a restaurant and they felt attracted to each other. In his book *Arcane 17* Breton writes about the death of Elisa's daughter. They married in 1945 and moved back to Paris in 1946.

Breton died in 1966, but Elisa continued to be active in the surrealist movement. She didn't create a lot of work and didn't exhibit her work very often. She is therefore not so well known. However, an American artist who was active in Paris in the 1950s once said about her *"Elisa*

Breton is the most remarkable woman in the group... a marvellous woman, who contributed enormously to the evolution of Surrealism".

After Breton's death, Elisa and Aube tried to establish a surrealist foundation to protect his large collection, but this didn't work out and eventually it was auctioned off. And right now, we are standing in front of the wall of his apartment. Breton was buried in Cimetière des Batignolles in Paris.

Like him or not, he was a man who will continue to inspire people. There is so much more to find out about him, but I think we should mention a few more amazing artists such as Frida Kahlo, Dora Maar and Claude Cahun and their association with the surrealist movement."

Watching this wall is rather special and after what you've just told us, it certainly is more meaningful. I have to say though, interesting as he is, I wouldn't have liked to meet Breton. Learning about him makes me think that he's not the type of guy I would have got on with.

"Let's talk a bit more about the artist Dora Maar. I've already told you about her as one of Picasso's women, but she was not only a really significant photographer but also a painter. Unfortunately, she is largely unknown due to being the muse of Picasso. I say unfortunately because this has somewhat obscured her own work.

To me she was a very important surrealist photographer who also used to hang out with the great photographers of the time, and was closely associated with the works of Brassaï, Cartier-Bresson, and Man Ray, yet she was not really appreciated. Dora Maar was an artist who published in fashion magazines and frequented the surrealist movement. It must be said that the first major exhibition of her work was at the Residencia de Estudiantes in Spain, 1997, which was at the end of her life. So she wasn't given recognition until then, until her death, really.

Her real name was Henrietta Theodora Markovich. Her father was an architect. Throughout her childhood, they lived in Argentina until the twenties when they came to France, to Paris. She was a very beautiful woman; it was difficult to determine the colour of her eyes. It was one of the characteristics and important aspects of her beauty; they were green, blue, brown, depending on the light.

Dora did become quite well-known in the world of fashion photography and advertising cosmetics and she did a lot of photomontages, which gave her images a certain charm, a dreamy impression. She also documented the misery of Barcelona at the time, as well as the suburbs of Paris, whilst publishing in important magazines.

In 1930, she met Brassaï in Montparnasse, and they shared a studio. Later on, she supported Man Ray. She joined the surrealist group, but this group was also profoundly sexist, meaning it was a movement dominated by men and with very special personalities, such as Breton.

Dora Maar also began to have political commitments; she was a progressive feminist who joined the 'October group' with the poet Jacques Prevert and others. She was deeply anti-fascist. I forgot to mention that around 1923, she attended various academies, including Academie Julien, which was important in the world of painting and culture. This is where she met Cartier-Bresson, as we've already talked about, one of the important photographers of that time.

After Picasso had left her, she began to isolate herself in a certain mysticism and moved away from Paris. Her work changed as she was now painting landscapes and taking photographs in the countryside."

It's interesting how many of these artists knew each other. We know that she became friends with Frida Kahlo who only visited Paris for a short period. So was Frida a surrealist as well?

"Wassily Kandinsky, who saw Frida Kahlo's work during a Mexican art exhibition, said that she was very charming and that her art had a strong surrealist tone. She is considered to be a surrealist artist by many, which I understand as she uses symbolism in her storytelling art.

Frida Kahlo was invited to participate in an exhibition in Paris by André Breton who had seen her work during his trip to Mexico. They included eighteen of her paintings which had previously been shown in an exhibition in New York. She wasn't happy at all. When she arrived in Paris, she saw it was a group exhibition of Mexican art, she had expected it to be a solo exhibition. Also, Breton was supposed to have picked up her paintings from the customs office which he hadn't done.

While she was in Paris Frida got sick and was able to stay for a while at the house of Marcel Duchamp. She wrote a letter to her friend Nickolas Muray in New York, saying that she felt Breton was a cockroach. She actually wrote that she didn't like most of the surreal artists as they were insulting, gossiped a lot and there were a lot of conflicts happening. She wrote that Duchamp was the only one of the artists who had his feet on the ground and his brain in the right place."

How interesting Mario, I remember you telling me that Frida Kahlo didn't like Paris and the artists scene there very much. Nowadays I think most people have heard of her as she has become a real icon and is even highly fashionable at the moment. She is painted by many, including me. But do you know more about that letter?

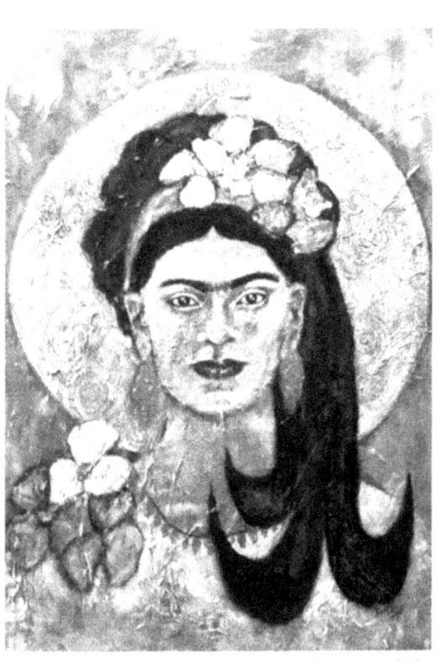

Frida Kahlo

"I don't think we need to talk extensively about Frida Kahlo as her story, which is indeed very interesting, is well known. But she has artwork in the Centre Pompidou, in fact a rather well-known painting called *El marco*. Perhaps we can take a look at it.

About the letter, yes apparently, she wrote something along the lines that the surrealist artists she had met made her feel sick, with their intellectual pretences sitting in cafés for hours, talking about art and culture, revolution and thinking of themselves as the gods of the world.

There was another fascinating surreal artist in Paris. She was known as Claude Cahun, but her real name was Lucy Schwob. She was a French photographer, writer and sculptor, a surrealist. Although she is referred to as a woman, she claimed she was 'gender fluid and said "*Neuter is the only gender that always suits me*" and she is well-known for challenging the strict gender roles with her androgynous appearance.

She started experimenting with self-portraits when she was eighteen years old and is known for having created many portraits throughout her career, in which she poses as all sorts of different figures, for example, a vampire, an angel, a dandy, and a doll.

In the beginning of the 1920s Claude Cahun settled in Paris with her partner Suzanne Malherbe, who used the pseudonym, Marcel Moore. They stayed together for the rest of their lives, but they curiously also became step-sisters in 1917 when Claude's father, who was divorced and Marcel Moore's mother, who was widowed, married. They published articles and novels and also worked on sculptures, collages and photomontages together. They liked using mirrors and some of Claude Cahun's portraits show her with her head shaven, without her body and looking the viewer in the eye. You could say that she had a unique way of showing herself. Claude and Marcel also started hosting artists' salons at their home.

In the Second World War Claude was active as a resistance worker and also founded *Contre Attaque*, which was a union of communist writers, among whom was Breton. An example of Claude Cahun's writings is *Heroines*, which is a collection of monologues of fairy tale style female characters which are compared, in a witty way, to contemporary women of her time.

At a later stage of her career, she also participated in various surrealist exhibitions, including in London and Paris. Thanks to her writings, photographs and other artistic endeavours she was, and still is, internationally acknowledged. And you could say also very much appreciated by fellow artists, such as Breton, who called her *"one of the most curious spirits of our time"* and more recently, David Bowie who, in 2007 created a multi-media exhibition of her work in New York.

He said *"You could call Cahun transgressive or you could call her a cross-dressing Man Ray with surrealist tendencies. I find this work really quite mad, in the nicest way. Outside of France and the UK she has not had the kind of recognition that, as a founding follower, friend and worker of the original surrealist movement, she surely deserves.*" That's not a surprise to me, but yet pretty special."

We are walking through the museum and are now viewing one of Wassily Kandinsky's works. A big name in the art world and seen as one of the pioneers in abstract art in the western world. I personally very much like some of his earlier artworks, for example *Couple on horse back*, *Blue mountain* and some of the paintings he did in Munich in Germany, but the more abstract works don't do much for me, although I can appreciate them. I know that many love his work and that's fair enough. It's still interesting to know a bit more about him.

"Yes, I like his work and how he became such an established artist and art theorist, considering that he only began studying art, attending life-drawing classes and learning how to sketch anatomy when he was thirty years old. Although he had studied art in Odessa, he actually was born in Moscow. He later studied law and economics at the University of Moscow and was successful in his profession.

He went to live in Munich in 1896 where he studied art at the Academy of Fine Arts, but after the outbreak of the First World War he returned to Moscow, this was in 1914. He went to Germany again in 1920 and started teaching art and architecture at the Bauhaus school from 1922 till the nazis closed it in 1933. He moved to France, became a French citizen and stayed in France for the rest of his life and this is where he created his most prominent art.

He once said that he remembered feeling stimulated by colour when he was a small child. He also loved psychology and felt that painting was like composing music; he said "*Colour is the keyboard, the eyes are the harmony, the soul is the piano with many strings. The artist is the hand which plays, touching one key or another, to cause vibrations in the soul*".

For Kandinsky to go from his earlier style to abstract was an evolution of his artistic experiences and his thought process in which he felt a spiritual desire to find inner beauty. Although some say that one day, when he got home, one of his paintings was hanging upside down and this created in him the interest in abstraction.

He usually painted landscapes, and already in his earlier works we can see a lot of colour. They certainly would fall in the Fauvism category and you can already notice a tendency towards more abstract work. For example, in his *Blue Mountain* from 1909.

In 1902 he met Gabriele Münter who came to his summer painting classes in the Alps, south of Munich. She was born in Berlin and was eleven years younger than Kandinsky. She was twenty-five years old at the time and had already lived in, and travelled through America for a period of two years. At the time they met Kandinsky was married with Anna Chemyakina, which was a cousin on his father's side, who was actually six years older than him.

Gabriele and Kandinsky at first were kindred spirits and developed a friendship, this then grew into a love relationship. Even though Kandinsky was married, they got engaged in 1903, but it was a secretive relationship. This was the time when Kandinsky started painting more post impressionistic and there are two rather beautiful portraits, he created of Gabriele."

We take a moment to look at Gabriele Münter's work on our mobiles and I have to say, I really like it. Her use of strong colours in many of her artworks, but also the strong lines and yet simple compositions that tell a story.

"Yes, it's nice work. She used to create her art from life scenes. In the summer of 1906, they stayed in Paris for a while, although Kandinsky wanted to leave as he felt out of place, but Gabriele wanted to stay. She enrolled in an art course and they say it was here that she found her unique style. Gabriele and Kandinsky stayed together for five years even though he was still married. They returned to Germany in 1908 which is where Kandinsky started painting abstract. They even bought a house together where they could live without being secretive about it.

Finally, Kandisky divorced his wife Anna, this was in 1911. When the first World War broke out, he and Gabriele went to Switzerland, but soon after, he left her there on her own, and he went to Moscow. They met again in Stockholm in the winter of 1915, but he left Gabriele again in the spring of the following year. He didn't officially leave her, but he did not tell her that he married Nina Andreevskaya in 1917, who he had met on the phone, apparently. He had fallen in love with her voice.

Gabriele still wrote to him, but he ignored her and she couldn't find him. Four years later, she got a phone call from his lawyer as Kandinsky demanded her to send him his belongings and paintings. She kept some for moral damages according to what I've heard.

Gabriele Münter abandoned art, which I think is a real shame. During the war, when modern art was outlawed, she hid Kandinsky's art and archive that was still in her possession in her basement, which was seriously risky. She donated it to the Städtische Galerie im Lenbachhaus in Germany in 1957. She herself passed away in 1962.

Nina Andreevskaya was from Moscow and her love for art, music and poetry made her frequent Moscow's cultural life. After having heard her voice on the phone Kandinsky created *To the Unknown Voice*. When they finally met, he was fifty, and she was only seventeen; she later said it was love at first sight. They married only one year later. She became a devoted wife and stayed with him till he died, after twenty-eight years together. They also had a son called Wsevolod, but he died when he was only three years old. They had no more children.

In 1921 they left Russia to go to Berlin and this is when Kandinsky was offered a job in the Bauhaus, which was a well-known modern art and design school, and they moved to Weimar, a small provincial town. This was artistically one of Kandinsky's most prolific periods. But then Hitler came to power and everything changed. The Bauhaus was closed, and they moved to Paris. Kandinsky was already sixty-seven at the time.

However, making a living from art was very hard. They stayed in Paris during the war and Kandinsky continued working on his art. He died in 1944, in Neuilly-sur-Seine when he was almost seventy-eight years old.

Nina Andreevskaya was convinced that the value of his art would go up and she didn't sell his work immediately. After the war she stayed in Paris and lived in their home, selling his art to various museums and organising exhibitions of his work. She also published a book of memoirs called *Kandinsky and me*. In the beginning of the seventies, she bought a chalet in Switzerland where she lived. Sadly, in 1980, she was robbed of all her jewellery and she was killed. A crime that was never solved. Kandinsky's art lives on and it's special to look at his work here, now.

There is another famous abstract painter though and you will both know him for sure. I'm talking about Piet Mondrian. He was actually born as Pieter Mondriaan, but he later changed his name to Mondrian. He was of course a Dutch painter and is thought of as one of the greatest artists of the twentieth century. He was one of the pioneers of abstract art.

He created the term Neoplasticism, a non-representational form of art, as he explained was necessary to create universal beauty. In 1914 he said *"Art is higher than reality and has no direct relation to reality. To approach the spiritual in art, one will make as little use as possible of reality, because reality is opposed to the spiritual. We find ourselves in the presence of an abstract art. Art should be above reality, otherwise it would have no value for man."*

Katherine Dreier, co-founder of New York City's Society of Independent Artists once said that The Netherlands produced three great artists, Rembrandt, Van Gogh and Mondrian."

I don't think you would be surprised to hear that it is surprising to me. I do sort of agree with what Mondrian said about art being higher than reality, but for me, in his work he takes it quite far. Like with Kandinsky, I rather like his early work, for example *View from the Dunes with Beach and Piers,* and I also really like *Evolution,* which he painted in 1911, in Paris I believe. I do think his story is extremely interesting, how he came to create the style in the primary colours that he is so famous for. It is certainly interesting to study that. But where was he born and how did he get to Paris, what did he do here?

"Mondrian was born in Amersfoort in The Netherlands and his father was a qualified drawing teacher so he learned to paint and draw from a very young age. He was raised in a strict protestant environment which some say had quite a profound effect on him. Later his art became very much about spiritual and philosophical studies. Mondrian himself at first worked as a teacher in a primary school, but he also painted a lot. The work from this period is best described as impressionistic with landscapes showing the typical Dutch countryside with fields, rivers and windmills, but it already shows a search for a personal style and includes touches of Pointillism and Fauvism.

He arrived in Paris for the first time in 1911 and it was, I believe, the beginning of a profound change in his work. Meeting cubist artists like Picasso and Braque certainly influenced his work.

But there is something that influenced his work even more. Mondrian had already become interested in Helena Petrovna Blavatsky's work, who launched the 'Theosophical movement' and also in Rudolf Steiner's Anthroposophy, before he came to Paris. Much of Mondrian's work was inspired by a search for spiritual knowledge.

During the first World War he went back to the Netherlands, but returned to Paris in 1919 when he was forty-seven years old. He created a studio that, to him, was a nurturing environment for the paintings he had in mind, and that would express the principles of Neoplasticism which he had studied and written about for quite some time. It is a philosophy that, in art, you reject a naturalistic representation of things and strip it down to straight lines, rectangular shapes and only using primary colours. I think when you look at the artwork he became so famous for, you understand this.

What I find remarkable as well is that while he was developing his almost scientific method to paint and as he said *"directed and led by the intuitive and driven by unknown forces"*, he also painted flowers, something he had started around the beginning of the new century. He did so in a rather secretive manner and into the 1920s, telling friends that this was only for commercial reasons. I have to say that to me the evolution into abstraction at the time was an evolution of liberation."

I personally am very much interested in Steiner's work and I even used to see a doctor in the Netherlands who practiced this theory with his patients. I loved that. I also believe that the more knowledge you get about certain aspects of life and about various theories, the more this will filter into your artistic work, as in my case as well. Although you could say that my art has some abstraction in it, I think I prefer to remain a fauvist, or perhaps I should refer to myself as an expressive colourist. Anyway, what about the women in Mondrian's life Mario, do you know something about that?

"I know he was never married, and some portray him or refer to him as a bit of a hermit, living a solitary life on his own, but this wasn't all true. During the 1920s Mondrian loved going out and regularly visited the Parisian clubs and also restaurants as he was a real foody. He was a great fan of jazz-music and the Charleston as well, and he himself used to enjoy dancing.

He certainly enjoyed the company of women and apparently had different relationships. One notable affair was with a girl called Lily Bles, who came to Paris and stayed with Mondrian. He was thirty years her senior but their affair lasted for quite a few years. He also asked her to marry him, but she refused, telling him she wanted to marry someone of her own age.

Many of the women he dated throughout his life were his lovers and inspired him, but they also helped spread his work. We know this because quite a few letters of Mondrian and these women have been saved. He felt increasingly attracted to younger women, but many of his affairs turned into platonic friendships, as Mondrian was known to feel uncomfortable by the intimate desires of these women.

Possibly this was because he was raised in such a strict religious family, where sex was only meant to produce children within a marriage. He frequented some prostitutes, but did stop this out of fear for venereal disease. As we know, syphilis in that time was widespread.

You can see his relationship to women in his work. He created a lot of portraits, showing women as almost mystical beings with large innocent eyes, but later they became more and more angular and sharp, as if their real presence was fading. He did have female artist friends as well and we do know that, at the time, Mondrian encouraged female artists to further develop themselves in modern art and he was thus a true inspiration to many of them.

Apart from his affairs there were women in his life that were important to his career, for example Peggy Guggenheim, an American art collector. She was born into the wealthy Guggenheim family. She collected art in Europe between 1938 and 1946 and settled in Venice in Italy, where you can still visit the Guggenheim Museum today. Some refer to her as an art addict. She organised an exhibition of Mondrian's work in America and partially thanks to her his work became known abroad.

Another crucial fact I think was when Katherine Dreier visited Mondrian's studio and purchased one of his paintings. This painting was exhibited in the first major modern art exhibition in America, in the Brooklyn Museum.

When fascism was rising in Europe, Mondrian moved to London. But after both Paris and his home country, The Netherlands, were invaded he left London and moved to New York's Manhattan. This was in 1940. His work seemed to change, his paintings became visually busier, with more lines. Some of the paintings he worked on were started years before, in Paris or London.

Visitors to his last studio were often astounded as his apartment looked like a painting, as if he was living in his painting, something he had done when he lived in Paris as well. He said it was good for his inspiration as well as serene. In his place in Manhattan, he first used the same off-white he always used in his canvases on the walls and then attached large compositions of coloured paper to the walls. All his furniture was square and painted in primary colours. According to Mondrian this was the best space he had ever lived. Sadly, he only lived there for a few months as he died of pneumonia in February 1944."

Again, I've learned so much and Jeanette agrees, it's been very interesting this visit to the Musée National d'Art Moderne in the Centre Pompidou. Just before we leave, we are going to see *Les mariés de la Tour Eiffel*. It depicts Chagall and Bella in front of a blue Eiffel Tower and a giant cockerel. It was created in 1939, just before the Second World War started. This is also the moment when our journey to Paris comes to an end.

I feel it's wonderful we end our journey with Chagall and with this painting. An ode to the great love of his life, Bella. And Chagall, he will continue to inspire, as he has inspired Cubism, Orphism, Dadaism, Symbolism, Surrealism and perhaps even Abstract art.

This art journey to Paris has moved me in an almost overwhelming way I should say. I have loved, admired, wondered about and appreciated all the fascinating stories that I've heard. And I feel great respect for all the women who made this trip to Paris during this period, bubbling with creative and artistic vitality and new inventions.

Thanks to Mario and Jeanette I can now continue to turn this journey into a written testimony, revisiting my memories that will perhaps invite others to dive into this world of the evolution of art in Paris and thus spreading it all over the world. This could not have existed without the women who inspired, educated, loved, suffered and were creative in a world of art. Let's acknowledge and honour these women who trod this path first, making it easier for other women artists to come. I certainly feel inspired.

May we have inspired you to create your own memories.

About the author

Internationally exhibited artist and published writer Renate van Nijen was born in The Netherlands. In 2004 she settled in Andalucía, southern Spain where she continues to paint, teach art classes and above all, to embrace her passion for writing.

Her first book 'Secret Thoughts', a collection of quirky, sensual short stories, was published in 2000. She went on to publish eight more books with quite a variety of subjects, among which *Cheers, breaking the silence…one voice at a time*, *Reflections from La Herradura* and *Memories of World War II seen through the eyes of a Dutch teenager* – telling the story of her father.

'The HeArt of Paris' is her tenth book. Inspired by this book Renate has created a collection of portraits of a number of the inspirational women who are described in this book. Some of which are included in this book in black and white.

More information about Renate's books and art can be found on her website www.renatevannijen.com

Cover Art

The art on the cover of this book was created by Renate van Nijen, the author.

'Selfie' is the name of the painting on the cover of this book. It is an acrylic painting inspired by a photo of Renate when she was younger. She purposefully used some Art nouveau touches in this artwork. It is a captivating painting, rendered in a vibrant and expressive style. The background is inscribed with words of positivity and affirmation, adding layers of meaning to the visual experience. The eyes, subtly highlighted, gaze out with a sense of calm and introspection, inviting the viewer into her serene world. The words in the background apply to most of the women that are described in this book. For the viewer, this painting serves as a source of inspiration and contemplation. It beckons one to embrace their own inner beauty and strength, encouraging a journey of self-discovery and acceptance.

Note from the author

I wrote 'The HeArt' of Paris from my home in La Herradura. It's a story about two friends, Mario and I, visiting Paris. A memory lane trip honouring the women who struggled to survive and to be recognised in the art world of that era. Telling their stories in this book was a special journey in itself and paying homage to these incredible women was a moving experience for me. I wish you the same joy reading it as much as I did writing it.

My journey hasn't finished, as I will continue to share my own, and the stories of incredible women who have put their stamp on the art world. You can find out more via the QR code below or on my website www.renatevannijen.com.

Acknowledgements

I want to express my special gratitude to Mario Aguilar, the co-writer of this book, for his invaluable contribution to its creation.

I am also deeply appreciative of the assistance provided by Jeanette Bos, Glen Ladegaard, Susie James and Jane Sparks in making 'The HeArt of Paris' a reality.